OXFORD POLITICAL

Series Editors: David Miller and

CIVIC VIRTUES

OXFORD POLITICAL THEORY

Oxford Political Theory presents the best new work in contemporary political theory. It is intended to be broad in scope, including original contributions to political philosophy, and also work in applied political theory. The series will contain works of outstanding quality with no restriction as to approach or subject matter.

Rights, Citizenship, and
Republican Liberalism

CIVIC

VIRTUES

RICHARD DAGGER

New York   Oxford
OXFORD UNIVERSITY PRESS
1997

Oxford University Press

Oxford   New York
Athens   Auckland   Bangkok   Bogota   Bombay   Buenos Aires
Calcutta   Cape Town   Dar es Salaam   Delhi   Florence   Hong Kong
Istanbul   Karachi   Kuala Lumpur   Madras   Madrid   Melbourne
Mexico City   Nairobi   Paris   Singapore   Taipei   Tokyo   Toronto

and associated companies in
Berlin   Ibadan

Published by Oxford University Press, Inc.
198 Madison Avenue, New York, New York 10016

Oxford is a registered trademark of Oxford University Press

Library of Congress Cataloging-in-Publication Data
Dagger, Richard.
Civic virtues : rights, citizenship, and republican liberalism /
Richard Dagger.
p.   cm.—(Oxford political theory)
Includes bibliographical references and index.
ISBN 0-19-510633-4 (cloth)—ISBN 0-19-510634-2 (paper)
1. Civil rights.   2. Liberalism.   3. Citizenship.   4. Community.
5. Political obligation.   6. Republicanism.   I. Title.   II. Series.
JC571.D14   1997
323—DC20   96-28697

1 3 5 7 9 8 6 4 2

Printed in the United States of America
on acid-free paper

For Barbara, finally

ACKNOWLEDGMENTS

This book began to take shape about seven years ago when Terry Ball and I were hiking the A. B. Young Trail to the rim of Oak Creek Canyon in central Arizona. We were talking shop as we hiked, at least when we had breath enough for talking, and somewhere near the top of the trail Terry suggested that I publish a collection of my essays on citizenship and related topics as a book. He soon persuaded me that this was a good idea. But I eventually came to think that an even better idea would be to use those essays as the basis for a book that would be more than a collection of essays. So I began to examine the essays to see where they would need revision, what new material would need to be written, and how the new and the old could be stitched together into what I hoped would be a seamless whole. Concluding that all of this could be accomplished in a year or two, I set to work on what I came to think of as *Civic Virtues*.

The path to completion of this book has been much longer than I thought it would be—and longer by far than the A. B. Young Trail. Other projects intervened and other duties interrupted progress time and again. And much more work was involved in converting a handful of essays into a book than I had anticipated. Others will have to judge how worthwhile that work has been, but I am happy to report, now that the end is near, that the effort of putting my thoughts into order has been personally quite rewarding. Not the least of these rewards has been the opportunity to benefit from the knowledge, critical acumen, and generosity of scholars and friends who have helped me, whether they knew it or not, to write this book. I take great pleasure in thanking them here for their assistance. I take less pleasure in absolving them of any responsibility for the remaining defects of this book, but honesty as well as tradition compel me to shoulder that burden myself.

First among those whose help I am pleased to acknowledge is Terence Ball. From that day in Oak Creek Canyon to the present, Terry's advice and encouragement have sustained my work on this book. I am especially grateful for his chastening comments on the first draft of *Civic Virtues*.

Much of this book originated in papers presented to meetings of the American Political Science Association, the Midwest Political Science Association, and the Southern Political Science Association. For their comments on those papers, I am grateful to Hadley Arkes, Richard Battistoni, Lawrence Biskowski, Keith Fitzgerald, William Galston, Emily Gill, Russell Hanson, J. Donald Moon, James Rhodes, Michael Smith, Rogers Smith, David Speak, and Leslie Paul Thiele. I am also delighted to record my thanks to Shelley Burtt, Alfonso Damico, and George Klosko, each of whom graciously read drafts of a chapter or more at my request and provided valuable criticisms. Professor Burtt's extensive comments on a draft of Chapter 12 were especially useful in helping me to decide how to bring this book to a conclusion.

At Arizona State University, I have been fortunate to have several colleagues, scattered among the philosophy and political science departments and the College of Law, who meet regularly to discuss one another's work in moral, political, and legal philosophy. In addition to the general stimulus this group has provided, I am indebted to its members—Jack Crittenden, Peter de Marneffe, Charles Dresser, David Kader, Joan McGregor, Jeffrie Murphy, Avital Simhony, Fernando Teson, Cynthia Ward, James Weinstein, and Michael White—for their comments on two papers that eventually found their way into this book. I owe a special debt of gratitude to Jeff Murphy for many discussions over the years that have spurred my thinking and lifted my spirits. I owe similar debts to Jack Crittenden and Avital Simhony, whose incisive comments on an earlier draft of this book helped me to strengthen several arguments and, I hope, avoid several mistakes. My erstwhile colleague in ASU's Department of Political Science, John Geer, also deserves special thanks for allowing me to include in Chapter 9 some of the fruits of our combined labor. I am also pleased to acknowledge the assistance of Eddie Genna, Daniel McDermott, and Mary Sigler, with special thanks to Dan and Eddie for compiling the index.

At Oxford University Press, I have had the benefit of the efficient editorial direction of Gioia Stevens and Thomas LeBien and the copyediting skills of Danielle Alexander and Paula Wald. The editors of the Oxford Political Theory series, David Miller and Alan Ryan, gave an earlier draft close readings, as did a peer reviewer who must, alas, remain anonymous. Whatever its failings, the book is much the better for their efforts. I am especially grateful to David Miller for a lengthy critique that forced me to rethink many points, large and small.

Finally, I must thank my daughters, Emily and Elizabeth, for their tolerance and support, and my wife, Barbara, for all that and more. Among her many virtues, civic and otherwise, is the ability to rescue a spouse who is more comfortable with words than with word processors.

In writing this book, I have drawn upon (and often extensively revised) material previously published in the following essays. I am grateful to the publishers for allowing me to use this material here:

"Understanding the General Will," *Western Political Quarterly* 34 (1981): 359–71. Reprinted by permission of the University of Utah, Copyright Holder.

"Metropolis, Memory, and Citizenship," *American Journal of Political Science* 25 (1981): 715–37. Reprinted by permission of The University of Wisconsin Press.

"Computers, Cables, and Citizenship," in *Dissent and Affirmation: Essays in Honor of Mulford Q. Sibley,* ed. A. Kalleberg, J. D. Moon, and D. Sabia (Bowling Green, Ohio: Popular Press, 1983).

"Rights, Boundaries, and the Bonds of Community: A Qualified Defense of Moral Parochialism," *American Political Science Review* 79 (1985): 436–47.

"Politics and the Pursuit of Autonomy," in *NOMOS XXVIII: Justification in Politics,* ed. J. R. Pennock and J. W. Chapman (New York: New York University Press, 1986).

"Rights," in *Political Innovation and Conceptual Change,* ed. T. Ball, J. Farr, and R. Hanson (Cambridge: Cambridge University Press, 1989). Copyright 1989 Cambridge University Press. Reprinted by permission of Cambridge University Press.

"Education, Autonomy, and Civic Virtue," in *Higher Education and the Practice of Democratic Politics,* ed. Bernard Murchland (Kettering, Ohio: Kettering Foundation, 1991).

Tempe, Arizona   R. D.
December 1996

CONTENTS

PART II. CITIZENSHIP

PART III. REPUBLICAN LIBERALISM

CIVIC VIRTUES

CHAPTER 1

Introduction

Since at least the seventeenth century, the concept of rights has figured prominently in political debate, especially in the English-speaking parts of the world. It is no surprise, then, to find individuals and groups of almost every persuasion stating their cases nowadays in terms of rights. What is surprising is the growing reaction against these ubiquitous appeals to rights. According to a number of commentators, popular as well as scholarly, people have become too concerned with rights. In the United States in particular, they argue, we are caught in the grip of a crippling preoccupation with rights.

This reaction grows out of three different complaints about the superabundance of appeals to rights. One is the complaint that rights are by their nature intransigent. When individuals insist on advancing and defending their *rights*, they resort to a concept that leaves little room for compromise and makes it difficult to reach agreement with others—especially when the others are insisting with equal vehemence on *their* rights. If "rights are political trumps," as Ronald Dworkin has said, then it is easy to see how a situation in which everyone is trying to play a trump card is likely to end in deadlock.[1] The more we appeal to rights, it seems, the less likely we are to find mutually satisfactory solutions to our social and political problems, for "part and parcel of rights discourse is a tendency towards forms of social life that are excessively adversarial, litigious, and geared towards modes of self-assertion, whether of individuals or collectivities."[2]

A related complaint is that the concept of rights is too one-sided and individualistic. When we talk and think in terms of rights, the argument goes, we set ourselves apart from others. Rights belong to individuals, so the appeal to rights encourages us to think of ourselves as apart from and threatened by a society, state, or government that is constantly seeking to intrude upon or invade our rights. But thinking in this way blinds us to the extent of our reliance upon others. As we regard ourselves more and more as self-constituted individuals, we fail to realize how we depend upon communities that not only give meaning to our lives but also largely constitute our identities. So preoccupied are we with our rights that we lose sight of our responsibilities and the need to act virtuously, with the good of the community in mind.[3]

The third complaint is that the ceaseless clamoring for a right to this and a right to that will inevitably weaken all appeals to rights. A kind of "conceptual inflation" is at work, in other words.[4] Just as the casual use of profanity robs it of much of its emotive force, so the constant invocation of rights threatens to deprive the concept of its power. If everyone claims to have a right to everything, then the appeal to rights will become almost as meaningless as in Thomas Hobbes's state of nature, in which everyone's right to everything effectively leaves no one with a right to anything.

Are these complaints justified? The last certainly is, in my view, and the other two contain more than a grain of truth. Political disputes, particularly in the United States, reduce too quickly to contending claims over rights, which means not only that they are difficult to resolve but also that they often must be adjudicated by the courts; and that means that the composition of the courts is increasingly a matter of open political dispute. This is not a healthy situation. If we are to overcome it, we must find some way to restore a sense of common purpose to civic life.

But restoring a sense of common purpose does not mean abandoning our concern for rights. We could not do this if we wanted to, for the concept of rights is too deeply engrained in our thinking simply to be abandoned. Nor *should* we want to even if we could. There is too much of value in the idea of rights—an idea rooted in firm and widespread convictions about human dignity and equality—to forsake it. The task, instead, is to find a way of strengthening the appeal of duty, community, and related concepts while preserving the appeal of rights.

One way to accomplish this task is to invent or revive forms of political thought that place civically oriented concepts at the center of their vocabularies. This is what the recent spate of communitarians have sought to do, as have those who have looked to a revival of the classical republican or civic humanist tradition. Too often, however, these writers have based their claims on a sharp distinction between communitarianism or republicanism on the one hand and rights-based liberalism on the other. These distinctions typically rely on a misleadingly narrow conception of liberalism as an atomistic theory that encourages people to conceive of themselves as rights-bearing individuals who are bent on protecting themselves against the depredations of others while furthering their own interests as best they can. Many liberal writers, of course, exhibit traces of this kind of thinking, but these are threads woven into a far richer garment that also includes more civically oriented concerns. In John Locke, Montesquieu, James Madison, Immanuel Kant, John Stuart Mill, T. H. Green, and others, the "republican" tendency is interwoven with the "liberal."[5]

From the historical point of view, then, there is reason to believe that a concern for rights need not be hostile to the desire to promote civic virtue. Whether a satisfactory marriage of the two is possible, however, is another question. It is the question that I try to answer, affirmatively, in this book. As I see it, republican liberalism promises to strengthen the appeal of duty, community, and the common good while preserving the appeal of rights. Rather than provide an account of how this doctrine has developed historically, however, I take a different tack. There are two reasons for doing so. The first is that republican liberalism has not truly *developed* historically. The ideas we now identify as republican and liberal have been woven together in the works of a number of writers, as I have noted, but none of them was consciously involved in developing a set of ideas that could be called republican liberalism. It is only the backward gaze made possible by those who have tried to disentangle republicanism from liberalism that allows us to conceive of such a theory.

The second reason for eschewing the historical approach is that it is not adequate to the task at hand. It is only recently that the complaints about the too-frequent appeals to rights have appeared. These are contemporary complaints, then, and they must be addressed in contemporary terms. If the claim is that republican liberalism affords a way of tying together a concern for rights with a sense of community or civic orientation, then one must show how this can be done. The task is to demonstrate that republican liberalism is a plausible and attractive political position now, at the end of the twentieth century and the beginning of the twenty-first.

I attempt to do this in the three parts of this book. In Part I, I show how a theory that takes rights seriously can lead beyond the isolated individual to a person who is embedded in significant social relations that require his or her attention and care. Because so many of the objections to rights-based liberalism rest on unduly narrow conceptions of rights and of liberalism, I begin in Chapter 2 with a preliminary analysis of three key concepts: autonomy, civic virtue, and rights. As this analysis reveals, these concepts, properly understood, are complementary, which means that it is possible to construct a political theory—republican liberalism—that links autonomy to civic virtue to rights. In Chapter 3, I argue that there is indeed a fundamental right—the right of autonomy—that is grounded in moral equality. In Chapter 4, I consider the implications of this right for the sense of community. A natural or human right must belong to all people, regardless of their citizenship or membership in a community, so one must wonder whether the right of autonomy will weaken or dissolve the bonds of community. My claim is that this right, properly understood, actually strengthens civic or political bonds. It does this through its reliance on the reciprocal rights and obligations that join the members of a political society, at least when that society may reasonably be regarded as a cooperative body governed by the principle of fair play. This principle provides the basis for an account of political obligation, which I set out and defend in Chapter 5.

Part I, then, attempts to draw out the connections between rights, obligations, and membership in a political society. In Part II I explore various ways of cultivating the sense of obligation and the desire to act for the common good that seem to so many commentators to be lacking in rights-obsessed societies. Much of the problem, I claim, is that people have obligations to one another as citizens that they fail to perceive because of the size and complexity of the modern state. The chapters of Part I are meant to explain how these obligations arise; the chapters of Part II explain why they are so hard to see and what might be done to make them more visible, and thus to encourage active, public-spirited citizenship. Chapter 6 thus begins Part II with a discussion of Jean-Jacques Rousseau, a philosopher who offers valuable insights into the problem of encouraging people to set aside their personal interests and act to promote the common good—to follow, in his words, the general will. Chapter 7 extends these insights with an analysis of rival conceptions of citizenship and of the conditions that foster the willingness to act as virtuous citizens. In Chapters 8, 9, and 10, I explore three areas in which there seem to be opportunities for cultivating civic virtue: education, political participation, and cities. These chapters constitute neither a comprehensive program for change nor a republican-liberal manifesto, but I do venture some prescriptions in the hope of provoking further thought on the merits and possibilities of republican liberalism.

Finally, I return in Part III to the general question of whether a marriage of republicanism and liberalism will yield a plausible and attractive political theory. I approach this question in Chapter 11 by way of two challenges posed by appeals to plurality and neutrality. According to the first challenge, republican liberalism is inherently hostile to cultural pluralism; in the name of citizenship or civic virtue, it threatens to ignore the differences between groups of people and to impose an artificial homogeneity on them. I respond to this challenge by arguing that republican liberalism promotes autonomy and solidarity—two goods that any defensible version of cultural pluralism must also endorse—rather than homogeneity. But this leads to the second challenge, which grows out of the debate between the "neutralists" and "perfectionists" within liberalism. If a liberal doctrine must be neutral with regard to conceptions of the good life, as some political philosophers have maintained, then my arguments and ideas may be republican, but they cannot be liberal. What I try to show, in response, is that liberalism necessarily contains its own standards of excellence—standards that prevent it from being neutral in any robust sense and that comport well with a republican interest in civic virtue. This argument carries over to Chapter 12, in which I conclude with a further examination of civic virtue. I argue that, more than being a single virtue, civic virtue comprises a set of related virtues, among which respect for the rights of others and of oneself plays a central role.

What the reader will find in these pages is not an exhaustive attempt to work out the theory of republican liberalism in all its details. My aim is more modest, yet it is ambitious enough. It is to demonstrate the possibility and desirability of a form of liberalism that is capable of overcoming the complaints of those who believe that liberals and liberal societies are obsessed with rights. If I can show that republican liberalism is worth developing into a full-fledged theory of politics, then others ought to be willing to help with the details.

PART I

RIGHTS AND OBLIGATIONS

CHAPTER 2

The Possibility of Republican Liberalism

To make the case for the desirability of republican liberalism, it is necessary first to show that republicanism and liberalism are not altogether incompatible with each other. If they are—if republican liberalism is an oxymoron, a contradiction in terms that simply cannot form the basis of a political theory—there is no point in trying to establish its worth.

Nor will it suffice to appeal to history. Even someone who believes that liberal and republican ideas and arguments have been historically intertwined may doubt that they share enough features to make republican liberalism either possible or plausible as a political theory. Lance Banning provides a case in point in the course of an argument that reaches this conclusion: "Logically, it may be inconsistent to be simultaneously liberal and classical. Historically, it was not."[1] According to Banning,

> modern liberalism and classical republicanism are distinguishable philosophies. *Liberalism* is a label most would use for a political philosophy that regards man as possessed of inherent individual rights and the state as existing to protect these rights, deriving its authority from consent. *Classical republicanism* is a term that scholars have employed to identify a mode of thinking about citizenship and the polity that may be traced from Aristotle through Machiavelli and Harrington to eighteenth-century Britain and her colonies. The two philosophies begin with different assumptions about human nature and develop a variety of different ideas.

The "incompatibility" of liberalism and classical republicanism "will seem much more pronounced," Banning continues, if we follow those who take liberalism "to encompass capitalism or imply a bourgeois attitude and set of values."

> Liberalism, thus defined, is comfortable with economic man, with the individual who is intent on maximizing private satisfactions and who needs to do no more in order to serve the general good. Classical republicanism regards this

11

merely economic man as less than fully human. Assuming a certain tension between public good and private desires, it will identify the unrestrained pursuit of purely private interests as incompatible with preservation of a commonwealth.[2]

Even if it is true, then, that earlier political thinkers have mixed republican with liberal ideas—as Thomas Jefferson and others surely did, according to Banning—this mixture provides no reason to believe that a republican liberalism is possible. The mixture may prove only that these thinkers were confused, guilty of logical errors, or, more charitably, simply unable to see a distinction between these "distinguishable philosophies" that has since become clear.

Are liberalism and classical republicanism really "distinguishable philosophies," as Banning says? Are they "inconsistent" and "incompatible" with each other? The answers, in my view, are yes to the first question and no to the second. If they were utterly indistinguishable, then presumably one of the two concepts would not have taken hold and we would now be able to talk about republicanism *or* liberalism, but not both. Even so, it does not follow that they are inconsistent or incompatible with each other. Bread and butter are distinguishable, but hardly incompatible, and the same may be true of liberalism and republicanism. Much depends on how one defines "liberalism" and "classical republicanism," of course, and it sometimes seems that scholars have defined those terms with an eye to drawing as sharp a distinction as possible between the two.[3] Yet neither term lends itself to precise definition. "Liberalism" is especially troublesome in this regard.[4] Indeed, Banning's brief definition—"a label most would use for a political philosophy that regards man as possessed of inherent individual rights and the state as existing to protect these rights, deriving its authority from consent"—suffers the embarrassment of excluding such prominent liberals as Jeremy Bentham and John Stuart Mill from the liberal fold.

For present purposes, however, I shall set definitional difficulties aside and begin by accepting the challenge posed by a sharp distinction between liberalism and republicanism. I shall assume, that is, that liberals place the greatest value upon individual rights and personal autonomy, classical republicans upon civic virtue and public responsibility. If I can show, even on these terms, that republicanism and liberalism are compatible with each other, then I can establish the case for republican liberalism on a firm foundation. To lay that foundation, I shall first examine the relationship of autonomy and civic virtue, then follow with a brief exploration of the concept of rights.

Autonomy and Civic Virtue

Autonomy and civic virtue are often taken to be at odds with each other because one has to do with individual liberty, the other with collective responsibility. Personal autonomy requires people to look inward so that they may govern themselves, while civic virtue demands that they look outward and do what they can to promote the common good. The two *are* different from each other, of course; they are even in tension with each other at times. But they appear to be incompatible only to those who conceive of autonomy as a purely individualistic notion and civic virtue as a strictly collectivist or communitarian ideal—and these are really misconceptions, as I shall try to demonstrate briefly here and more fully in later chapters. We will do better to look, instead, to the union of autonomy and civic virtue as part of what Charles Taylor has called *holist individualism:* "a trend of thought that is fully aware of the (ontological) social embedding of human agents, but at the same time prizes liberty and individual differences very highly."[5] The first step toward that union is to take a closer look at the concepts in question.

Civic Virtue

Unlike personal autonomy, which relates to the abstract notion of the self, civic virtue refers to a particular role that a person may occupy—the role of citizen. Someone exhibits civic virtue when he or she does what a citizen is supposed to do. In this respect civic virtue is like the other virtues, which typically relate to the performance of some role or the exercise of a certain skill.

The concept of virtue derives from the Greek *aretē,* or excellence, by way of the Latin *virtus,* which carried from its association with *vir* (man in the gender-specific sense) the additional connotations of strength and boldness. These connotations certainly persisted in the classical republican theorists' use of "civic virtue"; indeed, they often described men who lacked virtue as "effeminate."[6] Gender aside, however, even a person of a republican disposition could say that anyone who exhibited excellence in a particular skill or craft, or performed admirably in a particular role or occupation, possessed virtue of some sort. Such a person could also discern a more general form of virtue in those who manifested to a high degree the qualities of a good person. This was (and is) possible only when there was (and is) some fairly clear notion of what a person is supposed to be. Personhood, in other words, must be conceived of as a role that one may play, complete with criteria for determining when one is playing it properly. In this sense a virtuous person is like a virtuoso musician, who does with great skill what a musician is supposed to do.

As this simile suggests, there is a connection between the concept of virtue and the concept of good. Just as it would be absurd to say that Jones is a virtuoso pianist but not a good one, so it would be absurd to say that she is a virtuous person but not a good one. Such a connection does not hold between the idea of autonomy and the idea of good. We may think that autonomy itself is good, but there is no contradiction in saying that Smith is an autonomous person but not, all things considered, a good one.

As a role-related concept, virtue refers to the disposition to act in accordance with the standards and expectations that define the role or roles a person performs. The more sharply defined the role, the clearer the virtues associated with it will be. A steady hand may be among the virtues of a carpenter and a surgeon, for instance, but not of an accountant or poet. Some character traits or dispositions seem useful to almost everyone, however, and these are what we sometimes think of as *the* virtues—including the classical virtues of wisdom, courage, temperance, and justice. These qualities—along with honesty, loyalty, compassion, and others—are virtues not so much because they work to the advantage of the person who possesses them but because they work to the advantage of the people with whom that person associates. Virtues are valuable because they promote the good of the community or society, not because they directly promote the good of the individual.

To be virtuous, then, is to perform well a socially necessary or important role. This does not mean that the virtuous person must always go along with the prevailing views or attitudes. On the contrary, Socrates and John Stuart Mill have persuaded many people to believe that questioning and challenging the prevailing views are among the highest forms of virtue. In making this case, though, they rely on the claim that the social gadfly and the unorthodox thinker are really promoting the long-term interests of society and thereby performing a social role of exceptional value.

Even if it might be shown that some virtues have no social value at all, it is clear that *civic* virtue will not be among them. Civic virtue simply *is* the "disposition to further public over private good in action and deliberation."[7] Understood in this way, civic virtue was the key concept in classical republican thought. It survives today in various forms, such as the exhortations to do one's civic duty that regularly appear at election time. The suspicion that public officials are prone to corruption and conflicts of interest also betrays its traces.

Fear of *corruption* is one of three basic elements in civic virtue as the classical republicans conceived it. They took corruption to be the great enemy of virtue, for it leads to the neglect of one's duty as a citizen. Corruption could take the passive form of shirking one's civic duties in favor of personal pleasures, such as indolence or the pursuit of luxury, or it could take the active form of advancing one's personal interests at the expense of the common good. This active form of corruption was most likely to occur when ambition and avarice—the overweening desire for power and wealth—tempted a citizen to overthrow the rule of law and install a tyranny in its place.

The second key ingredient in the classical republican conception of civic virtue is fear of *dependence.* For republicans, the citizen is someone who rules and is ruled in turn, following Aristotle.[8] The person who is completely dependent on another person may be ruled, but is surely in no position to rule. The rule of law is essential, therefore, as a means of avoiding *personal* dependence. In a government of laws, not of people, the citizen is subject to laws, not to the demands and whims of rulers who act without restraint. The republicans also typically defended private property as a way of guaranteeing that the citizen would not be dependent on others for his livelihood. Some, notably James Harrington and Jean-Jacques Rousseau, went further, suggesting that property should be distributed in such a way as to prevent anyone from being so wealthy as to render other citizens dependent. As Rousseau put it, everyone should have something, but no one should have too much.[9]

The fear of dependence indicates, finally, the importance of *independence,* or *liberty,* in the republican conception of civic virtue. The virtuous citizen must be free, but not simply free to go his or her own way. Instead, the citizen is free when he or she participates in the government of his or her community. As part of the community, the citizen will recognize that the government of common affairs is more or less directly *self*-government. If self-government requires the occasional sacrifice of one's personal interests, so be it, for the sacrifice is necessary not only in the name of civic duty but also in order to preserve the liberties of the citizen of a self-governing polity.

That, then, is what civic virtue was—and still is, according to those theorists who want to revive the republican spirit in contemporary politics. The question to consider now is whether the revival of civic virtue is compatible with the desire for personal autonomy.

Personal Autonomy and Civic Virtue

The autonomous person adopts the principles by which he or she will live, which implies some degree of critical reflection on the principles available. With civic virtue, however, the emphasis is on acting, perhaps without reflection, to promote the common good. The unquestioning soldier who makes the "ultimate sacrifice" for his or her country provides a striking example, as do the virtuous Troglodytes of Montesquieu's *Persian Letters.*[10] It is easy enough to see, then, how autonomy and civic virtue can seem to be at odds with each other, for it is certainly possible for someone to exhibit civic virtue without being autonomous, just as it is possible for an autonomous person to act in a thoroughly selfish manner.

But this is to say that civic virtue and personal autonomy are different from each other and that they sometimes tug us in different directions, not that they are incompatible. Properly understood, autonomy and civic virtue turn out to be related concepts that can and should complement each other. Another look at the three principal elements of the classical republican conception of civic virtue should begin to make their compatibility clear.

First, the republicans' fear of corruption is largely a fear of human weakness. Indolence and love of luxury, ambition and avarice—these vices constantly beckon people to forsake their civic duties and disregard the claims of the common good. The threat of corruption is graver at some times than at others, they believed, but it is always a threat. Staving off corruption requires mixed government and the rule of law and, according to some republicans, even the rotation of public offices among the citizenry and measures to prevent the concentration of wealth and property in the hands of a few. But these devices will never eradicate the threat of corruption, which stems from selfish and ultimately self-defeating desires implanted in human nature. The best hope lies in "the education of desire" or, more optimistically, in an appeal to "the compulsion of duty."[11] To teach people to hold their passions in check and to cultivate devotion to the common good is therefore to achieve a form of self-governance. In this respect, civic virtue and autonomy have something in common.

The second element in the republican conception of civic virtue exhibits another connection with autonomy. In this case, the republican distinction between dependence and independence has a direct counterpart in the distinction between heteronomy and autonomy. The connection is probably clearest in the works of Rousseau, who inspired Immanuel Kant, the philosopher most often identified with the distinction between autonomy and heteronomy. In *Emile,* Rousseau draws a distinction between

> two sorts of dependence: dependence on things, which is from nature; and dependence on men, which is from society. Dependence on things, since it has no morality, is in no way detrimental to freedom and engenders no vices. Dependence on men, since it is without order, engenders all the vices, and by it, master and slave are mutually corrupted. If there is any means of remedying this ill in society, it is to substitute law for man and to arm the general wills with a real strength superior to the action of every particular will.[12]

Here Rousseau proclaims that the only way to overcome "dependence on men," and thus to promote freedom, is to rely on the impartial rule of law and the general will. If the rule of law frees people from their dependence on others, they will be free to make laws in accordance with the general will that they share as citizens. This freedom, as Rousseau says in the *Social Contract,* is "moral liberty," that is, living in accordance with laws that one prescribes for oneself.[13] And Rousseau's "moral liberty" bears a striking resemblance, as I shall show in Chapter 6, to what Kant and others call autonomy.

The connection between autonomy and civic virtue is perhaps most obvious with regard to the third element of civic virtue: the idea that liberty is participation in government and therefore is self-government. Since autonomy means self-government, one might say that the concept of civic virtue entails a commitment to autonomy, in some sense of the word. Again, this commitment is probably clearest in Rousseau's writings, as in the fundamental problem he sets himself in the *Social Contract:* "'Find a form of association that defends and protects the person and goods of each associate with all the common force, and by means of which each one, uniting with all, nevertheless obeys only himself and remains as free as before.' "[14] For Rousseau, in fact, it seems not only that civic virtue entails self-government but also that autonomy is possible only when civic virtue prevails. Unless the general will of the *citizen* takes precedence over the particular will of the *man,* to use his terms, no one can experience moral liberty.

From the perspective of the classical republican conception of civic virtue, in short, autonomy and civic virtue are far from incompatible ideals. The same result emerges from a preliminary analysis of the concept of autonomy. Autonomy "has to be worked for," which leads some philosophers to regard it as "a *character ideal* or *virtue.*"[15] But autonomy is not something that one can achieve solely through individual effort. It may have to be worked for, but it also has to be cultivated and developed. An infant may have the innate capacity to lead a self-governed life, but this capacity must be nourished and developed by others before he or she can ever hope to be autonomous. Recognizing this, the autonomous person should also recognize a duty of some sort to those whose help has made and continues to make it possible for him or her to lead a reasonably self-governed life. If this help sometimes takes the form of more or less impersonal public assistance or cooperation, then the corresponding duty is a civic duty. Thus the autonomous person has a reason to exhibit civic virtue, at least when the community or polity as a whole plays a significant part in fostering personal autonomy.

Perhaps the best way to put the point is to say that autonomy and civic virtue are complementary because both concepts help us to see how independence is related to dependence. The person who is completely dependent on others cannot be independent, yet even the independent person remains dependent on others in various ways. We are *interdependent,* in other words, and a proper understanding of autonomy and civic virtue leads us to recognize and appreciate this basic fact of life.[16]

Interdependent people do not always agree with one another, however, and their relationships are sometimes strained by tension. This is also true of autonomy and civic virtue. They sometimes pull in different directions, with autonomy leaning toward individual rights and civic virtue toward public responsibility. Yet even this tension is healthy. When autonomy pulls too hard in an individualistic direction, the appeal to civic virtue reminds us that both the development and the exercise of autonomy require the assistance and cooperation of others; when appeals to civic virtue threaten to jeopardize individual rights, the claims of autonomy remind us that the body politic ought to be a cooperative enterprise composed of individuals who have a right to lead a self-governed life. In this way the tension between autonomy and civic virtue leads to a healthy balance. This is the kind of balance that is reflected in the attitude of citizens who are willing to do their part for the common good as long as others are willing to do theirs. These citizens know that they and the other members of the body politic are interdependent: their cooperation helps to enhance others' autonomy, just as the cooperation of others helps to enhance theirs. They have a reason to exhibit civic virtue, then, at least when the body politic as a whole plays a significant part in fostering personal autonomy.

How might a body politic do this? Maintaining the rule of law is certainly one way, as I shall argue in Chapters 4 and 5. Providing for the common defense is another, as is providing protection from diseases and disasters. Education, the subject of Chapter 8, is yet another. The most direct way in which a polity can foster personal autonomy, however, is to show respect for individual rights.

Rights

At the beginning of this chapter, I noted that Lance Banning's definition of liberalism—"a label most would use for a political philosophy that regards man as possessed of inherent individual rights and the state as existing to protect these rights, deriving its authority from consent"—fails to encompass such prominent liberals as Jeremy Bentham and John Stuart Mill, who had little use for the idea of "inherent individual rights." Yet there is no doubt that Banning's definition captures what many people have in mind when they think of liberalism. If it does not require a belief in "inherent individual rights," liberalism certainly accommodates those who share this belief. But can it also accommodate those who share the republican concern that too many liberals give too much attention to the rights "possessed" by individuals? To answer this question—and to strengthen the case for the possibility of republican liberalism—a closer look at the concept of rights is necessary.

Rights, the Individual, and Society

Given his interest in "Jeffersonian ideology," it should not be surprising that Banning's definition of liberalism is almost a paraphrase of the second paragraph of the Declaration of Independence of the United States: man is "possessed" of "inherent individual rights," and the state, "deriving its authority from consent," exists "to protect these rights." But such ideas, as Jefferson himself later insisted, were part of the "harmonizing sentiments of the day."[17] Similar arguments characterize John Locke's *Second Treatise of Government,* Thomas Paine's *Common Sense,* the French Declaration of the Rights of Man and of Citizens, and many other tracts and treatises of the seventeenth and eighteenth centuries. Man, the individual, shorn of status, role, and often cultural identity, had become the center of the moral and political world for these thinkers, and the chief task of government, in their eyes, was to secure his "natural" or "inalienable" rights.

The extent to which Locke, Jefferson, and others conceived of rights as the exclusive property of individuals—as a kind of shield that surrounded each man and protected him against the depredations of others—can easily be exaggerated. As Banning and others have pointed out, "republican" appeals to duty and virtue were commonly intertwined with "liberal" appeals to the natural rights of man in the seventeenth and eighteenth centuries. Still, it is clear that complaints about the abstract and individualistic nature of rights claims began to appear even as Paine was celebrating "*the indefeasible hereditary Rights of Man*" during the French Revolution.[18]

Two of the early critics of rights theories, Edmund Burke and Jeremy Bentham, started from much the same point—condemnation of the French revolutionaries' appeal to natural rights. For both, the danger of the natural-rights approach was its tendency to substitute abstract rhetoric for sensible, practical thinking. "*Natural rights* is simple nonsense," according to Bentham's judgment on the French Declaration of Rights, and "natural and imprescriptible rights, rhetorical nonsense,—nonsense upon stilts."[19] Rights are conventional, not natural, in Bentham's view, and if we enjoy them at all, it is only because we are subject to a legal system, for to have a right is merely to be the beneficiary of a relationship sanctioned by law. Because there are no rights without law and government, law and government cannot possibly be justified by an appeal to rights. Instead, we should look directly to utility, understood most simply in terms of the "two sovereign masters," pain and pleasure, under which nature has placed us.[20]

For Burke, the French appeal to natural rights was dangerous not be-

cause it was nonsensical but because it was blind to circumstance and tradition. He acknowledged that there *are* natural rights, abstract rights that do
not depend for their existence on government, "but their abstract perfection is their practical defect." [21] To his mind, the French were elevating a
fiction, Man, to the status of a god, and proclaiming a new religion, the
Rights of Man, in his name. What they and their sympathizers in other
countries should be concerned with, Burke argued, is men as they are, in
all their variety and particularity, whether they are French, English, or
Chinese, peasants, merchants, or craftsmen, nobles or commoners, masters
or apprentices, for "I may assume that the awful Author of our being is
the Author of our place in the order of existence,—and that, having dis-
posed and marshalled us by a divine tactic . . . He has in and by that
disposition virtually subjected us to act the part which belongs to the place
assigned us." [22] We have rights, then, and they are a kind of property, but
a kind that attaches to whatever station in life we may happen to occupy.
Those who set the individual against others—those who talk of rights
against society and government—understand neither rights nor the order
of things.

The complaint that natural-rights theories are too abstract—that they lift
"man" from his social and historical context—became a common ground
of criticism in the nineteenth century, uniting writers as different from
Burke, and one another, as G. W. F. Hegel, Karl Marx, and T. H. Green.
For Marx,

> None of these so-called rights of man goes beyond the egoistic man, beyond
> man as a member of civil society, as man separated from life in the community
> and withdrawn into himself, into his private interest and his private arbitrary
> will. These rights are far from conceiving man as a species-being. They see,
> rather, the life of the species itself, society, as a frame external to individuals,
> as a limitation of their original independence. [23]

Rather than retreat with Burke toward status concepts and a notion of
an objective order, however, Marx looked forward, late in his life, to the
transcendence of the rights of man in "a higher phase of communist society," for "only then can the narrow horizon of bourgeois right be crossed
in its entirety and society inscribe on its banners: From each according to
his ability, to each according to his needs!" [24] Once that horizon is crossed,
presumably, human potential will flower forth and the concept of rights,
now rendered useless, will wither and die.

For Green, the liberal, criticism of the asocial and ahistorical views of
the natural-rights theorists led to an attempt at accommodation. Rights are
valuable not in themselves, in his view, but only insofar as they serve to
promote the "moral vocation" or "moral personality" of the individual.
Yet Green also believed that rights are absolutely necessary to the pursuit

of this vocation, so for him rights proved to be very valuable indeed. "There ought to be rights," he insisted,

> because the moral personality,—the capacity on the part of an individual for making a common good his own—ought to be developed; and it is developed through these rights; i.e. *through the recognition by members of a society* of powers in each other contributory to a common good, and the regulation of those powers through that recognition.[25]

Green's attempt at accommodation is thus an attempt to tie the rights of the individual to the good of the society to which he or she belongs. Our rights are not merely rights *against* others; they are also rights *to* the positive aid of others—aid we need in order to develop our powers so that we may contribute to the common good. As another of the British Idealists, D. G. Ritchie, put the point in 1894, "The person with rights and duties is the product of a society, and the rights of the individual must therefore be judged from the point of view of a society as a whole, and not the society from the point of view of the individual."[26]

Analyzing Rights

Where do we stand now, a hundred years after Green and Ritchie, with regard to rights? A survey of the intervening century suggests that two developments have been especially important.

First, philosophers and legal scholars have devoted considerable attention to the analysis of the concept of rights, one result of which is an abundance, perhaps a superabundance, of often disputed distinctions: between active and passive rights, positive and negative rights, welfare and option rights, special and general rights. By general consent, the most impressive of these was set out in 1919 in Wesley Hohfeld's *Fundamental Legal Conceptions.* Hohfeld's concern as a legal scholar was that the concept of rights and its correlative, the concept of duties, were too broadly and indiscriminately construed. A more careful analysis of rights and duties reveals, he explained, four distinct and fundamental relations under law: rights (i.e., rights in the strict sense) and duties; privileges and no-rights; powers and liabilities; and immunities and disabilities.[27]

From the standpoint of social and political philosophy, the principal value of Hohfeld's categories seems to lie in the distinction between *rights,* also called *claims* or *claim-rights,* and *privileges,* now better known as *liberties* or *liberty-rights.*[28] On Hohfeld's distinction, claim-rights entail a correlative duty on the part of at least one other person, but liberty-rights do not. The difference may be brought out by a pair of familiar examples. If Jones borrows $10 from Smith, Smith then has a claim-right to the return of the money and Jones has a duty to repay her, but if Jones and

Smith both see a $10 bill in the street and no one else is around, then each has a liberty-right to the money even though neither has a duty, ceteris paribus, to let the other have it. By distinguishing rights from liberties in this way, Hohfeld stresses the relational aspect of rights. Whereas the rights-theorists of the seventeenth and eighteenth centuries tended to regard a right as a faculty or possession, Hohfeld encourages us to conceive of a right as a kind of standing, a relationship between one person—the right-holder—and others. It may not have been his intention, but in this sense Hohfeld's analysis reinforces the efforts of the nineteenth-century writers who sought to endow rights with a social dimension.

Much the same could be said for the second notable development of this century in the concept of rights—the popularity among philosophers, political figures, and common people throughout the world of the notion of *human* rights. As the direct descendant of natural rights, of course, human rights is not an entirely new notion. But the shift from "natural" to "human" rights betokens a significant change of emphasis. Arguments from natural rights typically proceeded from the idea of self-possession, from that of a property in oneself that must be defended against others; arguments about *human* rights, however, usually rest on some conception of a human or (perhaps more precisely) a person as a being with needs and interests that must be met if he or she is to live a fully human life. Thus the *rights against* others of the natural-rights theorists tend to become the *claims upon* others of the human-rights theorists.[29]

This different emphasis is manifest in the Universal Declaration of Human Rights adopted by the United Nations in 1948. There, alongside such familiar proclamations as Article 3—"Everyone has the right to life, liberty, and security of person"—we find such novel assertions as that of the right to marry and found a family, the right to rest and leisure, the right to an adequate standard of living, and the right to participate in the cultural life of the community.[30] Whether these really are or ought to be regarded as rights, human or otherwise, is open to dispute, but the important point here is that these putative rights are put forward as vital ingredients in a fully realized human life. In that sense, the popularity of the appeal to human rights reveals a concern not for what we are but for what we can and presumably should be.

Efforts to secure rights for specific groups of human beings—women's rights, "gay" rights, the rights of national or cultural minorities, and so on—also display this concern. In each of these cases, the core argument is that the members of the relevant group suffer because they are neither accorded the same respect nor afforded the same opportunities as other persons. They are prevented from realizing their capacities or from acting autonomously and denied the consideration to which human beings are entitled—to be treated with full respect for their dignity as persons.

Perhaps this is why we seem to live in an age of rights. No other concept seems to capture so well the idea that every person, regardless of his or her place in society, is worthy of respect *as a person.* The concept of human dignity, despite the power of *dignitas* in ancient Rome, certainly lacks the conceptual force that the appeal to rights now exercises.[31] With the field left to rights, it begins to seem, as Joel Feinberg puts it, that

> respect for persons . . . may simply be respect for their rights, so there cannot be the one without the other; and what is called "human dignity" may simply be the recognizable capacity to assert claims. To respect a person, then, or to think of him as possessed of human dignity, simply *is* to think of him as a potential maker of claims.[32]

Individual Rights and Republican Liberalism

To think of a person as "a potential maker of claims" is to employ a richer conception of what it means to be a person than the phrase may initially suggest. There is, to begin with, the idea that one who *makes* claims is to speak for himself or herself—even when he or she is speaking on behalf of others. There is also the idea that we, as persons, have the *potential* to make claims, and this potential, like others, requires exercise and cultivation. In both of these respects, the "potential maker of claims" bears a strong resemblance to the autonomous person.

That should not be surprising, for individual rights and personal autonomy are widely associated with liberalism. But there is another aspect of the conception of the person as a "potential maker of claims" that serves to connect rights and autonomy to concerns more often associated with republicanism. For one to be an effective "maker of claims," someone else must be capable of responding, one way or another, to one's claims. A baby's cry may be understood as a claim to nourishment or attention, for instance, but it can be effective only when there are others present who are capable of responding. A person can be a "maker of claims," then, only when others are "responders to claims." Those who respond to claims, of course, will have claims of their own to make, which means that the rights-bearing person—the "potential maker of claims"—is entangled in a network of social relationships.[33]

As Green and others have argued, the appeal to individual rights can serve to strengthen as well as to weaken these relationships. In keeping with Taylor's account of holist individualism, the appeal to rights, properly couched, acknowledges the "social embedding of human agents, but at the same time prizes liberty and individual differences very highly." There is no reason to believe, then, that the appeal to individual rights is necessarily hostile to virtue, citizenship, or the common good—the concerns of *repub-lican* liberalism.

There is some reason to believe that it is growing out of control, how-ever. According to Mary Ann Glendon, "rights talk," at least as it is spo-ken in the United States, threatens to impoverish political discourse "by its starkness and simplicity, its prodigality in bestowing the rights label, its legalistic character, its exaggerated absoluteness, its hyperindividualism, its insularity, and its silence with respect to personal, civic, and collective re-sponsibilities."[34] Even some rights theorists now worry about "the escala-tion of rights rhetoric" that threatens either to overwhelm other valuable moral and political concepts and considerations or, by a process of concep-tual inflation, to rob the appeal to rights of much of its value.[35] These concerns are well founded; if not, there would be little reason to explore the possibility or plausibility of republican liberalism. But they should not lead us to conclude that we must attempt to abandon or eradicate the con-cept of rights. On the contrary, the lesson to be drawn is that we should appeal to rights more sparingly. We should recognize, that is, that the con-cept of rights has its place and its work to do, just as other concepts— autonomy and civic virtue among them—have theirs. As I shall try to show in the next chapter, it certainly has a place, complementary to civic virtue as well as to autonomy, in the theory of republican liberalism.

CHAPTER 3

A Fundamental Right

To believe in natural rights is to believe in nonsense, according to Jeremy Bentham. Belief in human rights "is one with belief in witches and unicorns," according to Alasdair MacIntyre.[1] Yet each in his own way is an egalitarian, Bentham as a utilitarian and MacIntyre as a professed "Augustinian Christian."[2] Can they have it both ways? Can they maintain that every person is in some sense morally equal to every other yet deny that people have natural or human rights?

Bentham's egalitarianism is particularly instructive here, for according to his theory rights exist only when the law of the land says they do. "What you have a right to have me made to do (understand a political right) is that which I am liable, according to law . . . to be *punished* for not doing."[3] If we have rights, Bentham insists, it is only because we have instituted them through legal practices—practices that derive their own justification from their ability to promote the greatest happiness of the greatest number. Yet Bentham also insists that everyone is to count for one, and no one for more than one, when utility is calculated. But why should this be? Why shouldn't *my* interests, *my* pains and pleasures, count for more than anyone else's? Appeal to the principle of utility cannot help us here. Indeed, we cannot even proceed with a calculation of utilities until we know how much weight to attach to each individual's pains, pleasures, or preferences. Nor will an appeal to social or legal conventions help since those conventions must be justified in terms of utility, which we cannot calculate until we know how much weight to attach to each person's pains, pleasures, or preferences.[4]

It seems, then, that Bentham must believe that everyone is *entitled* to be counted as (and no more than) one, and the source of this title can only be something more fundamental than the principle of utility itself. It must be, indeed, a fundamental right to be treated as an equal.

The claim that everyone has rights of some sort simply because he or she is a human being, or a person, entails a belief in equality—a belief that gives the notion of human rights much of its conceptual force. In this chap-

ter I examine and elaborate the connection between these two powerful
concepts. My argument is that anyone who believes that all people are in
some sense morally equal must also believe in human rights. Neither Ben-
thamite utilitarians nor Christians nor anyone else committed to human
equality can reasonably dismiss the notion of human rights *if these rights
are properly conceived.* What I shall need to set out, then, is not only the
relationship between equality and rights but also the proper conception of
human rights—a conception that rests on the claim that there is a fundamental right of autonomy.

Rights and Equality

Of the many arguments devised to justify the claim to human rights, the
most persuasive, to my mind, is the one H. L. A. Hart provides in "Are
There Any Natural Rights?"[5] If we have any moral rights at all, Hart contends, we must then have at least one natural right; otherwise the rights
we acquire from promises, contracts, and laws would have no ground or
foundation. These are all *special rights,* to use Hart's term, because they
arise from special relationships between specific individuals—relationships
in which one person, Jones, may confer on another person, Smith, the right
to limit Jones's liberty in one way or another. Jones may promise to take
Smith to the concert, for example, thus giving Smith the right to have a say
in (some of) Jones's conduct on the day of the concert. But Smith acquires
this right only because Jones grants it to him, and it is hers to grant because
she, Jones, is a free agent capable of choice, a person entitled to live free
from the unwarranted interference of others. If we have any moral rights
at all, therefore, we must also have what Hart calls an equal right to be
free.

This argument is strictly conditional, of course, and some may regard
this as a weakness.[6] Yet in two respects the conditional nature of Hart's
argument actually lends it power. The first is that Hart's analysis helps to
explain how we can confer rights on another, as we do when we make
promises. What, after all, gives us the right to give rights to others? If we
say that the institution of promising itself rests on a more fundamental
contract or convention into which we tacitly or hypothetically enter, we
must then ask what gives us the right to confer, through this convention,
rights upon others. There seems, in other words, to be a fundamental right
to which we must appeal—as Hart's conditional argument helps us to see.
We can confer rights upon others only because we have a fundamental
right to govern our own conduct, which is to say that special rights presuppose a natural or human right to liberty. In short, we must *have* a right
in order to *grant* a right.

The conditional nature of Hart's argument also reveals what is at stake in disputes about the existence of human rights: not only human rights—abstract, metaphysical, and overblown as the claims of their proponents may sometimes make them seem—but *all* moral rights, even the petty rights we assign one another in the course of our daily lives. If Hart is correct, the price of denying that there is at least one human right, the equal right to liberty, is greater than most people will want to pay. Those who think themselves willing to pay it should try to conceive of a society without rights—one in which promises, vows, and pledges have no place.[7]

In both of these respects, the conditional nature of Hart's argument seems to contribute greatly to its strength. This may be granted, though, without granting that Hart's reasoning is completely persuasive. A critic, noting that Hart's "natural right" is an *equal* right to liberty, might go on to question whether this is indeed a right everyone possesses equally or whether some people possess it at all. Perhaps, the critic might say, some people have a right to liberty—masters, let us call them—while others, whom we shall call slaves, have only those special rights that the masters choose to confer on them. This move would allow the critic to acknowledge that special rights do exist and that they do presuppose a fundamental right to be free, but this fundamental right, from the critic's point of view, would belong only to the masters. In this interpretation, the right to be free is not a *human* right at all, for it is the right of only some persons, not all.

Whatever else the merits of this objection may be, it does serve to reveal the importance to Hart's argument, and, mutatis mutandis to any argument for human rights, of the belief that in some morally relevant sense all human beings are equal. Anyone who denies this will also deny that mere humanity, or personhood, is the foundation for rights of any sort.[8] If we are to make a case for human rights, then, we must also make a case for human equality, understood as the view that every person is entitled to equal concern and respect *as a person*.

So far as I can see, there is no way to *prove* that we are all equal in this sense. But neither is there any way to prove that we are not. Human beings are unequal in many ways, certainly, but none of them bears on the question of whether we are all entitled, as human beings, to equal concern and respect. As Gregory Vlastos notes, those who argue against human equality tend to conflate two distinct concepts: human worth and human merit.[9] Merit is a grading concept, and even the staunchest egalitarian can readily admit that degrees and differences of merit exist among human beings. But, Vlastos points out, we cannot grade people according to their *worth* because human worth is something that must inhere in each individual as a person without regard to his or her merits. Thus the indisputable fact that some people are superior to others in some way, or even a number of ways, cannot count against the claim that all human beings are entitled by virtue of their equal worth to be treated as equals. By conflating merit and worth, those who argue from unequal merit to unequal rights simply miss the point.

Important as this distinction is, it is still not sufficient to establish the case for equality, for it remains possible for someone simply to deny that there is such a thing as human worth. Human beings exist, according to this argument, but human worth does not. If one accepts this view, there then seem to be only two ways to proceed. One is to take a position similar to Plato's Thrasymachus and maintain that what we think of as good or bad, right or wrong, just or unjust, is really nothing more than a matter of interest, advantage, or power. If this seems too extreme and too narrow, then one may take the other tack and argue that, in the absence of any proof of the existence of human worth, some other human property must provide the foundation for rights—some property not found in equal measure in all men, women, and children.

Although it is less extreme, this second way of proceeding is no more persuasive than the first. In this case the problem is settling on the property or capacity in terms of which merit leads to rights. Is it intelligence or rationality? Race or nationality? Gender? Strength? Intuition or insight of some sort? Whatever one chooses, one will have to demonstrate that this is *the* property that confers the fundamental right to liberty on those who possess it—a daunting task, surely. Perhaps such a property may someday be identified, but the history of attempts to do so, from that of Aristotle onward, seems to warrant skepticism. Indeed, the very attempt to find a property or capacity of this sort, and to trump up "evidence" to prove that some people or peoples lack it, testifies to the strength of the conviction that every person is in some sense equally worthy of respect and concern.

In the absence of any conclusive negative arguments, I believe that we are entitled to retain this conviction. There is a case for human equality, and that means that there is also a case for Hart's *equal* right to be free. But this leaves another matter to resolve before I turn to the explication of the right of autonomy, one that concerns a possible discrepancy between Hart's position and mine. I have tried to show that Hart's argument in "Are There Any Natural Rights?" provides a justification for a human right of autonomy. But Hart refers to an equal right to be free, not to a right of autonomy. The question, then, is whether Hart's argument supports the right of autonomy as well as it supports the right to liberty or freedom.

"Liberty," "freedom," and "autonomy" are closely related words, but they are not interchangeable. The difference between "liberty" and "freedom," on the one hand, and "autonomy," on the other, is especially pronounced. "Autonomy" carries a connotation of consciousness, of the capacity to make choices upon reflection, that is absent in many uses of "liberty" and "freedom."[10] We may speak of a lion that is "born free," for instance, or of a horse that gains its liberty by escaping from a corral, but the only animal we commonly characterize as autonomous is homo sapiens. This is an important difference. But does it mean that Hart's argument for an equal right to be free cannot be converted into an equal right of autonomy?

The answer is no, for reasons implicit in Hart's argument. When we make promises and pledges, according to that argument, we give others the right to interfere with our freedom—to have a say, at the least, in what we shall and shall not do—and we can give them this right only because we have a fundamental right to be free. In conferring such a right upon others, we simultaneously bind ourselves and empower them. But the bond and the power both relate to the right to govern our own conduct. When Jones promises to take Smith to the concert, for example, she exercises her right to govern her own conduct by granting Smith a right to govern part of her conduct on the day of the concert. Jones's obligation and Smith's right thus rest on Jones's fundamental right to exercise her capacity to lead a self-governed life—the right of autonomy.

If this seems to be mere wordplay, it may help to consider what the act of promising presupposes. People sometimes make promises thoughtlessly, and they often regret it when they do. People sometimes make promises that they simply cannot keep, and other parties often regret it when they do. We can blame, condemn, and hold these people accountable, however, only because we have reason to believe that they are able to engage in the practice of promising—and thereby govern their conduct. This means, at least, that someone must be able to look ahead, to recognize and weigh some of the available options, and to follow words with deeds. Someone who can say "I promise" but who is utterly incapable of forethought, reflection, or action can no more make a promise than a parrot can. That is why we attach less significance to the "promises" of a three-year-old child than to those of a six-year-old, and less to the six-year-old's than to an eight-year-old's, and so on, until that indeterminate age when the child's capacity for self-government seems sufficiently developed for his or her promises to be fully effective.

Promises, pledges, contracts, and vows commit us to act in certain ways. But they are commitments we enter into in order to govern our own conduct. They may limit our freedom to act in certain ways, but these are self-imposed limits that manifest and presuppose our ability to lead a self-governed life. If the rights and obligations created by promises, pledges, contracts, and vows must derive from some fundamental right, it must be more than the mere right to be free from interference. It must be a fundamental human right of autonomy.[11]

The Right of Autonomy

It may seem redundant to speak of the right of autonomy, for "autonomy" is sometimes taken to mean the right of self-government. This seems to be what we have in mind when we say, for instance, that a nation-state is autonomous. But there is also a stronger sense of the word, a sense that better fits our use of "autonomy" to characterize individual women and men. In this stronger sense, autonomy is the ability or capacity to govern oneself—an ability or capacity that someone who is free (from external restrictions) to govern himself or herself may not always enjoy. This is why we say that insane people are not autonomous, for it is not the right to rule their lives that they lack but the capacity to do so.[12] Thus there is no redundancy, in this stronger sense of "autonomy," in maintaining that women and men have a right, understood as a claim upon others, of autonomy. To say that everyone has a right of autonomy, then, is to say that every person is entitled to exercise his or her capacity to lead a self-governed life.

This does not mean that the right of autonomy is nothing more than the right to be left alone or nothing less than the right to do whatever one wishes. Autonomy, like other abilities, is not something we either do or do not have; it is something we may possess to a greater or lesser extent, just as the ability to speak English or play chess varies considerably among English speakers and chess players. Autonomy resembles other abilities in another respect, too, for it may be cultivated, neglected, or impaired. Its cultivation demands some effort on the part of the individual, of course, but it also requires the aid of parents, friends, teachers, and others—perhaps even therapists of one kind or another. No one becomes or remains autonomous solely through his or her own efforts. Everyone needs the assistance of others at times, and the right of autonomy establishes a claim to this assistance. It is more than merely the right to be left alone, therefore, because it is the right to the protection and promotion of one's ability to lead a self-governed life.

The right of autonomy is also less than the right to do whatever one wishes. Because it is a human right, it is a right that every person shares with every other person, and this limits what we may do *as a matter of right.* Jones may have the right to live as she chooses, but this does not entitle her to violate others' rights to live as they choose. This limit on our conduct follows from the logical correlativity of rights (in Hohfeld's strict sense) and duties. If Jones has a right to do something, then there must be someone who has a duty to assist her, or at least not to interfere with her, when she sets out to do it. When the right in question is one that every person has, furthermore, rights and duties are *completely reciprocal.* By this I mean that every person has both a *right against* and a *duty to* every other person. Thus Jones's right to autonomy implies that everyone else has a duty to respect her choices, but everyone else's right of autonomy implies a correlative duty on Jones's part. Given this complete reciprocity, it is clear that the right of autonomy is no warrant to do whatever one may wish.

This limitation notwithstanding, the right of autonomy is the fundamental right because all others follow from it. Recognizing autonomy as a right requires us to respect the dignity of the person: to treat others not as playthings or objects or resources that we may use for our own purposes but as individuals who are capable, at least potentially, of forming plans, entering into relationships, pursuing projects, and living in accordance with an ideal of the worthwhile life. Everyone possesses this right simply because he or she is a person, moreover, so the right of autonomy is also a right everyone shares equally. This is not a right to equal treatment but a right, as Ronald Dworkin says, to be treated as an equal: "the right, not to receive the same distribution of some burden or benefit, but to be treated with the same respect and concern as everyone else."[13]

This is all very general, of course, and one may wonder whether the right of autonomy is too vague, too lacking in content, to be of any practical significance. I shall now try to show that it is not.

Autonomy as the Fundamental Right

If autonomy is the fundamental right, then every other right either derives from or is in some sense a manifestation of our human right of autonomy. The right of autonomy must necessarily be formal and abstract, in other words, with special and general rights supplying its content. *Special rights*, again, are those that arise from special relationships between specific individuals, with promises and contracts providing the standard examples of these relationships. Special rights may be said to manifest the right of autonomy in the sense that they are created through the exercise of that fundamental right. Without the right of autonomy, there could be no transfer of rights in a promise or contract, for we must have a right to govern our own lives before we can grant someone else a right against us. Hence each right we receive from or confer upon others indirectly manifests the autonomy of the person who confers the right.

General rights, the second of Hart's categories, also manifest the right of autonomy, but they do so more directly. General rights—Jones's right to be free from assault, for instance—are known in legal terms as rights *in rem:* rights that hold against everyone rather than rights against specific, identifiable persons (rights *in personam*). Because they hold against everyone, general rights do not grow out of special relationships involving two or more people. Instead, they are instances, or direct manifestations, of the right of autonomy. Jones's right to be free from assault does not follow from any pledge or promise she exacts from other people; it is her right simply because the right of autonomy is the right to govern our own lives, and if assault on our persons threatens our ability to be self-governing, then assault violates the human right of autonomy. It follows that the right to be free from assault is one instance of the right of autonomy. In this way general rights, whether as widely recognized as the right to be free from assault or as controversial as the right to medical care at public expense, grow directly out of—and, with special rights, supply the content for—the human right of autonomy.

This may solve, or at least rationalize, the problem of vagueness, but the solution immediately prompts another question: Just how are we to know what special and general rights follow from the human right of autonomy? Questions of this sort cannot be answered easily, but I believe that we can at least discern the leading features of an adequate response. The point of departure is the right of autonomy itself, which I have defined as the right to the protection and promotion of the ability to lead a self-governed life. From this point we may go on to identify four questions we should raise, or four tests we should apply, whenever we need to decide whether a putative right should be regarded as a special or general manifestation of the fundamental right of autonomy.

First, we should ask whether the "right" in question does indeed protect individual autonomy. The rule of thumb here is that men and women should ordinarily be left to decide what is in their own interests.[14] Autonomy is the ability to govern one's life, and the direction of that life should be left to the individual as long as he or she respects the autonomy of others. This means that we must ordinarily respect the choices of individuals, including the choices they make when they confer rights on, and thereby undertake obligations to, other men and women. Special rights thus present no problem, not even in those cases in which one party to a special relationship is defrauding, exploiting, or coercing other parties, for in these cases the fraud, exploitation, or coercion violates the victim's right of autonomy and prevents any special right or obligation from arising from the relationship. Some general rights will also fall under the heading of rights that protect our autonomy, with the right to freedom from assault once again providing a clear example. Other general rights, such as the right to speak freely, also follow from the right of autonomy, although these rights will often prove troublesome when their exercise threatens to violate the rights of others. But trouble of this sort cannot always be avoided.

The second test goes beyond the first because it leads us to ask whether a putative right will actually promote, and not merely protect, individual autonomy. If it will, then it ought to be regarded as a right, positive and general, that flows directly from the fundamental right of autonomy.[15] The stronger sense of "autonomy" as the ability to govern one's life seems to require positive rights of this sort. This point is illustrated by the claim that members of linguistic minorities often make to the right to speak a particular language. When these people—the Québécois, say, or Latinos in the United States—lay claim to this right, they ask for more than protection against those who might wish to prevent them from speaking French or Spanish; they also ask for bilingual education and other forms of positive aid that will help them to sustain the use of their language. In this fashion, the right of autonomy, through such general rights as the right to speak a particular language, imposes a duty of assistance on those who are in a position to encourage, cultivate, or foster the autonomy of other men, women, and children. Because the right of autonomy is a human right, moreover, it is characterized by what I have called complete reciprocity: every person has a right to the assistance of others in projects that will promote his or her autonomy, and every person also has a reciprocal duty to provide similar assistance to those who will benefit from it.

This begins to sound as if we must devote our entire lives to service to others. That is not the case—indeed, I shall note shortly some limitations on what may be demanded in the name of autonomy—but there is no denying that this is a stringent conception of human rights. If we are truly concerned with the autonomy of the individual, however, such a conception is inescapable. Autonomy admits of degree, and this means that the right of autonomy is a right to widen one's range of choice in order to gain greater control of one's life. But rights also entail duties, so that those who are in a position to promote the autonomy of others will share a duty to help widen the right-holder's range of choice. A healthy person has a wider range of choice than someone who is unhealthy, for instance, so it seems reasonable to say that, other things being equal, the healthy person is more autonomous, or in greater control of his or her life, than one who is ill. Hence the right of autonomy seems to entail a general right to health care, a right that holds against anyone who is able to help provide this care. In much the same way, an educated person usually commands a wider range of choice than the uneducated man or woman, and this again seems to imply a right to schooling of some sort, even if this right imposes certain costs on those who are in a position to help provide the schooling. Thus we may conclude that the rights to health care and schooling pass the second of the four tests because they are among the rights that promote individual autonomy.

Even a stringent theory has its limits, however, and the remaining two tests define these for the right of autonomy. The third test recognizes that a project or action that promotes or protects the autonomy of some individuals may well narrow the range of choice for others. The question we must pose, then, is whether the "right" at issue, assuming it either protects or promotes someone's autonomy, infringes or violates the rights of others. If it does not, then we may pass on to the fourth test. But if it does entail a conflict of rights, we must then decide whether the proposed right ought to override a right already recognized. Something of this sort happens with both the right to health care and the right to schooling, for both may come into conflict with the right to live one's life as one chooses. Acknowledging a general right to health care or schooling will almost certainly require a diversion of resources from some people to others, and there is some truth to the claim that the person who is required to surrender some of his or her wealth for these purposes suffers a loss of autonomy; certainly the transfer of wealth can diminish one's range of choice. How, then, can we resolve this conflict?

There are at least two promising ways to reach a resolution when a conflict of this nature arises. The first is to establish either a floor or a ceiling for autonomy. We might say, in other words, that a transfer of resources is just whenever it helps to bring one or more persons up to a certain standard of autonomy—that is, to a point at which the range of choice is at least wide enough to begin to resemble true autonomy. Or, conversely, we might consider a transfer to be just when it does not lower those who must surrender resources below a certain level—a level that seems as high as we can reasonably go in the name of autonomy. In the first case, the man or woman who lives in poverty, with little chance for decent food, schooling, or medical care, is able to make some choices, but these are so limited that we are hardly likely to say that he or she is truly autonomous. In the second case, the person who must settle for a Mercedes-Benz because he or she can no longer easily afford a Rolls-Royce may suffer a diminished range of choice, but the diminution hardly represents a real loss of autonomy. Autonomy admits of degree, to be sure, and it is related to the range of choice we enjoy in governing our lives. But this is not to say that every change in our range of choice represents a notable extension or diminution of autonomy. In this respect, additions to our range of choice exhibit some of the features of diminishing marginal utility. This is why the floor or ceiling schemes may well provide a satisfactory method for resolving conflicting claims with respect to individual autonomy.

The second approach involves the application of something like John Rawls's difference principle to the right of autonomy.[16] In this case the intent is to promote the autonomy of the least autonomous people, even if this comes at the expense of those who enjoy greater autonomy. Following this approach, the ideal is to insist on providing everyone with as nearly equal a range of choice as possible unless there is reason to believe that an unequal distribution will somehow extend the range of choice for the least autonomous beyond what they would be likely to achieve with an equal distribution. Applying this principle to wealth, we might say that an unequal distribution is just only if such a distribution somehow provides those at the low end of the distribution with a broader set of choices, perhaps through incentives and trickle-down effects, than they would enjoy if wealth were divided equally.

These proposals are nothing more than tentative suggestions, but they do indicate how conflicting claims arising from the fundamental right of autonomy might be resolved. They bring us, finally, to the last of the four tests, and the second limiting test, for the special and general rights that supply the content for the right of autonomy. Here we must employ a variant of the maxim "ought implies can" and ask whether a putative right can indeed be realized.[17] If it can, and if it passes the other tests, then it should be acknowledged as a right deriving from the right of autonomy. If it cannot, it must be dismissed, even if it passes the other tests. The ability to fly by flapping one's arms might enhance one's autonomy—certainly it would add to a person's range of choice—but it would be silly to claim this as a right for the simple reason that we know of no way to cultivate this particular ability. Or, to take a more serious example, we cannot reasonably acknowledge a right to health, but only to health *care* of the best sort available. This is to say that we cannot recognize a right unless we have the means to perform its correlative duty or obligation.

This conclusion implies that the rights we may acknowledge as genuine instances of the fundamental right of autonomy will vary from place to place and time to time. That is, everyone possesses the right of autonomy, and everyone may also share some (very) general rights, such as the right to be free from unwarranted assault, but nesting within these rights will be a number of more specific rights that will differ from one set of circumstances to another. Thus it may be reasonable to maintain that the residents of Canada have a right, say, to the use of a hemodialysis unit because this particular right derives from the general right to health care, which derives in turn from the fundamental right of autonomy. We could not have asserted this right a hundred years ago, though, and we may not be able to attribute it now to millions of people throughout the world who have no reasonable access to hemodialysis units. If everyone has a right to the best health care available, and if hemodialysis devices are part of the best health care available anywhere on earth, then a proper concern for human rights requires us to strive to make these devices available to everyone who needs them, either by taking the device to the patient or bringing the patient to the device. This concern also provides grounds for criticizing those who would block or ignore the effort to make hemodialysis more widely available. But limited resources and other circumstances may prevent the accomplishment of this goal for some time, so that the right to the best health care available may not always entail a right to hemodialysis. Cultural and economic conditions, available technology, the institutions under which we live, even geography—all of these will help to determine the particular rights to which we may be entitled under the right of autonomy. Indeed, these various circumstances will even affect the kinds of claims men and women put forward as rights.

There is a sense, then, in which most of the specific rights we enjoy are social in character. All moral rights presuppose the right of autonomy— directly, if they are general rights, and indirectly, if they are special rights. But what counts as protecting or promoting autonomy cannot always be determined without reference to the particular circumstances of particular people. When we refer to these circumstances in order to decide whether a putative right passes the fourth test, we are acknowledging that the human right of autonomy may appear in different guises under different conditions. We are also supplying the content of the right of autonomy when we do this, thus defeating the charge that the right is too vague to be of practical significance.

Autonomy, Individuals, and Community

Another complaint that may be brought against the claim that there is a fundamental human right of autonomy has nothing to do with worries about vagueness or lack of utility. In this case the complaint follows from the concern that I noted on the first page of this book: that an appeal to autonomy as a fundamental right simply reinforces a tendency too prevalent in the world, especially in the United States. This is the tendency to exalt the rights and liberties of the individual at the expense of the needs and interests of the community. As Mary Ann Glendon puts it, "The exaggerated absoluteness of our American rights rhetoric is closely bound up with its other distinctive traits—a near-silence concerning responsibility, and a tendency to envision the rights-bearer as a lone autonomous individual."[18] "By making a radical version of individual autonomy normative," she adds, "we inevitably imply that dependency is something to be avoided in oneself and disdained in others."[19] Anyone who finds these charges compelling will have reason to doubt whether it is wise or salutary to insist on a fundamental right of autonomy.

Rather than dismiss Glendon's charges, which I find plausible as an account of the way in which many people nowadays conceive of their rights, I shall try to dispel the doubts she and others have about the value of autonomy. In particular, I want to show that the autonomous person, properly conceived, is quite different from "the lone rights-bearer"—a "self-determining, unencumbered, *[sic]* individual, a being connected to others only by choice."[20] To make this difference clear, we shall have to look more closely at the concept of autonomy.

"Autonomy" is one of those words that is both easy and difficult to define. It is easy to provide a superficial definition of "autonomy" as self-governance, self-rule, or self-legislation. But then one must proceed to explain what self-governance, self-rule, or self-legislation consists of, and that is where difficulties definitely arise. The difficulties lie on both sides of the hyphen, as it were, for any attempt to make sense of the notion of autonomy will lead not only to the question of what it means for a man or woman to govern or legislate for himself or herself but also to questions about the nature of the self. Perhaps the best way to uncover these difficulties is to examine the conception—or misconception, in my view—of autonomy that Glendon deplores.

According to this "radical version of individual autonomy," autonomy is best understood as strict independence, self-control, or self-sufficiency. As an ideal, however, this leads away from autonomy properly conceived. On the "radical version," if I wish to control my life and be the master of my fate, I must strive to allow no one else a chance to interfere with my control, with my authority over myself. Unless I can find some way to dominate everyone else, this means that I must withdraw from society. This withdrawal may be literal, as in the case of the hermit who goes to live in a cave or a cabin in the hills, or it may be figurative, as in the case of the person who withdraws into himself or herself. If I then find that I desire far more than I am able to provide for myself, the solution is to desire less. This requires self-mastery, for I must suppress and deny those desires that I cannot fulfill within myself; but I can do this if I can come to regard these desires as accidental, distinct from my essential self, or as part of a "lower" self that I must transcend.

Taken to its extreme, this notion of autonomy as self-sufficiency leads to what Isaiah Berlin has called "the retreat to the inner citadel":

> the traditional self-emancipation of ascetics and quietists, of stoics or Buddhist sages, men of various religions or of none, who have fled the world, and escaped the yoke of society or public opinion, by some process of deliberate self-transformation that enables them to care no longer for any of its values, to remain, isolated and independent, on its edges, no longer vulnerable to its weapons.[21]

The problem, of course, is that this attempt to become sufficient unto oneself is likely to leave one with a self that is shriveled and miserable. What begins as a quest for self-sufficiency ends in self-denial or even self-destruction. As Berlin says, "If I go too far, contract myself into too small a space, I shall suffocate and die. The logical culmination of the process of destroying everything through which I can possibly be wounded is suicide."[22]

To conceive of autonomy as total independence or self-sufficiency, then, is to misconceive it. Autonomy is self-rule, but it is rule that aims at the realization, not the constriction or destruction, of the self.[23] In this respect it is, as I suggested earlier, an ability or capacity that needs to be cultivated—the ability or capacity to lead a self-governed life. From this follow the two implications I mentioned in the second section of this chapter. The first is that autonomy, like other abilities, is something we may enjoy to a greater or lesser extent. Autonomy is a matter of degree, which means that we can draw comparisons between persons, or even between one's self at different times, as being more or less autonomous. There may be a sense in which we think of someone as an autonomous person *simpliciter,* but this is probably because we have some threshold in mind. Once a person acquires a sufficient, but indefinite, level of skill at playing the violin or shortstop, for example, we say that he or she *is* a violinist or shortstop. The same holds true for the person who reaches a threshold of proficiency in leading a self-governed life. But this does not mean that the person we call autonomous cannot become even more autonomous, any more than it means that our hypothetical violinist or shortstop cannot become more proficient at the instrument or position he or she plays.[24]

The second implication is that the cultivation of autonomy, like that of other abilities, requires the efforts not only of the individual in question but also of others. Rather than being a form of rigid control we impose on ourselves by relentlessly denying our appetites, affections, and inclinations, autonomy is the ability to control our lives through reasoned choice. This ability grows out of our needs and desires, our talents and limitations, and the opportunities and obstacles in the world around us. And no one can develop this ability without the help of others.

If this seems to stray from the usual understanding of autonomy as self-legislation, then one ought to consider what self-legislation entails. People are self-legislating, autonomous rather than heteronomous, to the extent that they choose the principles by which they live. But if they truly *choose* the principles that guide their conduct, autonomous people must *be aware* of the alternatives from which they can choose and *be able* to think critically about them. Someone who does the right thing instinctively, without reflection, in the manner of Herman Melville's Billy Budd, is a good and decent person but not an autonomous one. Autonomy requires awareness: an awareness of the choices available to us, to begin with, and an awareness of our capacity to choose. If we are to lead self-governed lives, we must first be able to think of ourselves as something more than objects at the mercy of outside forces, like so many leaves tossed about in the wind. Yet we cannot acquire the knowledge necessary to choice, and therefore to the ability to legislate for ourselves, without the assistance of parents, teachers, friends, and many others.

Once we have acquired this knowledge and ability—once we have graduated from autonomy school, so to speak, and become self-legislating— may we then properly conceive of ourselves as "lone autonomous individual[s]"? The *development* or *cultivation* of autonomy may require the assistance of others, in other words, but its *exercise* does not. Once we have achieved autonomy, then, we no longer rely on others to remain autonomous.

There is some merit to this view. Robinson Crusoe on his island, even before Friday appeared, may have been able to reflect on the choices available to him, and perhaps even to think critically about his aims and desires, in a way that we can call autonomous. Nevertheless, the range of choices available to him was narrower than it would have been in society. Those of us who are not stranded on an island will find that the exercise as well as the development of autonomy depends in many ways upon others. Even a person who wants only to maintain his or her present degree of autonomy will sometimes find it necessary to call on the aid of others. Being able to read is vital to the exercise of my autonomy, for example, but my continued ability to read is something I owe not only to my parents and teachers but also to various optometrists, opticians, writers, publishers, and providers of light, electrical and otherwise. Being able to enter into promises and contracts is also vital to the exercise of autonomy, to guiding the conduct of one's life, for reasons I explained earlier in this chapter. But promises and contracts are practices that require the cooperation of others—and not the only ones that do so, as I shall explain in the next two chapters. Without this cooperation, it would be virtually impossible to exercise one's autonomy, no matter how well developed it might have been.

When we conceive of autonomy as the ability or capacity to lead a self-governed life, then, we are led to the paradoxical conclusion that we cannot govern ourselves without the assistance of others. Instead of "the lone rights-bearer," the autonomous person turns out to be someone who *depends upon* others to help him or her achieve and maintain a substantial measure of *independence.* In this respect, autonomy entails *inter*dependence.[25] Another way to put this point is to say that autonomy requires community.

Autonomy requires community because the awareness of ourselves *as selves capable of choice* is something that others teach us, wittingly or not. This self-conception or self-identity develops together with those capacities, such as reason, language, judgment, and the ability to defer gratification, that make autonomy possible. Yet we must recognize that the individual does not develop these capacities through his or her efforts alone.

Whether we think of it as developed identity or developed capacities, in short, self-development is a social process.[26] Because there is no self-legislation without some degree of self-development, there is apparently no autonomy without community. It may cramp and constrain the individual in a number of ways, but the community is also a force that fosters autonomy by helping to constitute the self.

Conclusion

There is no reason, in sum, for the appeal to autonomy to take the excessively individualistic turn that Glendon and other communitarians deplore. Such a turn, as I have tried to show, would in fact betray autonomy as well as community. Nor must the appeal to human rights always be couched in the universal and abstract terms that seem so empty to Alasdair MacIntyre. On the contrary, we must often look to cultural traditions and community loyalties in order to see what a person is entitled to do or enjoy under the fundamental right of autonomy.

Yet there is no denying that the right of autonomy has its cosmopolitan aspect as well. It may not allow us to divorce ourselves from the conditions and traditions in which real people really live, but it also does not allow us to accept every tradition or way of life simply on its own terms. If we encounter a society in which slavery is taken to be part of the natural order, for example, we should not allow sensitivity to cultural differences to prevent us from protesting the violation of the human right of autonomy. Cultures and communities do deserve our respect—they must, if personal autonomy depends upon community—but their practices must not be exempt from our criticism. It would be wrong to expect every society to protect and promote the ability to lead a self-governed life in the same way or to the same extent. It would be a greater wrong to turn a blind eye to those that smother or crush the attempt to lead such a life.

CHAPTER 4

The Right of Autonomy and the Bonds of Community

Any appeal to human rights must in some way act as a solvent on more particular or parochial loyalties and attachments. Those who appeal to human rights, and particularly to the right of autonomy, should certainly expect to find themselves criticizing and opposing social and political practices, at home and abroad, that violate these rights. So the question must arise: Are we giving up too much when we accept a fundamental right of autonomy? Are we surrendering an equally fundamental belief in the importance of belonging, of membership in a particular group or community or society—a belief that seems essential to a *republican* liberalism?

In this chapter I approach this question by considering a widespread intuition or belief that grows out of the conviction that shared membership is of great value. This is the belief, as Henry Shue has put it, that "compatriots take priority."[1] My claim is that this belief, at least when it is suitably qualified, is consistent with the right of autonomy. If it is, then it follows that human rights and communal ties need not be hostile to each other.

Communities take a variety of forms, of course, and so do communal ties. As the connection with "patriot" suggests, compatriots are people who believe that they share a common home- or fatherland or think that they belong to the same country. What a person takes to be his or her homeland or country need not match the political boundaries of a state, however. Two people may therefore regard themselves as compatriots even when they are not, in the legal sense, fellow citizens. Conversely, two other people may be fellow citizens but not, in their own eyes, compatriots. To avoid these complications, I shall focus here on shared citizenship as a communal tie and ask whether our fellow citizens should indeed take priority.[2]

41

Human Rights and the Significance of Citizenship

To say that fellow citizens take priority is to say that we stand in a special relationship to those men, women, and children who share membership with us in a political community. This relationship is special because it requires us to attend to their needs and interests before we attend to the needs and interests of foreigners. We may have some responsibility to others, but our first responsibility is to the people of our own state, especially the poor, the hungry, and the homeless. In a sense, this is the political analogue of the belief that "charity begins at home," except that the requirements involved, duty and obligation, are more stringent than the requirements of charity.

This view—perhaps because compatriots and fellow citizens are often so closely related—seems to be both widely and firmly held. But should it be? Perhaps it is only a form of chauvinism or moral parochialism that cannot withstand critical scrutiny. Perhaps an examination of our political and moral relationships from a cosmopolitan point of view will reveal that there is no good reason to give priority to fellow citizens.

This seems to be an implication of the human rights perspective in moral and political philosophy. If people have rights by virtue of the fact that they are human beings, or persons, then one may wonder whether any moral significance attaches to the fact that almost all human beings are thought to be members (in one way or another) of political communities (of one sort or another). By definition, a human right must be universal and equal, a right that all persons possess in equal measure; it must also entail a correlative duty that falls equally on all persons who are in a position to discharge it. If there is a human right of autonomy, as I have argued, it follows that every person has an equal right of autonomy and a correlative duty to respect the autonomy of every other person without regard to race, nationality, or citizenship. A starving person would have a claim against those who are in a position to meet his or her needs, then, even if those who are subject to the claim are citizens of a distant country. Nor is there anything in the bare notion of a human right that would lead one to think that his or her first responsibility, as far as the protection and promotion of rights is concerned, is to his or her fellow citizens and those resident aliens who may also be considered members of his or her body politic. In this respect human rights seem to be neutral: the rights of fellow citizens are to count for neither more nor less than the rights of others. And in this respect neutrality seems to be hostile to the belief that fellow citizens take priority.

Does this mean that we must either abandon the human rights perspective or surrender the intuition that we stand in a special moral relationship to our fellow citizens? Not if our argument from rights is properly conceived. If it is so conceived, I shall argue, the appeal to rights actually requires us to recognize that a special relationship obtains between the members of a political community. This is not to say that no changes are necessary, however, for the intuition in question will have to be qualified by the addition of a ceteris paribus clause: that is, citizens take priority *when other things are equal.* Because other things are seldom equal in these matters, what follows may well be regarded as a qualified defense of moral parochialism. This defense begins with an examination of the arguments that might be mustered on behalf of this intuition, arguments from necessity, efficiency, side effects, and reciprocity.

The *argument from necessity* rests on what some regard as a psychological truth about human beings. Samuel Gorovitz puts the point neatly when he says that "one defense of what might be called our moral parochialism is the claim that it is a psychological necessity; that the scope and complexity of the world's population of individuals is such that a person would likely become dysfunctional in attempting to deal with more than a restricted subset—indeed, a very carefully restricted subset—of that population."[3] We might conclude, then, that fellow citizens take priority because human beings are too limited to cope with a wider range of responsibilities than that defined by national boundaries. Any attempt by individuals to undertake to provide aid to everyone who needs it would end by destroying the persons, or at least the personalities, of those who make the attempt. In short, we should give our fellow citizens priority for the simple reason that our psychological limitations will not allow us to do otherwise.

We need not dismiss this view of human psychology in order to reject the argument from necessity, for even if we grant that "a person would likely become dysfunctional in attempting to deal with more than a restricted subset" of the world's population, we cannot simply assume that this subset conveniently comprises one's fellow citizens. Many countries are now so large that it seems likely that anyone who seriously attempts to identify and sympathize with all of his or her fellow citizens will be rendered every bit as dysfunctional as the person who takes on the burdens of the entire world. There may be some truth to the claim that psychological necessity requires us to restrict our concerns to a subset of the world's population, but perhaps this subset consists of a province, city, town, or neighborhood—or, for that matter, a group, such as a religious sect or nationality, that spills across geographical and political boundaries. We will, in any case, need an independent argument demonstrating that the boundaries of the state also set the boundaries of this subset before psychological necessity can have a part to play in this context. I doubt that such an argument can be found.

Another reason for rejecting the argument from necessity is that it seems to assume that we must actively identify and sympathize with others before we can recognize that they may have a right to our aid. Although we may be more likely to go to the aid of those with whom we strongly identify and sympathize, I do not believe that we can or will acknowledge a duty to aid others *only* when we feel a bond of this sort. We know that there are men, women, and children in this world who are living, and dying, in desperate poverty. We also know that we can take some steps to help them. And if my account of the right of autonomy is correct, we know, too, that we have a responsibility to go to their aid. Yet all that this requires in the way of identity and sympathy is the simple recognition that these people have a right, as human beings, of autonomy. Certainly we may feel some anguish when we consider the plight of these unfortunate people, or some distress at the thought of what we may have to give up in order to help meet their needs. But this need not render us dysfunctional. In the end, the argument from psychological necessity seems to miss the point.

If necessity will not justify the belief that fellow citizens take priority, perhaps the *argument from efficiency* will. Here the claim is that we ought to aid the needy among our fellow citizens before we look to the needs of foreigners because this is simply the most efficient way to meet human needs. We can satisfy more needs at less cost when we begin at home, as it were. It costs less for Australians to supply food, shelter, and medical care to the needy within Australia than to supply the same goods to the people of Bangladesh or Ethiopia, so Australians will provide the most aid for their money if they first take care of their own citizens.

There is something to be said for efficiency, surely, and, other things being equal, we should prefer an efficient way of achieving a goal to an inefficient one.[4] That is not enough to lead us to conclude that fellow citizens should take priority, though, for in some cases it may be more efficient to aid foreigners than fellow citizens. For instance, if I know that there are people who need clothing in New York and others with similar needs in Nogales, Mexico, and if I have some clothing that is suitable, mere efficiency may require me to take or send the clothing the 180 miles from my home to the people in Mexico. Or if I am traveling in a foreign country and come across people who need aid that I am able to give, efficiency will hardly require me to find some U.S. citizens whose needs I might satisfy first. As these examples demonstrate, the argument from efficiency does not accord any special status to our fellow citizens, nor does it recognize that we stand in a special relationship of any sort to them. Propinquity seems to be all that matters.

But propinquity is not enough. If we assume that as a matter of fact we may more efficiently attend to the needs of fellow citizens than to those of people in some distant land, we must still go on to assess the extent and severity of the various needs. To take a very simple example, we might face a situation in which we can provide either a hearing aid for a fellow citizen with a partial loss of hearing or food for a month for a starving child in a foreign country. The argument from efficiency presumably requires us to balance the good we can do against the costs we incur while doing it, and in this case it seems that the citizen would not take priority. Important as it is, efficiency is not enough to establish the priority of compatriots.

Another consequentialist argument, the *argument from side effects,* may come closer to providing a justification for the belief that our first responsibility is to those who share membership with us in a political community. This is because the consequences taken into account here are broader than the argument from efficiency allows. The argument from efficiency requires us to identify our goal—providing aid to those who have a right to it, in this case—and then to take the course of action that will reach that goal at the least cost. The argument from side effects, however, asks us to consider what the indirect consequences of our actions will be. If these prove to be valuable, then we may have reason to follow a course of action that appears to be less efficient in terms of the original goal than another course of action that produces side effects of less value. In the present context, this might mean that we should grant priority to fellow citizens because doing so not only leads to the fulfillment of some vital needs but also promotes solidarity, fraternity, or the sense of community. In caring first for our own, we may help to strengthen the bonds of community by affording special recognition to our fellow citizens. Acting as if shared membership and mutual aid are important, in other words, may help to make them so. Anyone who wishes to foster the sense of community among citizens will thus have a reason to believe that fellow citizens should take priority.

The problem with this argument is that it provides a reason for according fellow citizens priority only under certain restricted conditions. To begin with, we must have grounds for believing that the policy of attending first to the needs of citizens really will strengthen the bonds of community or produce other valuable side effects. Assuming that the policy does this, we next have to consider whether these side effects might not be outweighed by the positive side effects of a different policy, such as providing aid to as many people as we can without regard to their nationality or citizenship. Someone who takes a cosmopolitan view might maintain, for instance, that a policy of the latter kind will promote feelings of universal fellowship and thus combat chauvinism, jingoism, and racism. Since the argument from side effects is a consequentialist argument, the case cannot be settled in favor of fellow citizens until all of the side effects are taken into account and balanced against one another, and I see no reason to expect that citizens will always win this test of consequences. If they do win, one may still object that these positive side effects simply do not deserve to be weighed in the balance with the fulfillment of human rights. Solidarity and community may be good things, in this view, but rights always take priority, and meeting the needs of starving people must take priority over goods to which we have no right, no matter how desirable these goods may be.

Both efficiency and side effects count, to be sure, and both may lead us to conclude that *in certain circumstances* we ought to grant priority to our fellow citizens. But both arguments are strictly contingent. They tell us that we ought to take care of fellow citizens first not because they have a right to this priority—not because they stand in a special relationship to us—but only because this policy sometimes may be the way to do the most good. For a stronger justification, we must look to the argument from reciprocity.

Stated simply, the *argument from reciprocity* holds that we should grant priority to fellow citizens because there is a special relationship, entailing special rights and obligations, among those who share membership in a political community. All human beings have general rights against and corresponding duties to all other human beings; this follows directly from the right of autonomy. But we also enjoy special rights and incur special obligations when we enter into special relationships, such as those created by a promise or by participation in a cooperative enterprise. The parties to these relationships are doubly bound, for they are related to each other both as human beings, with general rights and duties, and as participants in a special relationship, with special rights and obligations. Although they may be overridden by more compelling moral considerations, the rights and obligations that follow from these special relationships normally take priority over others. In the case at hand, this means that we can justify the intuition that fellow citizens take priority if we can show that citizens do indeed share this kind of special relationship.

A straightforward way to do this would be to demonstrate that the people of a state have somehow consented to enter into a special relationship, thereby gaining rights against and undertaking obligations to one another. But the telling criticisms of the different forms of consent theory seem to doom an effort of this sort.[5] A more promising alternative is to argue that the members of a body politic stand in a special relationship to one another because they are engaged in a cooperative enterprise. If a body politic is a cooperative enterprise—a just, mutually beneficial venture that produces one or more public goods through the cooperation of the people who participate in it—then it must fall under the principle of fair play.

According to this principle, anyone who takes part in and enjoys the benefits of a cooperative practice must contribute to the production of these benefits even when his or her contribution is not necessary to their production. To fail to contribute is to act unfairly, for the person who shares the benefits without sharing the burdens is taking advantage of those who cooperate. Thus the principle of fair play demands what H. L. A. Hart calls a "mutuality of restrictions": "[W]hen a number of persons conduct any joint enterprise according to rules and thus restrict their liberty, those who have submitted to these restrictions when required have a right to a similar submission from those who have benefited by their submission."[6]

To say that a political community is, or can be, a cooperative enterprise, and therefore subject to the principle of fair play, is to draw attention to two of the features it may exhibit. First, a political order typically provides benefits for those who belong to it, for it enables them to work together for common purposes and pursue in peace their personal interests. If nothing else, the rules established and enforced by the body politic—at least when the rule of law is in force—make it possible for citizens to coordinate their affairs and order their lives with a confidence that would be utterly inconceivable in a state of nature, whether it be Hobbes's brutish state of war or Rousseau's brutish state of peace. Moreover, these benefits are provided through the cooperation of the citizens, which is the second feature of the political community *qua* cooperative enterprise. Citizens' ability to form and act on expectations about the conduct of others—the expectations we rely on when driving, for example—may depend upon the rules of the political order, but these rules would be useless if the members of the body politic did not cooperate with one another by obeying them. Obedience need not be unanimous, of course, but the political order will cease to provide benefits, and perhaps cease to exist, when its rules are widely disobeyed.

When the political order does constitute a cooperative venture of this kind, everyone who joins in that venture incurs an obligation to the others to bear a fair share of the burdens of the enterprise in exchange for a fair share of the benefits. This means that every member of the enterprise is under an obligation, other things being equal, to obey the laws of the body politic. Because rights and obligations are correlative, those who take part in the enterprise have rights against as well as obligations to one another. If the law of Jones's state stipulates that drivers must drive on the right-hand side of the road, for example, then Jones has an obligation—and her fellow citizens a right to require her—to drive on that side. But Jones has this same right against her fellow citizens and they have the same obligation to her. In this way there is a reciprocity between the members of a cooperative enterprise. We have, in these circumstances, an obligation to obey the law because we owe it to the cooperating members of the body politic to do so. They have a right to our obedience because they, through their obedience, enable us to enjoy the benefits of the political order. They have a claim on us, in other words, as long as the body politic may reasonably be regarded as a cooperative enterprise.

The argument from reciprocity leads, then, to two important conclusions. First, because they have this claim on us, our fellow citizens should take priority. Their claims may be overridden in extraordinary circumstances, as I have indicated, but the bond that grows out of the special relationship of the cooperating members of a political order gives their rights and interests priority over others. Second, the appeal to human rights, when couched in terms of the right of autonomy, does not dissolve the bonds of community. In fact, it should strengthen these bonds insofar as it leads people to recognize that a special relationship obtains between them and the cooperating members of their political community. Those who recognize this relationship are also likely to agree with William Galston when he suggests that

> *every community represents a cooperative endeavor in pursuit of shared purposes.* Each term of this proposition offers a key ingredient of community. "Cooperation" presupposes mutual benefit, rather than the exploitation of some members by others through force or fraud; "endeavor" implies that the good must be created, rather than passively received or consumed; and "shared purposes" define a common good the community seeks to bring into being and to sustain, not merely private individual advantage.[7]

As this sketch of the argument from reciprocity indicates, reciprocity connects the right of autonomy to the bonds of community. Yet the sketch will have to be filled in and some serious objections overcome before the connection is truly established. One kind of objection concerns political obligation. The argument from reciprocity traces political obligation to the principle of fair play, as we have seen, but several philosophers have argued that this principle cannot provide an adequate account of political obligation. Some philosophers have even gone so far as to claim that there is no general obligation to obey the laws of any state, no matter how just the state may be. If either claim is correct, of course, the attempt to link autonomy to community by way of reciprocity must fail. In the next chapter, therefore, I shall try to defeat these claims by presenting a direct defense of the fair-play account of political obligation.

Another objection might be that the argument from reciprocity succeeds in connecting autonomy to community, but only in a formal, legalistic, and attenuated sense of "community." Fair play may reveal how a person may have an obligation to his or her fellow citizens in a polity governed by the rule of law, in other words, but this polity may not be a true community. To this communitarian objection I shall now turn.

Community

Michael Sandel provides the best example of the objection I am anticipating when he criticizes the "weak" conceptions of community in liberal theory.

According to Sandel, liberal views of community have been "weak" because they are either "instrumental"—"where individuals regard social arrangements as a necessary burden and cooperate only for the sake of pursuing their private ends"—or "sentimental"—as in John Rawls's vision of community as a situation in which "the participants have certain 'shared final ends' and regard the scheme of cooperation as a good in itself."[8] Against these "weak" conceptions, Sandel proposes what he takes to be a truer conception of community:

> On this strong view, to say that the members of a society are bound by a sense of community is not simply to say that a great many of them profess communitarian sentiments and pursue communitarian aims, but rather that they conceive their identity—the subject and not just the object of their feelings and aspirations—as defined to some extent by the community of which they are a part. For them, community describes not just what they *have* as fellow citizens, but also what they *are,* not a relationship they choose (as in a voluntary association) but an attachment they discover, not merely an attribute but a constituent of their identity. In contrast to the instrumental and sentimental conceptions of community, we might describe this strong view as the constitutive conception.[9]

Although Sandel makes no mention of obligation here, his "constitutive conception" of community implies that those who are "bound by a sense of community"—a community to which they "discover" an "attachment"—certainly do have an obligation of some sort to the community and its members. But the *sense* of obligation seems to be more important than the obligation itself. Someone who sees himself or herself as a member of a community in this strong sense will identify so closely with it that questions of obligation—questions of *political* obligation, if we can ever think of a state as a community—are unlikely to arise. That one has an obligation to follow the customs, norms, or laws is, in these circumstances, something that goes without saying. Indeed, if the community largely constitutes my identity, then asking whether I have an obligation to obey its rules is as pointless as asking whether I have an obligation to obey myself.

Part of the reason that considerations of obligation are otiose in a strong community is that the members of the community are unlikely to regard themselves as being burdened when they act for the common good. In an instrumental conception of community, such as the one the principle of fair play seems to invoke, the members of the cooperative endeavor bear the burdens of cooperation in order to receive its benefits. In a strong community, by contrast, the members identify so thoroughly with the community that they hardly think in terms of personal gains or losses, benefits or burdens. From the standpoint of constitutive community, in fact, it seems reasonable to suppose that what at first glance appear as "my" assets are more properly described as common assets in some sense; since others made me, and in various ways continue to make me, the person I am, it seems appropriate to regard them, in so far as I can identify them, as participants in "my" achievements and common beneficiaries of the rewards they bring. Where this sense of participation in the achievements and endeavors of (certain) others engages the reflective self-understandings of the participants, we may come to regard ourselves . . . less as individuated subjects with certain things in common, and more as members of a wider (but still determinate) subjectivity, less as "others" and more as participants in a common identity, be it a family or community or class or people or nation.

One consequence of an enlarged self-understanding such as this is that when "my" assets or life prospects are enlisted in the service of a common endeavor, I am likely to experience this less as a case of being used for others' ends and more as a way of contributing to the purposes of a community I regard as my own.[10]

This vision of a constitutive community that simultaneously promotes and rests upon the "enlarged self-understanding" of its members is appealing in some ways but not in all. Its appeal resides mainly, I think, in two features. One is that individual identity does in some sense depend upon community. No one is an entirely self-created person, and the constitutive conception of community recognizes and builds upon our social or communal nature. The second source of its appeal is the bond the constitutive community forges between the purposes of the individual and those of the community. Where these are closely linked, there is little need for coercion. If the members of a cooperative venture see their relationship as merely instrumental, each of them will have a strong incentive to try to receive the benefits of the venture without bearing its burdens—to be a free rider. To prevent this from happening and to ensure that the venture succeeds in producing a public good, the threat of coercion is usually invoked—a point to which I shall return in later chapters. If the members of the venture see their relationship from the perspective of enlarged self-understanding, however, they will cooperate not only freely but also happily. The threat of coercion will not be necessary because they will see the public good simply as *the* good, with no consideration of how they might benefit personally by doing or giving less than the community expects of them.

In these respects, Sandel's strong sense of community is genuinely attractive. But that is not to say that it is unequivocally good or that it rules out the kind of community involved in the argument from reciprocity. I want to defend the connection between autonomy, reciprocity, and community, therefore, by establishing three points: (1) that we should not want to foster too strong a sense of community; (2) that communitarian appeals to the "obligation to belong" need the support that the argument from reciprocity provides; and (3) that the sense of community involved in reciprocity and fair play need not be merely or strictly instrumental.

How Strong Should Community Be?

Perhaps the best way to see the dangers as well as the attractions of San-del's strong community is to return to the virtuous Troglodytes of Mon-tesquieu's *Persian Letters* for a well-known, if fictitious, example of a con-stitutive community.[11] As Montesquieu's character Usbek describes them, every Troglodyte spontaneously did what he or she took to be best for others and for the community as a whole. No one asked whether he or she had an obligation to the community. No one even thought to raise such a question, for the Troglodytes were practically unable to distinguish per-sonal from public good. They were, as a result, a simple, virtuous, and flourishing people, until the desire for ease and riches led them to forsake self-rule, which they had come to perceive as burdensome, and to impose the responsibility for governing the community on a wise and reluctant old Troglodyte.

If the example of the Troglodytes is truly apposite, then it is easy to see the attractions of the constitutive conception of community. The Troglo-dytes lived, worked, and prospered together with no need for punishment or threats of coercion. But is this enough to recommend their way of life, or the constitutive conception of community, to us? The Troglodytes lived very simply, with little variety and little room for independent or critical thinking. Such a life may well foster a secure sense of self—of where and what and even who one is—but at what price? The person whose identity is so closely bound to the community that he or she is virtually incapable of questioning or challenging the community's norms, as seems to be the case with the Troglodytes, is someone whose rational faculties are stunted. Such a person may be happy—or at least satisfied, as John Stuart Mill argued—but he or she is stunted nonetheless by the inability to realize a capacity for rational thought and self-reflection, for this capacity cannot be fully employed unless a person is able to see himself or herself as somehow apart or separate from the community.

To be fair to Sandel, this criticism may link the constitutive conception of community too closely to Montesquieu's untutored and unreflective Troglodytes. Sandel probably prefers a more Aristotelian or Hegelian form of community than Montesquieu portrays. Yet he cannot justify this pref-erence simply by appealing to the constitutive conception of community. An Aristotelian community would constitute the identity of its members in one way, the Troglodyte community in another. Both would be consti-tutive communities, however, and judged by that standard one is as desir-able as the other. Even communities that have become notorious for smugness, intolerance, and superstition—Salem, Massachusetts, in Puritan New England, for example—seem to be models of consitutive community.[12]

A possible response to this complaint is in the appeal to membership that Sandel makes in the introduction to *Liberalism and Its Critics*. There he says that "the civil rights movement of the 1960s might be justified by liberals in the name of human dignity and respect for persons, and by communitarians in the name of recognizing the full membership of fellow citizens wrongly excluded from the common life of the nation."[13] In this case, Sandel says, communitarians and liberals agree on the policy to be followed, but the liberal conception of "unencumbered selves" misses the dimension of membership that communitarianism, with its conception of "situated" selves, captures. He is right about this dimension of membership, I think, as African Americans' complaints of being defined as "second-class citizens" suggested at the time. But there is another dimension of membership that does not support his position.

Membership is usually defined not only *inclusively*—that is, in terms of who the members are—but also *exclusively,* by ruling some people out. Thus one may appeal to membership in an effort to exclude as well as to include people. A self can be so situated, so imbued with a sense of membership in a community, that he or she will fail to acknowledge the claims to membership made by those he or she considers to be outsiders. Slavery and segregation laws encouraged people to think in this way in the United States, just as apartheid has done in South Africa. Thinking in terms of membership is thinking in terms of "we" and "they," in other words, and there is nothing inherent in the idea of membership that leads one to believe that "we" ought to be expanded to include "they."

For Sandel's example to work as he wants it to, in fact, the norms of the community must be open to either internal or external criticism or both. The stronger the sense of community, however, the less likely it is that anyone within it will challenge its norms. If the way of thinking that justified racial segregation had been even more pervasive, so that blacks and whites alike firmly and unanimously believed that their respective places in society were naturally fixed by race, then complaints about second-class citizenship would not have arisen and the civil rights movement would never have begun. A person must be able to rise above his or her situation in society, to gain a critical distance from community norms, before it is even possible to appeal to membership as Sandel does in his example. Without this distance, it would be impossible to see that "fellow citizens [were] wrongly excluded from the common life of the nation." In the case of the civil rights movement of the 1960s, liberal concern for human dignity and respect for persons—in concert with Christian notions of human equality and brotherhood—provided much of this critical distance.[14]

This seems to leave Sandel on the horns of a dilemma. If a community is tightly knit, as it presumably must be to satisfy the constitutive conception, its standards and practices will likely admit little or no challenge. This will leave little room for freedom, or for self-development in any rich sense of the term. The situated self may thus be as cramped and crippled as the Chinese lady's foot to which Mill referred in *On Liberty*. But if the community is open enough to allow or even encourage free and critical thinking, its standards and practices will be constantly challenged and possibly undermined. The unencumbered self may thus cut itself off from its moorings in community.

Is there an escape between the horns of this dilemma? Is there a way to encourage free and critical thinking—the kind that autonomy requires—within a community that fosters devotion to the common good? Such an escape may be possible by way of "holist individualism"—a view that Charles Taylor associates with thinkers as diverse as Wilhelm von Humboldt, Machiavelli, Montesquieu, and Alexis de Tocqueville.[15] The means of escape are not yet complete, however, for Taylor lacks an adequate account of political obligation.

Community and Obligation

Taylor's sympathies with communitarianism are evident, but his unwillingness to abandon the liberal concern for liberty, autonomy, and rights is equally clear. His strategy, it seems, is to show liberals how the realization of their hopes for individual rights and liberties fundamentally depend on certain social and cultural conditions. Moreover, he endorses these liberal aspirations, at least when they are understood as he thinks they should be. In "Atomism," for instance, Taylor rejects what he calls "the primacy of rights," but he does so not to dismiss or discount their importance. Instead, his purpose is to show that a commitment to the value of individual rights entails "an obligation to belong. This will be as fundamental as the assertion of rights, because it will be inseparable from it. So that it would be incoherent to try to assert the rights, while denying the obligation or giving it the status of optional extra which we may or may not contract."[16] Furthermore, in "Atomism" and in "What's Wrong with Negative Liberty," he makes the same move with regard to freedom. His argument is

> based on the notion, first, that developed freedom requires a certain understanding of self, one in which the aspirations to autonomy and self-development become conceivable; and second, that this self-understanding is not something we can sustain on our own, but that our identity is always partly defined in conversation with others or through the common understanding which underlies the practices of our society.[17]

For Taylor, then, the liberal emphasis on rights and liberty is not so much mistaken as misplaced. Liberals are right to value individual rights and liberty, but they need to see that these rights and liberties cannot be grounded in atomism and the "utterly facile moral psychology of traditional empiricism, according to which human agents possess the full capacity of choice as a given rather than as a potential which has to be developed."[18] On the contrary, the value of rights, liberty, and autonomy can only be grounded in and sustained by a community or culture that enables the individual to develop his or her capacity of choice.

If this is communitarianism, then it is a communitarianism of a decidedly liberal cast. Whatever we call it, the important point is that Taylor's "holist individualist" approach promises an escape from the dilemma that seems to confront Sandel. For my purposes here, moreover, Taylor's attempt to reconcile community and liberty is especially significant for what it implies for political obligation. Taylor does not speak directly to the question of whether there is an obligation to obey the laws of one's community, but he does invoke the language of obligation more often and more explicitly than Sandel, Alasdair MacIntyre, and other communitarians. Thus he speaks, as we have seen, of "an obligation to belong" that is "inseparable" from the assertion of rights. "I am arguing," he says,

> that the free individual of the West is only what he is by virtue of the whole society and civilization which brought him to be and which nourishes him; that our families can only form us up to this capacity and these aspirations because they are set in this civilization; and that a family alone outside of this context—the real old patriarchal family—was a quite different animal which never tended these horizons. And I want to claim finally that all this creates *a significant obligation to belong* for whoever would affirm the value of this freedom.[19]

Taylor's belief in this "obligation to belong" is, then, quite clear; the source and nature of this obligation, however, are not. If we have an obligation to belong, what does this obligation require us to do? To whom do we owe this obligation? How can we repay them? The furthest Taylor goes toward answering questions of this sort is in "The Nature and Scope of Distributive Justice," in which he says, "To the extent that we think of ourselves as already formed by the past development of these institutions and practices [that protect and sustain the sense of liberty], our obligation to maintain them springs from a principle of justice between generations, that the good we have received we should pass on."[20] This is helpful, but it hardly counts as a satisfactory answer to the questions raised above. If our obligation is to those who formed the institutions and practices that have formed us, how are we to identify them? Is this an obligation to the members of our community or more broadly an obligation to those who have formed our culture or civilization or tradition? If our obligation is to maintain these institutions and practices, how can it be an obligation to future generations? How do we repay those who have gone before us by passing on the good we have received to those who follow?

Here is where the principle of fair play can come to the aid of those who want to reconcile rights and liberties, on the one hand, with membership and community, on the other. Fair play offers a theory of political obligation that respects the rights and interests of individuals, but it does so by demonstrating how individuals benefit from and depend upon one another when they engage in cooperative practices. This is an aspect of fair play that communitarians should be glad to accept, for it requires us to think of ourselves to some extent as members of communities of some sort. They should also be happy to note that the obligations following from the principle of fair play are owed not to the state or government or some other impersonal entity but to the cooperating members of a common endeavor. The principle, in short, can provide the account of obligation that appeals to community and belonging have lacked.

Still, one might object that the principle of fair play is too narrow to do all of the work required to sustain Taylor's "obligation to belong." That is probably true. Fair play can certainly account for the connection Taylor draws between the assertion of rights and the obligation to belong, but it cannot account for the "significant obligation to belong" that the "free individual of the West" apparently owes to "the whole society and civilization which brought him to be and nourishes him." Perhaps one can make a case for an obligation to a society or culture, but I doubt that it will rest on the principle of fair play.

In this context, however, acknowledging the limits of fair play is a way of indicating its strength. I say this for three reasons. The first is that we should beware of claiming that every person who is formed or constituted to a signficant extent by a community, culture, or civilization truly has an obligation to belong to it. Some people may be quite unhappy with their formation; others may think themselves quite happy yet seem to us to have been deformed—thwarted, stunted, oppressed, and abused. Did the *helot* in Sparta, the slave in the American South, and the concubine in Persia, to take some of the most dramatic examples, have an obligation to belong to the communities or cultures in which they found themselves? Could they best repay this obligation by passing their way of life on to others? The answer in both cases is no because the communities or cultures in question were fundamentally unjust. Because they were unjust, they could not have satisfied the requirements of fair play. To say that fair play cannot justify an obligation to belong in such cases, therefore, is to speak on behalf of this principle.

This defense of the argument from fairness seems to defeat the objection of anyone who wants to attach the obligation to belong to any kind of constitutive community. To be fair to Taylor, though, we must note that he is more selective. As he sees it, the obligation to belong apparently attaches only to those whose societies and civilizations have encouraged them to assert their rights and value their liberty. But this provides a second reason for acknowledging the strength of the principle of fair play. If fair play cannot account for the obligation Taylor perceives here, it is because it occupies a special place within a broader theory that can. Fair play applies only in cases of cooperative endeavors, and it is difficult at best to think of cultures and civilizations as endeavors or practices of this sort. But fair play provides an explanation for *special* rights and obligations within a broader concern for the right of autonomy. Thus we can capture Taylor's belief in an obligation to pass on to others the institutions and practices that promote and sustain liberty by invoking autonomy and fair play. The right of autonomy is a right to the protection and promotion of the ability to lead a self-governed life, so we must have a duty to help others develop and exercise that ability, and when we find ourselves in a special relationship with others as members of a cooperative endeavor, engaged in a practice that promotes and sustains liberty, we are doubly bound to respect their rights and interests. Fair play thus provides an account of political obligation—the form of obligation appropriate to the *political* community—within a broader theory that conforms to and helps to clarify Taylor's appeal to the obligation to belong.

Of course, one could try to avoid the problem of invoking an obligation to belong to, and presumably to support, an undesirable community simply by defining community, or true community, in such a way as to rule out the undesirable types. In this case, however, one would have to find a plausible basis for this definition. This will not be easy to do for "community"—a word, as one commentator has observed, with "a high level of use but low level of content."[21] In any case, the definition of community will not rest strictly on the degree to which putative communities constitute the identities of their members, for identity may be constituted in desirable or undesirable ways. We could follow Karl Marx and Friedrich Engels here and distinguish true from illusory communities by looking to see whether so-called communities provide their members with "the means of cultivating [their] gifts in all directions."[22] Setting aside other problems—Do we really want to cultivate *all* gifts in *all* directions?—this definition seems to lead to the conclusion that no *true* community has ever existed. There may be something to be said for that conclusion, but it can scarcely be said by someone who hopes to show that people nowadays have an obligation of some sort to their communities. A more attractive alternative is Galston's suggestion that *"every community represents a cooperative endeavor in pursuit of shared purposes."* But that effectively defines community as a cooperative enterprise, and community so defined would then be subject to the principle of fair play.

In the absence of a better way of distinguishing true from illusory communities, we must conclude either that it is a mistake to look for an obligation that always binds people to the communities in which they find themselves or that the obligation obtains only because all true communities are cooperative endeavors subject to fair play. Either way, we have a third reason for regarding the limits fair play sets on community as a strength, not a weakness. And that is all the more reason to believe that fairness or reciprocity supplies the basis for a political obligation that joins the right of autonomy to the bonds of community.

Reciprocity and the Constitution of Community

There is a final objection to consider, however. Here the complaint is that considerations of fair play or reciprocity rest on an instrumental and therefore unsatisfactory conception of community. Sandel charges, as we have seen, that liberal conceptions of community are either instrumental—where "individuals regard social arrangements as a necessary burden and cooperate only for the sake of pursuing their private ends"—or "sentimental"—where "the participants have certain 'shared final ends' and regard the scheme of cooperation as a good in itself." In either case, the conception of community is weak, according to Sandel, because it fails to recognize that "community describes not just what [people] *have* as fellow citizens, but also what they *are,* not a relationship they choose . . . but an attachment they discover, not merely an attribute but a constituent of their identity." The principle of fair play, with its emphasis on the benefits and burdens of participating in a cooperative enterprise, invokes an instrumental conception of community, or, perhaps in cases in which the participants are aware that the public good they are producing is a "shared final end," a sentimental conception. In either case, it must be unsatisfactory, for it is not a strong, or constitutive, conception of community.

One response to this objection is to accept the charge but to deny that the constitutive conception of community is superior to the instrumental or sentimental conceptions. I have some sympathy with this position, of course, as my earlier comments on the dangers of too strong a conception of community attest. Yet I have also noted some of the attractions of the constitutive sense of community. So I think that a better response to this third objection is to point out that Sandel's way of classifying conceptions of community is misleadingly tidy.

Sandel's three categories are too tidy because they suggest that we cannot or should not conceive of community in both instrumental and constitutive terms. Yet there is ample reason to believe that we do and should think of community in both ways. People who are born and raised in a small town may well see themselves as a part of that community, but that

need not prevent them from asking whether the community is treating
them fairly or providing them with opportunities they want to pursue.
When we conceive of community, we are not forced to choose between a
thoroughly instrumental vision within which everyone's sole concern is
"What's in it for me?" and a thoroughly constitutive vision within which
everyone's constant preoccupation is "doing what's best for the group."
There is a middle ground between these two visions, and it is likely to
provide a more solid foundation for a healthy community than either a
strictly instrumental or a strictly constitutive conception.

Less tidy but more helpful than Sandel's three categories is Michael Taylor's definition of community in *Community, Anarchy, and Liberty*. Like
autonomy, community, as Taylor conceives it, is a matter of degree. That
is, something can be more or less of a community, or approach or fall away
from the ideal of a community, depending on the degree to which it manifests the "three attributes or characteristics possessed in *some* degree by *all*
communities": "shared values and beliefs, direct and many-sided relations,
and the practice of reciprocity."[23] Together, these characteristics, but especially the second, serve to eliminate most of the candidates for the title of
community *in the strict sense of the word*, according to Taylor. The requirement that communities exhibit "direct and many-sided relations"
among their members disqualifies any association in which these relations
are mediated by "representatives, leaders, bureaucrats, institutions such as
those of the state, or by codes, abstractions and reifications"—or in which
they are "specialized, narrowly confined to one area" of life, as they are in
the "academic community."[24] For a collection of people to be more rather
than less of a community, it "must be relatively small and stable. In a large
and changing mass of people, few relations between people can be direct
or many-sided, and reciprocity cannot flourish on a wide scale, since its
continuation for any length of time requires *some* actual reciprocation,
which in turn requires stable relations with known individuals."[25]

Taylor's observations include some important points to which I will return in later chapters. For the present, their significance is twofold. First,
Taylor's conception of community embraces both instrumental and constitutive elements: "shared values and beliefs, direct and many-sided relations,
and the practice of reciprocity." Second, it helps to explain why the sense
of belonging may be so strong in some cases—perhaps in small and stable
communities such as *kibbutzim* or monasteries—that the members think
of reciprocity less as a matter of benefits, burdens, and fair treatment than
as a matter of contributing what they can to the community and receiving
what they need from it.[26] Where the sense of belonging is less powerful,
the community will be weaker, as a community, and the members will
look more closely to see who is receiving the benefits and who is bearing
the burdens out of fear of being double-crossed or being played for the

sucker. Either way, in the strong as well as the weak community, reciprocity plays an essential role in constituting the community.

There is no need to worry, then, that the argument from reciprocity succeeds in connecting autonomy to community only in a formal, legalistic, and weak sense of "community." It does apply to weak communities of this sort, including bodies such as the modern state that perhaps should not be considered communities at all. That is, reciprocity and fair play apply to all cooperative ventures, even those that are not characterized by "direct and many-sided relations" among their members. But they apply as well to communities in the strictest or strongest sense of the word. It is possible, therefore, to connect the right of autonomy to the bonds of community, for both are involved in considerations of reciprocity and fairness. With that established, we may now return to the intuition with which this chapter began.

A Qualified Defense of Moral Parochialism

Fellow citizens take priority, I have argued, because we owe it to them as a matter of reciprocity. Everyone, citizen or not, has a claim to our respect and concern—a claim founded on the right of autonomy—but those who join with us in cooperative enterprises have a claim to special recognition. Their cooperation enables us to enjoy the benefits of the enterprise, and fairness demands that we reciprocate. When the body politic may reasonably be regarded as a cooperative practice, then, we must accord our fellow citizens a special status, a priority over those who stand outside the special relationship constituted by the political enterprise.

In this way the argument from reciprocity supports the intuition that compatriots—or fellow citizens, to be precise—should take priority. As I have already noted, though, this intuition is acceptable only with the addition of a ceteris paribus clause. This is not a trivial modification, for the intuition in question holds only with three significant qualifications. The first is that the argument from reciprocity applies not only to the political order but also to any cooperative enterprise. This being the case, we may encounter situations in which members of two (or more) cooperative practices have claims against us, and it is hardly obvious that the claim of the fellow citizen must take priority over the claims of a foreign member of one's church, for instance, or of one's profession or political movement.[27]

The second qualification may be even more serious. If the belief that fellow citizens take priority rests on the extent to which a political community may reasonably be regarded as a cooperative enterprise, then there are likely to be some ostensible political communities that fall quite short of the mark. Where violence and terror take the place of the rule of law, we may well conclude that the "members" of a particular "body politic" have no special rights against or obligations to one another *qua* members. There may be good reasons in this situation for obeying the commands of those in power, but reciprocity or fair play will not be among them. Even where the rule of law seems to prevail, furthermore, the distribution of resources and opportunities among the members of a political community may indicate that their relationships are marked not by reciprocity but by exploitation. When access to property or wealth or positions of political power is effectively denied to some members, those without access will have little choice but to labor for the benefit of those who dominate their lives— hardly the hallmark of a cooperative enterprise that gives rise to special rights and obligations among its participants. There is a critical edge to the argument from reciprocity, then, an edge that suggests that fellow citizens in many cases simply have no moral claim to priority.

Finally, we must also qualify the intuition by noting that the priority we give to the rights of those who share citizenship with us is not absolute. Granting the priority of their claims does not entail that we must always honor their claims rather than those of someone who is not bound to us in a special relationship of one kind or another. We should grant fellow citizens priority in the sense that we look first to their claims—to what we can do to protect and promote their autonomy. But there may nevertheless be excellent reasons to decide to neglect a citizen's claim to our aid if we must do so in order to meet a foreigner's. Here, once more, the chief consideration is the severity or extent of the deprivation in question. If we face a hard choice between devoting resources to the attempt to promote the autonomy of some of our fellow citizens by providing them, say, with opportunities for physical therapy or to the attempt to promote autonomy by supplying food to starving people in a distant land, then we probably ought to decide in favor of the starving strangers.

For these three reasons, we must conclude that fellow citizens take priority, but only when other things are equal. Still, this modification leaves the core of the intuition intact. This is an important conclusion because it means that the adoption of a human-rights perspective does not force one to hold that the bonds of political community count for little or nothing. It also indicates how a concern for rights may be interwoven with a concern for civic responsibility. Indeed, if the arguments marshaled in this qualified defense of moral parochialism are correct, our task is to cultivate the place of community within a concern for human rights—and thus to formulate a *republican* liberalism. To determine whether these arguments are correct, we must now look to the objections raised to the fair-play account of political obligation.

CHAPTER 5

Political Obligation

Republicanism and liberalism share a fundamental commitment to the rule of law. This shared commitment may complicate the lives of those who want to provide a clear distinction between the two theories, but it makes matters easier for anyone who wants to show that republicanism and liberalism are compatible with each other. For the republican, the rule of law is typically regarded as an essential means of securing people from dependence on the arbitrary will of others. "A government of laws, not of men," was the slogan because dependence on the law was thought to be a form of independence—especially when one could take part in law-making. For the liberal, the rule of law is typically regarded as an essential means of giving people a secure set of expectations so that they may pursue their private projects. That is why John Locke's cure for the "inconveniencies" of the state of nature was a known and settled authority to make, enforce, and interpret laws.

For the republican liberal, then, the importance of the rule of law is a settled matter. Any well-ordered republican-liberal society will be one in which the rule of law is in force and the citizens will acknowledge a general obligation to obey the law. The republican side of republican liberalism will stress that mere obedience is not always enough to make one a good citizen, but obedience is, ceteris paribus, a requirement of citizenship. From the liberal side, however, questions about the nature and foundation of this obligation—and about the relationship between the rule of law and personal autonomy—are sure to arise. How can the individual be autonomous when he or she is subject to laws that may be in conflict with his or her beliefs, convictions, and desires? Can an autonomous person undertake a general obligation to obey the laws of a polity without thereby surrendering his or her autonomy? What is the source of this obligation?

In recent years, in fact, several political philosophers have concluded that there is no hope of providing a satisfactory account of political obligation. According to these philosophers, the typical citizen of any political society—even the best, the most just of such societies—has no general or prima facie obligation to obey its laws. The typical citizen may have good reasons, moral as well as prudential, for obeying the laws, and perhaps an obligation to obey this or that particular law, but no *general* obligation to obey the law of the land. The search for a satisfactory account of political obligation is simply bound to be fruitless.[1]

The arguments of these philosophers fall into two broad categories. Arguments of the first sort maintain that it is impossible in principle to provide a satisfactory account of a general obligation to obey the law. This is the position Robert Paul Wolff takes in his *In Defense of Anarchism*. Arguments of the second sort are more modest in their aims but nearly as devastating in their conclusions. In this case the aim is not to show that a satisfactory defense of political obligation is impossible but that such a defense, despite the efforts of some of the best minds in the history of philosophy, has yet to appear. Those who take this approach usually proceed by raising objections to the various attempts to justify political obligation, such as those based on consent or fair play. All of these attempts have failed, according to this second kind of argument, so we must conclude that only those relatively few people who have explicitly committed themselves to obey the law, perhaps by swearing allegiance as part of an oath of citizenship, have anything like a general obligation to obey the laws under which they live.

This is an unsettling conclusion. It is also wrong, as is Wolff's more sweeping conclusion about the impossibility of a satisfactory account of political obligation. It *is* possible to provide a satisfactory account of a general obligation to obey the law, and the foundation of that account is the principle of fair play—or so I hope to demonstrate in this chapter. Beginning with the first category, I will attempt to show that Wolff's arguments fail. In the second part of the chapter, I examine and respond to arguments of the second sort, concentrating on three apparently devastating criticisms of the principle of fair play. I conclude with some remarks about what we may learn from these attacks on the belief in a general obligation to obey the law, for, wrong as I think they are, these attacks still have something important to teach us about the relationships between citizens and laws in today's megalopolitan societies.

Authority, Autonomy, and Political Obligation

Is it possible to provide a satisfactory account of a general obligation to obey the laws? Not according to Wolff, who argues that any such obligation must violate the "primary obligation" of autonomy, "the refusal to be ruled."[2] To be precise, autonomy is the refusal to be ruled by anyone other than oneself: "[I]t is a submission to laws which one has made for oneself"

(p. 14). As Wolff defines it, then, autonomy is a combination of freedom and responsibility. A person can be autonomous because he or she has the capacity for choice, for freedom; but this carries with it the responsibility of exercising that capacity—the responsibility to act autonomously. Whenever someone fails to exercise this capacity, therefore, he or she fails to meet this "primary obligation" of autonomy.

This primary obligation dooms any attempt to develop a theory of political obligation, Wolff argues, except in the highly unlikely case of a unanimous direct democracy, in which case everyone subject to the law agrees that every law is indeed a binding law. Under any other form of government, autonomy and authority are simply incompatible. As Wolff defines it, authority is "the right to command, and correlatively, the right to be obeyed" (p. 4). Someone who has authority over us thus has the right to give us orders, while we have the correlative obligation to obey. But if we acknowledge such an obligation, we allow someone else to rule our lives, which is to violate our fundamental obligation to act autonomously. To fulfill this fundamental obligation of autonomy, then, we must refuse to acknowledge any obligation to obey the orders of anyone who claims to have authority over us.

Wolff qualifies this argument in two ways. He says, first, that an autonomous person need not disobey the "orders" of someone who is supposedly in authority. If we have good reasons for doing what the person who claims to have authority tells us to do—if we have independent reasons, that is, reasons that make no appeal to authority—then we should do what we are ordered to do. As autonomous persons, we may do *as* we are ordered so long as we do not do it *because* we are ordered. Autonomous persons will probably obey a police officer directing traffic at a crowded intersection, for instance, but they will do so because they believe their obedience will help to make the best of a bad situation, not because they believe that the police officer has authority over them.

Wolff's second qualification is that it is sometimes reasonable to forfeit one's autonomy. This may happen, to use his example, when someone in a physician's care simply follows "doctor's orders," for in this case the patient suspends his or her judgment and accepts the authority of the physician. To do this is to forfeit one's autonomy, at least to a limited extent, according to Wolff (p. 15). What makes it reasonable, apparently, is the presence of two special conditions: first, that the patient surrenders autonomy in only a limited area of his or her life, and second, that the surrender is to someone with technical expertise the patient lacks.

Whether Wolff believes that other considerations may sometimes make it reasonable to forfeit one's autonomy is not clear. What is clear is that he believes that neither of these two special conditions applies to our encounters with those who claim to hold political authority. We may often have good reasons to obey their commands, but on Wolff's account we never have an *obligation* to obey. "Insofar as a man fulfills his obligation to make himself the author of his decisions," as Wolff puts it, "he will resist the state's claim to have authority over him. That is to say, he will deny that he has a duty to obey the laws of the state *simply because they are the laws.* In that sense, it would seem that anarchism is the only political doctrine consistent with the virtue of autonomy" (p. 18; emphasis in original).

If Wolff is right, the search for a satisfactory theory of political obligation is futile, for there never can be a general obligation to obey the law in any political society that is not a unanimous direct democracy. But is Wolff right? There are two reasons, both of which relate to his understanding and use of autonomy, to believe that he is not.

Forfeiting Autonomy

The first reason is that Wolff is wrong when he insists that authority and autonomy are incompatible. He is wrong whether the authority in question is someone who is *in* authority or someone who is *an* authority, and his mistake is due largely to his failure to appreciate the ways in which law and authority can open options to us.[3] According to Wolff, the autonomous person cannot even take "because it's the law" as a reason to be considered when deciding how to act. But that, I hope to show, is an implausible conception of autonomy.

As Wolff sees it, we forfeit our autonomy, at least to a degree and perhaps with good reason, when we follow the orders of a physician or, by analogy, a lawyer, a financial counselor, a mechanic, or anyone who is *an* authority in an area of importance to us. It may well be reasonable to entrust our interests to those who speak with authority in these matters, as Wolff says, but it is hardly reasonable to regard this as a forfeiture of autonomy. On the contrary, someone who makes it a rule to seek and follow the advice of those who are experts in areas in which he or she is largely ignorant is exercising autonomy, not forfeiting it. Or would I be acting autonomously, as Wolff's argument implies, if I were to spend most of my time in medical libraries trying to diagnose and discover how to treat my ailments? Such an attempt to maintain absolute control over my life would probably leave me with no life worth controlling. This would certainly be unreasonable, as Wolff implies, but beyond that it could entail a far greater loss of autonomy than the forfeiture that supposedly results when we follow the doctor's orders. If autonomy is self-rule that aims at the realization rather than the constriction of the self, as I argued in Chapter 3, then the attempt to take complete control of my physical well-being would lead, through the neglect of my other interests, to the constriction of my self and the loss of autonomy. It is possible, to be sure, for one to decide that the best use of one's time and resources is to devote them to research that will promote one's physical well-being. If a person makes it a rule to live this way, then he or she is acting autonomously, if not wisely. But the person who makes it a rule to seek and follow the advice of experts in some areas of life in order to pursue a wide range of interests and realize more aspects of his or her self is acting autonomously as well.

This is to say that Wolff begins by misconstruing autonomy, then proceeds to base his argument against political authority and political obligation on this misconstruction. The autonomous person may comply with the laws, Wolff says, but he "will deny that he has a duty to obey the laws of the state *simply because they are the laws.*" Just as we forfeit our autonomy when we obey the man or woman who is *an* authority, so we forfeit our autonomy when we obey the men and women who issue orders simply because we believe them to be *in* authority over us.

Wolff's position here is attractive insofar as it draws on the notion that blind obedience—obeying the law *simply because it is the law*—is incompatible with autonomy. But acknowledging authority is not the same as blind obedience. To acknowledge that someone or something has authority over us is not to acknowledge an absolute or indefeasible obligation to do whatever the authority would have us do. We may typically believe that we have an obligation to obey those in authority, other things being equal, so there may be a presumption in favor of obedience. But it remains our responsibility to decide whether other things are truly equal or whether there are special circumstances that free us—or perhaps even require us—to disobey. This being so, it is certainly possible for someone to maintain that (1) the law has authority over him or her, so (2) he or she has an obligation to obey it, but (3) overriding considerations lead him or her to disobey. Such a person has acknowledged authority but has not surrendered his or her autonomy.

But what if this person decides to obey? What if he or she decides that the law, wrong as it is in the case at hand, is still the law and therefore ought to be obeyed? Has this person then forfeited his or her autonomy? Not necessarily. The person's obedience might well follow from the conviction that law and authority play positive roles in our lives. Without law and authority to enable us to coordinate our affairs and develop reasonable expectations about the actions of others, even so ordinary an activity as taking the bus to work would become virtually impossible. Yet law could not play this positive part in our lives if there were no presumption that it ought to be obeyed. Someone who recognizes the value of law might make it a rule, then, to obey the law *simply because it is the law,* unless there are special or extenuating circumstances that require disobedience. Such a person acts autonomously *by* acknowledging authority. Even in the case that looks most favorable to Wolff's position, then, autonomy and authority are not incompatible. Wolff's argument against the possibility of a general obligation to obey the law must therefore collapse.

Autonomy as a Capacity

This collapse becomes even clearer when we consider the second reason for believing that Wolff's understanding and use of autonomy have led him to the wrong conclusion about political obligation. In this case the problem is that Wolff does not take seriously enough his own definition of "autonomy." As we have seen, this definition includes the Kantian notion that autonomy "is a combination of freedom and responsibility" (p. 14). Our freedom resides in our *capacity* to choose; our responsibility, in our *obligation* to choose, and thus to exercise this capacity. Exactly how this obligation follows from this capacity is not clear, nor is it clear to whom this obligation is owed, but here the important point is that Wolff conceives autonomy to be, at least in part, a capacity. There is nothing wrong with this; indeed, I believe there is everything to recommend it, as I indicated in Chapter 3. The problem is that he fails to see what follows from this conception of autonomy.

To put it simply, Wolff overlooks the social dimension of autonomy. Autonomy is a capacity of individuals, in his account, and one that each individual has an obligation to exercise. Moreover, Wolff apparently thinks that each individual has "a continuing obligation to achieve the highest degree of autonomy possible" (p. 19). Despite a discussion of the importance of social roles in the third part of his book (pp. 72–78), however, Wolff argues as if the individual is to achieve the highest possible degree of autonomy solely through his or her own efforts. It is true, of course, that autonomy, like any other capacity, can be neither exercised nor developed without some effort on the part of the individual. But it is also true, as I argued in Chapter 3, that no one becomes or remains autonomous without the assistance and cooperation of other people.

This is true not only of the development or cultivation of autonomy but also of its exercise. In some cases this is plainly true. Someone who suffers so severely from headaches that he or she can no longer make choices may well believe that the physician who finds a way to stop the headaches or relieve the pain has enabled him or her to exercise autonomy once again. In much the same way, the person who overcomes disabling delusions may be able to act autonomously only because a psychotherapist helped him or her recover that ability. Behind the physician and the psychotherapist in these examples are other individuals and institutions, of course, such as the medical researchers whose discoveries make it possible for the physician to treat the person with crippling headaches. Whether there is one person responsible or one million, however, the point is the same: some people plainly owe the exercise of their autonomy to the efforts of others.

These are unusual cases, to be sure, but there are other, less obvious respects in which all of those who exercise autonomy do so only because they can count on the efforts of others. This is not to say that these "others" do what they do *in order to* enable the autonomous person to exercise his or her autonomy; in a great many cases, the "others" will not even know the person or persons whom they help to act autonomously. Yet that is just what these "others" do when they pass, enforce, or observe traffic laws, for instance, for laws and practices such as these enable us to do a number of things routinely, with almost no forethought, that we would otherwise hardly be able to do. When "others" observe traffic laws or wait their turns in line, they expand our opportunities, even if this is not what they specifically intend to do. By expanding our opportunities in these and numerous other ways, they enhance our capacities to choose— that is, they make it possible for us to do, and therefore to *choose* to do, far more than we could without their help, intended or not. In short, even if neither we nor they are aware of it, we often rely on the assistance of others when we exercise autonomy.

To say that Wolff fails to see the social dimension of autonomy, then, is to say that he fails to see, or at least to consider, how one person's autonomy depends upon the assistance and cooperation of others. This is a significant failure because the social dimension of autonomy strongly suggests that the autonomous person owes something to those who help him or her to develop and exercise autonomy. Precisely what this person owes them may vary from case to case—the person whose crippling headaches are cured probably owes his or her physician a fee, for example—but in most cases he or she will owe them reciprocity. Those whose assistance and cooperation help one person to act autonomously deserve that person's assistance and cooperation in return. When the people who help me are the cooperating members of a rule-governed practice that expands my range of choice, then fairness requires me to continue to cooperate when the burdens of the practice fall on me.

This argument succeeds only if one believes that autonomy is good or valuable, for we usually do not believe we owe anything to those who "enable" us to be or do something we do not want to be or do. But Wolff certainly seems to believe that we ought to want autonomy. More than that, he says that autonomy is our "primary obligation." If this is true, then surely we owe something to those whose assistance and cooperation help us to fulfill our "continuing obligation to achieve the highest degree of autonomy possible."

All of this indicates, again, that a commitment to autonomy is *not* incompatible with a general obligation to obey the laws. On the contrary, if

I am a citizen of a country whose laws and law-abiding citizens promote and protect my autonomy, then I am under an obligation, rooted in reciprocity, to obey the laws. I have an obligation to those who help me to be autonomous and to exercise autonomy. What I typically owe them is reciprocity—assistance in developing and exercising their autonomy. Those who follow the law help me, ceteris paribus, to be autonomous and/or to exercise autonomy, so I am under an obligation to them to reciprocate—to follow the law in turn. This cannot be an obligation to obey the law no matter what the law requires, for this would call for the blind obedience that Wolff rightly rejects as inimical to autonomy. But it is an obligation nonetheless.

So Wolff's project fails. The commitment to autonomy does not entail that we become philosophical anarchists who think that only those who rule themselves in a unanimous direct democracy have a general obligation to obey the laws. Instead, a proper understanding of autonomy as capacity—an understanding that draws on the social dimension of autonomy—leads to the conclusion that, under conditions far less restrictive than those that characterize a unanimous direct democracy, the commitment to autonomy entails political obligation.

But if Wolff's project fails, the second category of arguments against political obligation may still succeed. That is, even if it is not impossible in principle to provide a satisfactory theory of political obligation, it remains to show that a such a theory has been or can be provided. With that in mind, I turn now to the defense of the argument from reciprocity or fair play that I promised in Chapter 4.

Fair Play and Political Obligation

According to the principle of fair play, anyone who takes part in and enjoys the benefits of a cooperative practice must contribute to the production of these benefits, even when his or her contribution is not necessary to their production. This principle may be applied to a number of cooperative practices, large and small, including bodies politic when they really do seem to be cooperative practices. In such a case we have an obligation to obey the law because we owe it to our fellow citizens and the other cooperating members of the body politic to do so. They have a right to our obedience because they, through their obedience, enable us to enjoy the benefits of the political order. They have a claim on us and we on them, in other words, as long as the body politic may reasonably be regarded as a cooperative enterprise.

What if the body politic in which we live may not reasonably be regarded in this way? In that case the principle of fair play says that we have no *general* obligation to obey the laws. There may be particular obligations to obey particular laws, but no political obligation as such.

The fair-play account of political obligation is both plausible and attractive. Its critical edge is one of its chief attractions. Because the principle grounds political obligation not in any individual act, such as the expression of consent, but in the character of the body politic itself, those who follow the principle of fair play will need to subject the political order to scrutiny to see whether they can reasonably regard it as a cooperative enterprise that deserves their (continued) obedience. Another attraction is that the principle makes it clear that when there is an obligation to obey the law the obligation is owed not to some impersonal force—usually called the state—but to the cooperating members of the political society. Yet another attraction is its straightforward reliance on fairness, which gives the principle of fair play an intuitive appeal that is both broad and deep. Whether the principle of fair play provides a sound basis for political obligation is nevertheless the subject of a vigorous controversy, with critics raising three major objections.

Fair Play or Foisting Obligations?

The most sweeping objection has been advanced by Robert Nozick, who argues that the principle of fair play implies that others can place us under an obligation to them simply by conferring benefits on us. According to this principle, then, others may foist obligations on us. That is quite a departure from our usual way of thinking about obligations, however, so the principle must be wrong. As Nozick puts it, "You may not decide to give me something . . . and then grab money from me to pay for it, even if I have nothing better to spend the money on."[4]

Nozick's point here is surely correct, but it is not really pertinent. Fair play does not require us to reciprocate *whenever* someone does something that is to our benefit; it applies only to the benefits of a cooperative *practice*. But Nozick sees the same problem arising within such practices because the benefits may be nonexcludable and therefore impossible to avoid. Hence he offers the following example:

> Suppose some of the people in your neighborhood (there are 364 other adults) have found a public address system and decide to institute a system of public entertainment. They post a list of names, one for each day, yours among them. On his assigned day (one can easily switch days) a person is to run the public address system, play records over it, give news bulletins, tell amusing stories he has heard, and so on. After 138 days on which each person has done his part, your day arrives. Are you obligated to take your turn?[5]

Nozick's answer is "surely not," and it is difficult to disagree. But his claim, by implication, is that anyone who accepts the principle of fair play would have to answer affirmatively. Again, it is by no means clear that this is true, for those who accept the principle may say that the "you" in Nozick's example is under no obligation to take a turn as broadcaster. To see why this is so, we need only look to the principle as Nozick, following John Rawls, formulates it:

> This principle holds that when a number of persons engage in a just, mutually advantageous, cooperative venture according to rules and thus restrain their liberty in ways necessary to yield advantages for all, those who have submitted to these restrictions have a right to similar acquiescence on the part of those who have benefited from their submission. Acceptance of the benefits (even when this is not a giving of express or tacit undertaking to cooperate) is enough, according to this principle, to bind one.[6]

Nozick obviously believes that his example meets the conditions set out here. But one may wonder who has *engaged* in this venture. Perhaps those who found the equipment and began the broadcasts have engaged themselves, but it is far from evident that anyone else has or that anyone has a right to "assign" a turn at the microphone to others.

The problem is that Nozick interprets "acceptance of benefits" too broadly.[7] Merely receiving the benefits of a practice, especially when one cannot avoid them, is not enough to place one under an obligation to comply with the rules of the practice. There must be some sense in which one *takes part* in the enterprise or leads those who are participating to believe that he or she is taking part in it. Only in these circumstances can we say that someone is obligated to do his or her part. Indeed, it is only in these circumstances that we can sensibly talk about one's *part* in a practice.

No Benefit, No Harm, No Problem

The second objection, raised by M. B. E. Smith, is that "the obligation of fair play governs a man's actions only when some benefit or harm turns on whether he obeys."[8] According to Smith, the principle of fair play will generate an obligation to cooperate only when the cooperative enterprise in question is small enough that any participant's failure to obey the rules could reasonably be expected to harm it—perhaps "by diminishing the confidence of the other members in its probable success and therefore reducing their incentive to work diligently towards it." But this reasoning will not support a political obligation, Smith charges, for one can readily imagine cases in which someone's disobedience neither deprives anyone of any benefits nor harms the political enterprise in any noticeable way. If we accept Smith's claims as to when fairness is and is not a moral consideration, consequently, we must also accept his conclusion that fairness cannot require us to obey the laws of a state.

Smith presents three hypothetical cases to develop and support his position. In the first case A's compliance with the rules of a practice "will confer on B a benefit roughly equal to those *[A]* has received from B"; in the second, A's failure to comply will harm the practice and thus harm B indirectly "by threatening the existence or efficient functioning of an institution on which B's vital interests depend." In both cases, Smith says, fairness demands that A abide by the rules. But this does not hold for the third case, in which A is simply a free rider, for "if A's compliance with some particular rules does not benefit B and if his disobedience will not harm the community, it is difficult to see how fairness to B could dictate that A must comply. Surely, the fact that A has benefitted from B's submission does not give B the right to insist that A obey when B's interests are unaffected."

The problem with this argument is that it rests on an unduly narrow conception of fairness. As Smith sees it, one person cannot be unfair to another without directly or indirectly affecting the latter's interests. But if we think of fairness in this way, we can no longer criticize free riders for not playing fair—which is precisely the charge we ordinarily bring against them. We could no longer criticize the tax cheater, for instance. If he or she is like most citizens of modern states, the cheater's taxes constitute an insignificant portion of the state's total tax revenue. This being so, the cheater's failure to pay taxes will not bring about the downfall of the political order or put his or her favorite programs in jeopardy, or even affect any of his or her fellow citizens' interests in any perceptible way. Still, as much as we may admire some of them for their cleverness or audacity, we typically condemn tax cheaters because they do not play fair. Given his notion of fairness, however, Smith would have to say that the cheater is not acting unfairly unless there are some special circumstances—an open flouting of the law, perhaps, that threatens to encourage widespread tax cheating.[9]

What Smith overlooks is the consideration that itself underlies the notion of fairness: the conviction that everyone involved in a practice is to be treated as an equal. This holds even when the interests of the parties involved are not affected, directly or indirectly, for one may be wronged (deceived, treated unfairly) without being harmed.[10] Those who refuse to cooperate in a practice while they accept its benefits are acting unfairly and wronging those who do cooperate. They are making exceptions of themselves. They want others to cooperate—enough to preserve the practice, at least—but they are not themselves willing to bear the burdens of cooperation. By according themselves this special treatment and by exploiting the cooperation of others, they betray a lack of respect for other persons. They are, in Kantian terms, using others as means to their own ends when they should be treating them as ends in themselves.[11]

If Smith is wrong about fairness, as I have argued, his objection to the principle of fair play as the foundation for a general obligation to obey the law is also wrong. But another powerful objection remains to be considered.

The Limiting Argument

Those who raise the third objection against the principle of fair play do not reject the principle altogether, as Nozick seems to do. Instead, like Smith, they question the applicability of fair play to the political context. In this case, however, the complaint is that considerations of fair play apply only to cooperative schemes that produce benefits that one may refuse. If the enterprise produces *nonexcludable* goods—goods that everyone in a group or area receives regardless of whether he or she worked for them or wants them—there can be no obligation of fair play to bear a share of the burdens of the enterprise. The principle's range of application is severely limited, then, with the body politic falling outside those limits. Following George Klosko, I shall refer to this criticism as "the limiting argument."[12]

This argument rests on a distinction between two different ways of enjoying the benefits of a cooperative practice. One way is to accept these benefits; the other is merely to receive them. According to the limiting argument, we can rightly say that someone has an obligation of fair play to contribute to a cooperative practice only when he or she has *voluntarily accepted* the benefits of the practice. Mere receipt of benefits is not enough. It is always possible, after all, that the person who merely receives the benefits of a cooperative practice does not particularly want them, perhaps because he or she finds that the costs of cooperation outweigh the benefits. Even when the benefits do outweigh the costs, moreover, those who advance the limiting argument claim that no genuine obligation follows from the mere receipt of benefits, for obligations must be voluntarily undertaken. Perhaps someone who simply receives benefits *ought* to repay his or her benefactors in some way, in this view, but there is no reason to believe that he or she has an *obligation* to do so. If we are to charge a person with an obligation to contribute to a cooperative enterprise, we must show that he or she not only has enjoyed its benefits but also has accepted them. Only in this way can we say that the person has truly taken part in the practice and thereby incurred an obligation to do his or her part.

Do the members of a body politic have a general obligation, grounded in fairness, to obey its laws? They do, according to the limiting argument, only if the body politic in question may be reasonably regarded as a cooperative enterprise *and* its members accept the benefits it provides them. But most citizens merely receive these benefits. Only a handful take any steps that constitute genuine acceptance of benefits. It follows, therefore, that considerations of reciprocity or fair play are not strong enough to generate a general obligation to obey the law, not even for the citizens of a just political society.

This argument succeeds, of course, only if the distinction between acceptance and receipt of benefits holds. When cooperative practices producing public goods are involved, however, the distinction is not easy to draw. Yet A. John Simmons insists that the distinction holds. "To have accepted a benefit," he states, "an individual must either 1) have tried to get (and succeeded in getting) the benefit, or 2) have taken the benefit willingly and knowingly."[13] Someone may *receive* a benefit without satisfying either of these conditions, according to Simmons, but no one can *accept* a benefit without satisfying at least one. With regard to the benefits provided by the political order—public goods such as the rule of law—it seems clear to Simmons that most people have not accepted these benefits in either of the senses he sets out. Citizen Schwartz may receive the benefits of the rule of law, but if she never tried to obtain them or never took them willingly and knowingly, she has no general obligation to obey the laws. And most of us are like her in this respect.

Assuming that Simmons has correctly identified two sufficient conditions for acceptance of benefits, there appear to be three strategies available to anyone who wishes to maintain, against the limiting argument, that the principle of fair play does provide the foundation for a general obligation to obey the law. The first strategy, followed in different ways by Richard Arneson and George Klosko,[14] is to deny that acceptance of benefits is necessary. On this view, under certain conditions, including conditions that apply to the political order, "[m]ere receipt of benefits may suffice to obligate."[15] As Klosko argues, "the principle of fairness is able to generate powerful obligations to contribute to nonexcludable schemes" if the schemes produce goods that are "(i) worth the recipients' effort in producing them; (ii) 'presumptively beneficial'; and (iii) have benefits and burdens that are fairly distributed."[16] The second strategy, pursued by Thomas Senor, is to show that the consequences of the limiting argument are far more serious than the argument's proponents either intend or desire, for in undermining the citizen's political obligation, the limiting argument also undermines political authority.[17] Although I find considerable merit in both of these positions, I believe it is also important to challenge the claim that the typical citizen of the body politic *qua* cooperative enterprise does not voluntarily accept the benefits of the political order. Therefore, I shall pursue this third strategy here.

The challenge to the limiting argument proceeds on both empirical and conceptual grounds. Simmons offers an apparently empirical observation, first, when he asserts that most people fail to satisfy either of the two conditions for acceptance of benefits. Against this we may set the plausible counterassertion that, as a matter of fact, far more people than he recognizes satisfy one or the other of his two conditions. If we assume, for instance, that the United States and the United Kingdom are cooperative political orders insofar as each maintains the rule of law, it seems clear that a great many citizens of these polities have "tried to get (and succeeded in getting)" benefits made possible by the rule of law. Those who have taken a case to court have sought and presumably received such a benefit, as have those who have entered into a contract secured by law or a marriage recognized by law or those who have called on the police for protection. There is reason to believe, in fact, that almost all citizens of these states have taken some steps that count as accepting the benefits of the rule of law.

Simmons would respond, I suspect, with the conceptual claim that the steps I have just mentioned should not count as steps taken to accept the benefits of a cooperative practice, for he places considerable emphasis on "beliefs and attitudes" in his discussion of cooperative practice. "We must remember," he says,

> that where there is no consciousness of cooperation, no common plan or purpose, no cooperative scheme exists. I do not think that many of us can honestly say that we regard our political lives as a process of working together and making necessary sacrifices for the purposes of improving the common lot. The centrality and apparent independence of governments does [sic] not make it natural to think of political life in this way.[18]

Simmons is both right and wrong here, in my judgment. He is probably right to doubt that "many of us can honestly say that we regard" ourselves, as citizens of the United States, the United Kingdom, or other nation- or multination-states, as participating members of a cooperative political enterprise. But he is wrong when he takes this to mean that we therefore are not engaged in such an enterprise. To be sure, it would be odd indeed to say that a small group of people were cooperating with one another to produce certain benefits even though none of them was aware that he or she was cooperating. But what if the group is not small? As the size of enterprises grows, their rules of cooperation become more formal and their participants less familiar with one another. This certainly makes cooperation harder to see, but it does not mean that cooperation ceases. Indeed, in large enterprises it may well be that people are cooperating with one another in a common venture despite the fact that many or even most of them are not aware that that is what they are doing.

What of Simmons's second condition—that we "have taken the benefit willingly and knowingly"? Again, I do not believe it is as significant as he thinks. There are, to begin with, benefits that we receive, *and accept*, without thinking of them as benefits. When I ride my bicycle to work, for instance, I seldom reflect on the benefits I enjoy because my fellow citizens have cooperated in the production and maintenance of public streets, bicycle paths, and traffic signals—not to mention national defense and the rule of law in general. But does my failure to reflect on these benefits mean that I am not taking them willingly? Does it mean that I am merely *receiving* these benefits, not *accepting* them? I do not see how. After all, it is not as if these benefits have been laid in my lap. I do have to mount my bicycle and take to the streets in order to enjoy these particular benefits, so it seems fair to say that I have accepted them.

Simmons will not want to accept this conclusion, however. As he sees it, one cannot "willingly and knowingly" accept the benefits of a practice if one cannot avoid them. "Certainly," he says, "it would be peculiar if a man, who by simply going about his business in a normal fashion benefited unavoidably from some cooperative scheme, were told that he had voluntarily accepted benefits which generated for him a special obligation to do his part."[19] In response to my example, then, he might say that I cannot accept the benefits mentioned if I cannot avoid them. I may leave my bicycle at home, but I still have to use the public streets and traffic signals to get to work. Or I may simply stay at home in an effort to avoid receiving these benefits, but even then I will continue to receive others, such as the benefits of national defense and police protection. So if I cannot avoid receiving these benefits, how can I possibly say that I voluntarily accept them?

Here the best response seems to be, What else am I to say? That these benefits have been thrust upon me? That I have received them *unwillingly* and *involuntarily?* Neither of these responses seems to capture what happens when citizens enjoy the benefits of the political order. "Voluntary" and "involuntary" are not clear opposites, as J. L. Austin demonstrated, and it seems foolish to insist that everything people do must be either (and clearly) one or the other.[20] To say that obligations (if not duties) must be undertaken voluntarily need not mean that the person who undertakes the obligation must say, or even think, "By doing this I am undertaking an obligation." If we take "voluntarily" to mean something on the order of "with full awareness and conscious intent," however, we rule out many cases in which we attribute obligations to individuals who have not deliberately—that is, *with actual deliberation*—incurred those obligations. Colleges and universities hold students accountable to codes of conduct, including rules against plagiarism and harassment, for example, although many students apparently do not know what these codes require when they matriculate. Yet colleges and universities would not be able to do this if we restricted obligations to those that are undertaken with full awareness and conscious intent.

The alternative is to say that "voluntarily" should be taken to mean something on the order of "not under constraint or duress."[21] This definition recognizes that students, or any people in similar circumstances, are obligated to obey the relevant rules despite their failure to proclaim, or perhaps even to reflect upon, their acceptance of the obligation. Hard cases will arise, certainly, and we will then find it difficult to determine whether an action should be considered voluntary—that is clear from numerous legal cases that raise issues of personal responsibility and voluntary action. So far as obligation is concerned, however, the only way to avoid this problem is to limit obligating actions to express statements of consent, promises, contracts, and so on. But doing so is consistent with neither ordinary use of "voluntary" nor common practice.

My difference with Simmons on this point probably rests on a fundamental difference in the way we conceive of the relationship between the individual and the political order. We both agree that most citizens are born into political communities. For Simmons, though, this means that we are "dropped into" the cooperative scheme.[22] For my part, it seems more reasonable to say that we *grow into* it. On neither view is our entry into the political order a matter of choice. But beyond that, the implications are remarkably different.

Simmons's view falls squarely into the atomistic camp that Charles Taylor and the communitarians have criticized. When he says that we are "dropped into" a political community, he implies that the community is something external or foreign to us. We simply awake, as it were, to find ourselves in the midst of an ongoing scheme of cooperation—if that is truly what it is—that we did not choose to join and that gives us benefits we did not choose to receive. Furthermore, we are told that we must do our part by sharing the burdens of cooperation because we have somehow incurred an obligation to our fellow citizens to do so. Given this view of the matter, it is easy to understand why Simmons does not believe that most citizens voluntarily accept the benefits of the political order.

But this is a remarkably artificial way to conceive of the relationship. To say that we *grow into* the political community into which we are born is closer or truer to life. According to this view, the political order *qua* cooperative enterprise is indeed something that most of us do not choose to join, but it is not something foreign to us. On the contrary, we are who we are in part because of the protection and opportunities the body politic provides us—protection and opportunities made possible by the cooperation of the members of the body politic. Perhaps we merely receive these benefits when we are infants and youngsters, but as we grow older and gradually learn something about how our political community operates, most of us begin to take advantage of the opportunities the community offers to pursue our interests. We use public transportation; we begin to drive a car; we apply for admission to a public university or seek a state-funded scholarship; we vote in an election; we enter into a contract; we do a number of things that we can do because the cooperating members of the community enable us to do them. In doing these things—in *growing into* membership in the polity—we accept the benefits of the political order *qua* cooperative enterprise and undertake an obligation to obey its laws. No one of these actions is sufficient to establish our consent to the rules of the enterprise. But our continuing acceptance of the benefits that flow from cooperation places us under an obligation of fair play to the cooperating members. And if we fail or refuse to obey, we take unfair advantage, ceteris paribus, of those whose cooperation makes it possible for us to enjoy the benefits of membership.

A reconsideration of Nozick's example of the neighborhood public address system may help to clarify the importance of thinking of citizenship as a matter of growing into membership in a political body. As Nozick tells the story, a group of neighbors find some public address equipment and "decide to institute a system of public entertainment," which they then expect you to help sustain when, they say, *your turn* has come. The neighbors maintain that you have an obligation, grounded in fair play, to do your part, but Nozick argues that they are trying to foist on you an obligation that you have not undertaken. Suppose, however, that the system of public entertainment began before your birth, and as you grew up, it became clear to you that everyone in the neighborhood was expected to devote one day a year to running the system. It is also clear that everyone is free to campaign for the abolition of the system and to move from the neighborhood. Now that you are an adult resident of the neighborhood— now that you have *grown into* membership—do you have an obligation to spend a day a year operating the system? In these circumstances, and given Nozick's assumption that the public entertainment system is a cooperative practice producing a public good, the answer seems to be yes. Even if you have taken the public address operation for granted—and therefore have not *accepted* its benefits in Simmons's terms—you still have an obligation to do your part in this neighborhood practice that you have grown into. The obligation may be overridden, of course, and it holds only as long as the practice, and perhaps the neighborhood itself, may be regarded as a just, mutually beneficial cooperative venture. But it *is* an obligation, which is more than one who takes the artificial, "dropped into" view of membership can acknowledge.

We grow into membership in a political order, then, just as we grow into the exercise of autonomy, the capacity of choice. In neither case can we achieve this growth without the assistance of others. But these others are not only those fellow citizens who have formed the practices and institutions that protect and sustain the sense of liberty by protecting and sustaining the sense of community. They are also those whose cooperation continues to form, to preserve, and sometimes to reform those practices and institutions. To them we owe an obligation grounded in the principle of fair play.

It may be worth repeating here some of the qualifications I entered earlier. First, the principle holds only if the political order may reasonably be regarded as a cooperative practice or set of such practices. I do not mean that each and every member must clearly perceive it as such, although I shall shortly explain why it is desirable that they do. It is necessary, however, that the political order meet the requirements of the principle of fair play by being a just, mutually beneficial, rule-governed, cooperative enterprise. If it is, the members have an obligation to obey its rules. But this obligation, according to the second qualification, is not absolute; it may be overridden by more pressing moral considerations. Finally, the obligation is not to the laws or the state as such but to the cooperating members of the body politic. Reciprocity and fairness *to them* place us, other things being equal, under a general obligation to obey the law.

The Sense of Obligation and Civic Virtue

It seems, then, that neither of the two kinds of arguments against a general obligation to obey the laws succeeds. Not only is it *not* impossible in principle to devise a satisfactory theory of political obligation, one that does not require the surrender of autonomy, but also the principle of fair play provides the foundation for such a theory.

Yet there is still something valuable to learn from these two kinds of arguments. By calling into question the existence of the obligation to obey the law, they help us to understand why the *sense* of obligation seems to be growing weaker. This is particularly true of the challenge Simmons mounts against the principle of fair play when he says that many people "do not regard the benefits of government as the products of a cooperative scheme," for "even in democratic communities, these benefits are commonly regarded as purchased (with taxes) from a central authority, rather than as accepted from the cooperative efforts of our fellow citizens."[23]

As I have argued, the fact that people misperceive their relationship with their government and their fellow citizens does not speak against the existence of an obligation to obey the law. But this does not mean that these misperceptions should not concern us. Certainly we should expect those who misperceive these relationships to be mistaken about the existence and/or direction of their obligations—about what, if anything, they owe and to whom it is owed. When these misperceptions are widespread, the consequences can be very serious indeed; when people fail to realize that they have an obligation to bear their share of the burdens in a cooperative enterprise, largely because they do not perceive themselves to be participants in a cooperative enterprise, the enterprise itself is in jeopardy.

This is the predicament in which we too often find ourselves in modern states, in which the government of even one's own city often seems remote. In these circumstances it is all too easy to think of the government as some alien power ruling over us and much too difficult to think of the strangers about us as our partners in a cooperative venture. It then becomes increasingly likely that the individual will come to view

> what he owes the common cause as a free contribution, the loss of which will harm others less than its payment burdens him. And considering the moral person of the State as an imaginary being because it is not a man, he might wish to enjoy the rights of a citizen without wanting to fulfill the duties of a subject, an injustice whose spread would cause the ruin of the body politic.[24]

One way to avoid this outcome is to compel people to obey the law—to force them, if not to be free, then at least to bear their share of the burdens. In this way the practice of punishment seeks to ensure that "those who would voluntarily obey shall not be sacrificed to those who would not."[25] A more positive way to secure cooperation is to cultivate the desire to do one's part in the cooperative endeavor. This desire fosters a form of civic virtue—of acting for the common good even when it proves personally painful. The more we can rely on people to exhibit this virtue, the less we shall have to rely on punishment and other forms of coercion to secure their cooperation. Punishment may be a necessary evil, but civic virtue is a positive good.

The problem is that this form of civic virtue, or good citizenship, is tied to the members' perceptions of the political order. For people to think of obeying the law as an instance of the cooperation that preserves a cooperative enterprise, they must first think of themselves as citizens or members who have an obligation to their fellow citizens or members to obey. They must think of themselves, that is, as participants in a cooperative enterprise. Some citizens of modern states do think of themselves in this way, especially when a war or natural disaster leads them to recognize that "we're all in the same boat." The more people think in these terms, the more likely we are to find civic virtue in the form of a willingness to cooperate for the common good. But if the sense of obligation is weak, as Simmons suggests, and growing weaker, as I suspect, then we face the troubling prospect of more crime, more punishment, and a continued fraying of the bonds of community.

The best way to avoid this situation, I have suggested, is by cultivating civic virtue. But how are we to do this? How are we to bring people to see themselves, in relation to the political order, as citizens participating in a cooperative endeavor? These are the questions I shall address in a variety of ways in the five chapters of Part II. I begin with an examination of a philosopher whose plan for uniting autonomy and civic virtue in a just state is especially important in gaining an appreciation of republican liberalism.

PART II

CITIZENSHIP

CHAPTER 6

Citizenship and the General Will

Jean-Jacques Rousseau is not likely to be the first choice of anyone who canvasses the history of political thought in search of exemplars of republican liberalism. Rousseau's republican credentials are good enough, to be sure, as a number of recent studies attest.[1] The problem is that they may be too good to allow much hope of finding a significant strain of liberalism in his thought. Certainly his willingness to invoke a legislator who "should feel that he is capable of changing human nature," his call for a civil religion that requires "a purely civil profession of faith, the articles of which are for the sovereign to establish," and his declaration that people may "be forced to be free" seem to put him outside the bounds of most definitions of liberalism.[2]

In the end, one may decide that other important political philosophers—Montesquieu or Tocqueville, perhaps, or John Stuart Mill or T. H. Green—are better exemplars of republican liberalism than Rousseau. Yet none of these thinkers combined a republican commitment to civic virtue with the analytical device of the social contract—a device usually associated with liberalism. Rousseau did this, of course, and he did it in a way that is doubly valuable for the purposes of this book.

Rousseau's peculiar contractarian republicanism is valuable, first, because it suggests that republican ideals and liberal devices are not strictly incompatible. Quentin Skinner may be correct when he remarks that "the ideals of classical republicanism had largely been swallowed up by the rising tide of contractarian political thought" by the time of Montesquieu, at which point "the concept of individual rights attained that hegemony which it has never subsequently lost."[3] If contractarian thought did have this general effect, however, it was despite Rousseau's efforts. For Rousseau, the "rising tide of contractarian political thought" presented an opportunity to advance republican ideals, not engulf them. The idea of the social contract may have encouraged people to think of government as a guarantor of their individual rights and liberty, but Rousseau saw that the idea also offered a means of deepening their understanding of their duties and common interests.

By using the contractarian device in this way, Rousseau pointed to the reciprocity that should obtain between the members of a body politic. This concern for reciprocity or fair play is the second respect in which his brand of republican liberalism is worth exploring here. Rousseau recognized the need to make people aware of their reciprocal rights and obligations and to help them see the connection between their individual interests and the common good. He hoped to accomplish these goals—and thus to promote citizenship—by appealing to the idea of the "general will." Whether he succeeded or failed, there is much to learn about the plausibility of republican liberalism from a study of his attempt.

To see how Rousseau's political thought provides an example, albeit an imperfect one, of republican liberalism, we must therefore understand the general will. Much of what I shall have to say on this point is now fairly familiar; indeed, I begin with a general account of what Rousseau meant by "the general will" that largely follows Brian Barry's analysis of the concept.[4] I extend this analysis, however, to argue that Rousseau's attempt to formulate the general will is an attempt to provide the foundation for a body politic as a cooperative venture in which all citizens are treated fairly. More than that, Rousseau's polity would secure a substantial measure of autonomy for citizens in the form of "moral liberty." Whether they will recognize this, however, and sense that their rights and obligations are reciprocal—that their liberty as citizens rests on their duties as subjects—is another matter. Whether they will act on that sense is yet another. As Rousseau remarks in his *Letter to D'Alembert,*

> [W]hen our interest is involved, our sentiments are soon corrupted. . . . Is it not a necessary effect of the constitution of things that the vicious man profits doubly, from his injustice and the probity of others? What more advantageous treaty could he conclude than one obliging the whole world, excepting himself, to be just, so that everyone will faithfully render him what is due him, while he renders to no one what he owes? He loves virtue, unquestionably; but he loves it in others because he hopes to profit from it.[5]

Once he has formulated it, then, Rousseau's task is to find ways to secure the general will. One way, he argued, is to force people to be free. Another is to cultivate the desire to act in accordance with the general will.

The General Will and Moral Freedom

The idea of the general will rests on a fundamental distinction between two aspects of a person. In Rousseau's terms, every person may be thought of as a *man*—an actual, identifiable person—and, at least potentially, as a *citizen*. Insofar as we are men, we are each unique; each of us, that is, has a particular identity and set of interests. Insofar as we are citizens, however, we are alike in that we are members of the public, and as members of the public we share a common interest in the welfare of the body politic. Everyone, consequently, has both a *particular* interest as a man and a *general* interest as a citizen.[6]

From the distinction between man and citizen, Rousseau moves to a corresponding distinction between the *particular* or *private will,* on the one hand, and the *general will,* on the other. The private will aims at the fulfillment of the particular interest of a man, of an actual individual, while the general will seeks to further the interest of the citizen. Because the interests of all citizens are the same, the object of the general will is the common good or public interest—the interest all share as members of the public. Rousseau distinguishes the private from the general will in this manner: "[T]he private will tends by its nature toward preferences, and the general will toward equality" (II, 1:59). As men with private wills, we naturally tend to grant precedence to our own interests and desires. The private will is *partial* both because it is the will of an identifiable individual, one who is only part of the body politic, and because it places a higher value on one's personal interests than on the interests of others. The general will, in contrast, tends toward equality because it necessarily grants equal consideration to the interests of every member of the body politic. Because it focuses on the common interest we share as citizens, the general will is *impartial:* it considers only the interests of the abstract person Rousseau calls the citizen. Because we are all the same *qua* citizen, the general will is devoted equally to all.

A man who has the ability to be an adept burglar, for example, may well find it in his interest, as a man, to put his burgling skills to use. His private will may then be to steal from others in order to satisfy his own desires. The general will, however, directs the potential burglar to obey the law. As the will of the citizen, the general will requires us at times to ignore our particular interests and personal attributes—our possessions, our position in society, our abilities—and to think of ourselves *only* as members of the public. Laws against burglary are in the interests of all citizens, if not all men, and if our potential burglar thinks of himself only as a citizen, he will recognize that he ought to respect the law.

As the example illustrates, the general will performs much the same function as John Rawls's "veil of ignorance," which deprives the parties to a hypothetical social contract of most information about their personal identities.[7] Behind the veil, the parties do not know what their social or economic positions are, what abilities or disabilities they have, what religious or philosophical views they hold, or even what their ages or sexes are. The veil thus forces the parties to the contract to adopt a common, and presumably morally neutral, viewpoint. Or, to use Rousseau's terms, it leads the parties to promote their common interest as citizens rather than their private interests as men.

There is also a moral dimension to the general will, just as there is to the veil of ignorance. Rousseau does not invoke the general will simply as a counterweight to selfish interests. This would be futile, for one's interest as a man may well outweigh one's interest as a citizen. An industrialist may find, for instance, that it is not in his or her interest to install pollution-inhibiting devices in the factory's smokestacks, all things considered, even though it is in his or her interest as a citizen to reduce air pollution. Rousseau's claim, however, is that in some cases we ought to consider *only* our interests as citizens. The purpose of the general will, then, is to provide a principle that will lead to just public policy. If we consider the interests of citizens and not those of men, in other words, we will reach decisions that establish laws and policies in accordance with the common interest. From the standpoint of citizens—as members of the public—we share the same interests. Considered abstractly, as citizens, the burglar and his victim share a common interest in the enforcement of a law against burglary, just as the industrialist and the person who lives downwind of the factory share a common interest in eliminating air pollution. What Rousseau suggests, in sum, is that only the general will of the citizen and not the private will of the man should determine public policy.[8]

Understood in this way, the general will operates as a moral imperative or principle; its purpose is to guarantee that the claims of no particular individuals are given preference. Everyone receives equal consideration because public decisions take into account only the viewpoint of the citizen. Any other perspective is at best morally irrelevant. Here we see the emphasis on equality that is such a marked characteristic of Rousseau's political philosophy. "The social compact," according to Rousseau,

> established an equality between the citizens such that they all engage themselves under the same conditions and should all benefit from the same rights. Thus by the very nature of the compact, every act of sovereignty, which is to say *every authentic act of the general will, obligates or favors all citizens equally,* so that the sovereign knows only the nation as a body and makes no distinctions between any of those who compose it. (II, 4:63; emphasis added)

A further implication is that laws established in accordance with the general will do more than grant equal consideration to everyone: they truly are in everyone's interest, for a law sanctioned by the general will promotes everyone's interest *qua* citizen. Such a law may not be the first choice of many individuals, but it is acceptable to all because it makes some contribution to everyone's well-being. It is, in Barry's words, "a sort of highest common factor of agreement."[9]

According to Rousseau, moreover, the general will applies only to laws, not to decrees. A law is a general policy, a rule that governs the conduct of every member of the body politic, while a decree is an act that refers to particular, identifiable individuals. The general will "loses its natural rectitude when it is directed toward any individual, determinate object. Because then, judging what is foreign to us, we have no true principle of equity to guide us" (II, 4:62).[10] There is no principle of equity in these cases because flesh-and-blood men, in all their particularity, are involved, not abstract citizens. Instead of appealing to the general will, then, we must decide on the merits of the particular case—and these decisions are best left to executives and judges, not to the sovereign people as a whole.

Understanding the general will as a principle meant to guide public decisions is also consistent with what Rousseau has to say about groups within the body politic. There is a sense in which each of these groups, or "partial associations," has its own general will, for the individuals who compose each group share a common interest in their capacities as members of that association. These groups, in other words, may be considered publics. When we regard them from the perspective of the body politic, however, it is clear that the will of each association is a private will—one that may be antagonistic to the general will of the community as a whole. Rousseau consequently disapproves of these associations because he fears that they will divide and divert the loyalty of the people, who will be more likely to think of themselves as merchants or farmers, say, or Catholics or Protestants than as citizens. When this happens, Rousseau warns, the private wills of these groups will prevent the general will from prevailing when the people vote. "In order for the general will to be well expressed," he concludes, "it is therefore important that there be no partial society in the State, and that each citizen give only his own opinion."[11]

There is also a close connection between the general will and Rousseau's conception of moral freedom. There must be, if the social contract is to solve the "fundamental problem" that Rousseau sets himself: " 'Find a form of association that defends and protects the person and goods of each associate with all the common force, and by means of which each one, uniting with all, nevertheless obeys only himself and remains as free as before' " (I, 6:53).

How can a man who enters into a contract to place himself under law be as free as he was before the contract? Rousseau's answer relies on a distinction between three kinds of freedom: natural, civil, and moral. The man who enters into the social contract may surrender the natural freedom of the state of nature, but he gains civil freedom and the opportunity for

moral freedom in its place. Civil freedom, which secures "the proprietor-
ship of everything he possesses," is "limited by the general will"; moral
freedom, which overcomes the "impulse of appetite" and requires "obedience to the law one has prescribed for oneself," is expressed through it (I,
8:56). If the people are furnished with adequate information when they
meet to make laws, Rousseau says, and if they are not allowed to commu-
nicate when they deliberate—apparently to prevent logrolling and to encourage people to vote as citizens—the outcome of their vote will conform
to the general will. Their votes will thus establish laws that promote their
interests as citizens, and as citizens subject to these laws, they will have an
obligation to obey them. They will then be free when they obey, for they
will be obeying laws that they have prescribed for themselves.

This solution to Rousseau's "fundamental problem" is not, as we shall
see, free of difficulties. Nevertheless, it is a remarkable attempt to square
autonomy with authority. For Rousseau, as for Kant, there is a close connection between freedom and law.[12] Moral freedom consists of self-
legislation, of obeying laws that one gives to oneself. Natural freedom is
freedom from restraint, but moral freedom requires *self*-restraint. In order
to formulate the laws that are to govern one's conduct, one must reflect on
one's appetites, needs, and circumstances. To follow "the impulse of appetite alone is slavery," but the moral freedom that comes with self-
legislation "makes man truly the master of himself" (I, 8:56). Moral freedom, then, is a form of self-government or self-mastery—of autonomy—
that is available only to those who belong to a polity in which men act as
citizens by following their general will. In the state of nature, man may be
free in one sense, but he is subject to the impulses of his appetites and the
attacks of others. In the just society of the *Social Contract*, the individual
enjoys a different kind of freedom—the kind that allows him to obey only
himself, as a citizen, while uniting with others in a cooperative, law-
governed enterprise.

In this way the social contract and the general will, understood as a
principle akin to Kant's categorical imperative, represent what may be
called the liberal side of Rousseau's political thought. On the one hand, the
contract and the general will justify political authority by showing how it
can reconcile "what right permits with what interest prescribes, so that
justice and utility are not at variance" (I, Introduction:46); they also show
how the individual who enters the contract "obeys only himself and remains as free as before" (I, 6:53). Yet political authority is justified, on the
other hand, only when the general will is operative and citizens are obeying
laws that they prescribe for themselves. Thus Rousseau conjoins autonomy
with authority, moral freedom with political obligation.

There are, however, well-known problems with Rousseau's contractual
argument, especially where freedom and obligation are concerned. There

is, first, the complaint that he is self-contradictory, and perhaps tilts toward totalitarianism, when he claims that someone may be "forced to be free." How can one be forced to be free when freedom is the very absence of coercion?

The obvious answer is that Rousseau is talking about moral freedom here, and he merely means that one may be compelled to obey a law to which one has consented. But this explanation does not meet all objections, for why should one have to be forced to obey a law to which one has consented? Here the answer lies in Rousseau's distinction between private wills and the general will. The private will of the lawbreaker—of a man who cheats on his taxes, for example—is likely to be in conflict with his general will as a citizen. The cheater may "view what he owes the common cause as a free contribution, the loss of which will harm others less than its payment burdens him," and consequently "wish to enjoy the rights of the citizen without wanting to fulfill the duties of a subject" (I, 7:55). These two wills are in conflict because the cheater wants to enjoy the benefits of the social order—"the rights of the citizen"—without contributing his share to the maintenance of that order—"the duties of a subject." If he follows his private will, he acts against "the general will he has as a citizen" (I, 7:55). The spread of this kind of injustice, Rousseau observes,

> would cause the ruin of the body politic.
>   Therefore, in order for the social compact not to be an ineffectual formula, it tacitly includes the following engagement, which alone can give force to the others: that whoever refuses to obey the general will shall be constrained to do so by the entire body; which means only that he will be forced to be free. For this is the condition that, by giving each citizen to the homeland, guarantees him against all personal dependence . . . and alone gives legitimacy to civil engagements which without it would be absurd, tyrannical, and subject to the most enormous abuses. (I, 7:55).

The body politic, according to the view set out here, is supposed to be a cooperative enterprise, and the citizens are all pledged to share its burdens. Only those who try to evade this obligation—those who "wish to enjoy the rights of the citizen without wanting to fulfill the duties of a subject"— must be "forced to be free." These individuals are free riders. Like the tax cheater, they want to receive the benefits of social cooperation without contributing their fair share toward the provision of those benefits. If the number of free riders is relatively small, the benefits of social cooperation will still be provided, but when their numbers rise above a threshold, they may well render social cooperation impossible. In large groups the temptation to ride free is especially strong, and Rousseau recognizes that some means must be found to encourage men to honor their commitments. Otherwise, he says, the sovereign "would have no guarantee of the subjects' engagements if it did not find ways to be assured of their fidelity" (I, 7:55). The threat and perhaps the use of coercion are thus necessary to assure fidelity and fair play.

One may still wonder what all this has to do with freedom. Why not simply say that members of the body politic will not be allowed to take unfair advantage of one another? The answer is that Rousseau speaks of freedom here because he considers the polity or state—or at least the de jure state he sketches in the *Social Contract*—to be the realm of freedom. The just state grants equal rights and protection to all, thereby helping to secure everyone from personal dependence. Any man who accepts and follows social rules whenever they favor him, only to break them when it serves his purposes, is contributing to the destruction of that realm. Such a man is a parasite whose actions threaten his own freedom—his moral freedom—as well as that of others. That is why Rousseau says that the free rider must be "forced to be free"—forced, that is, to act in accordance with his own will as a citizen.[13]

Assuming that this response is satisfactory, there is still a second problem confronting Rousseau's attempt to join right and interest, freedom and obligation. This problem arises out of Rousseau's endorsement of majority rule, which appears to lead him again into a contradiction: How can someone remain as free as before he entered into the social contract if he is now subject to the will of the majority?

Rousseau is aware of this problem, as his brief discussion of majority rule makes clear. He begins by acknowledging that the social contract requires unanimous consent: "Since every man is born free and master of himself, no one . . . can subject him without his consent" (IV, 2:110). But he soon goes on to say that "[e]xcept for this primitive contract, the vote of the majority always obligates all the others" (IV, 2:110). The problem is obvious—"How can the opponents be free yet subject to laws to which they have not consented?"—and Rousseau quickly offers this resolution:

> When a law is proposed in the assembly of the people, what they are being asked is not precisely whether they approve or reject the proposal, but whether it does or does not conform to the general will that is theirs. Each one expresses his opinion on this by voting, and the declaration of the general will is drawn from the counting of the votes. (IV, 2:110–11)

These two sentences provide a good example of an important distinction, almost unmarked in Rousseau's writings, between *the* general will and *a* general will.[14] The proposal is to be approved if it conforms to *the* general will, that is, the principle that everyone should act as a citizen, not as a man; but *a* general will, a specific policy that satisfies this principle, is discovered only by counting votes. Votes are irrelevant to *the* general will, for principles are not discovered by voting, but *a* general will often cannot be ascertained without them.[15] Were it not for the difference between the general will *qua* principle and policies that conform to that principle, Rousseau would not even need to discuss voting.

The point of immediate importance, however, is brought out in the remainder of the paragraph.

> Therefore when the opinion contrary to mine prevails, that proves nothing except that I was mistaken, and what I thought to be the general will was not. If my private will had prevailed, I would have done something other than what I wanted. It is then that I would not have been free. (IV, 2:111)[16]

This explanation is complicated and paradoxical, but it is not simply nonsense. Rousseau admits that even the people as a whole may fail to discern the policy that accords with the general will (II, 6:67),[17] so the question here is, Why is the majority opinion less likely to be mistaken than that of the minority or of a solitary individual? It is certainly possible for one person to be right while everyone else is wrong. But if we make certain assumptions, as Barry has shown, then the opinion of the majority *is* more likely to be correct than that of the minority.[18] This occurs when we assume, as Rousseau seems to do, that (1) there is a uniquely right answer, a specific policy in conformity with the general will, to be found; (2) everyone has an equal, better-than-even chance of discerning the right answer; and (3) everyone wants the right answer to prevail. It may be difficult to accept all of these assumptions, but they do indicate how one might be glad, as a citizen, that his or her own point of view was not victorious. Rousseau's point, then, is not that whatever the majority wants is *eo ipso* the general will but that the majority is simply more likely than the minority to have discovered the policy that conforms to the general will.

One may wonder again what this has to do with freedom. How could a person possibly be less free if his or her opinion had carried the day? The answer here, as in the case of the "forced-to-be-free" passage, follows from Rousseau's conception of the just state as the realm of freedom. Rousseau assumes that *in this state* all voters want the policy that best satisfies the general will to prevail. If the majority is more likely to perceive that policy, then a person whose opinion is in the minority may be said to have voted against his will *qua* citizen. His will was to promote the common interest, but his opinion as to what policy would do so was mistaken. "The constant will of all the members of the state is the general will, which makes them citizens and free" (IV, 2:110). If people see, therefore, that the policy they favored actually (or ostensibly) is not in the common interest, they then recognize that their particular opinion differed from their constant will. Because the realm of freedom is preserved only through observance of the general will, freedom is diminished whenever a policy contrary to the general will is pursued. Those who had supported such a policy—along with everyone else—would then be less free than they would have been if their opinion had not prevailed.

All this presumes, of course, that people are voting as citizens rather than men, and Rousseau frequently testifies to the powerful impulse to place one's private interest above the common good. Forcing people to be free—or not to be free riders—may serve to secure compliance with laws that conform to the general will, but it cannot inspire in people the desire to find a general will by voting as citizens. Coercion may be necessary to guarantee that those who act as citizens are not double-crossed or exploited by those who act as men, but it cannot ensure that people will want to act as citizens when the threat of coercion cannot reach them. To see how Rousseau hoped to meet this problem—the problem, in republican terms, of promoting civic virtue and staving off corruption—we shall have to turn to the more republican side of his political thought.

Making Citizens of Men

Beginning with the liberal device of the social contract, Rousseau's argument leads to conclusions usually associated with republican theorists—and occasionally, some critics claim, with totalitarians.[19] His definition of citizens not as mere bearers of privileges and immunities but as "participants in the sovereign authority" already points in the republican direction (I, 6:54). So does his argument that people must sometimes "be forced to be free" in order to prevent them from disobeying laws they have prescribed, as citizens, for themselves. One might object that the man who resolves always to act as a man rather than a citizen is in fact obeying a law he has prescribed for himself and is therefore morally free in Rousseau's sense. But Rousseau's response is that no one can enter the social contract on these terms, for no polity could survive if it allowed its members to disobey the laws whenever it suited their personal interests to do so.

Rousseau's argument thus rests on his conception of the political order—the just or de jure state, at any rate—as a cooperative practice subject to the principle of fair play. He does not use these terms, to be sure, but the logic of his argument clearly points to this conception of the political order. One important aspect of this conception is his desire to promote the spirit of cooperation by encouraging people to think of themselves as subjects who have an obligation to obey the laws they make as citizens.

Rousseau's abiding concern for equality is evidence of this desire. The great possibility of a political society, according to Rousseau, is that it "substitutes a moral and legitimate equality for whatever physical inequality nature may have placed between men." In a footnote to this statement, he connects the distribution of wealth and property to this "moral and legitimate equality" by observing that "the social state is only advantageous to men insofar as they all have something and none of them has anything superfluous" (I, 9:58). In Book II, he goes on to argue for equality because "freedom cannot last without it." It is necessary, therefore, that "no citizen should be so opulent that he can buy another, and none so poor that he is constrained to sell himself" (II, 11:75).

Equality thus promotes freedom, largely by securing people from *personal dependence*. Throughout his writings, Rousseau makes plain his hatred for personal dependence, which, in true republican spirit, he deems a form of slavery. As he declares in *Emile,* to return to a passage quoted in Chapter 1, "Dependence on men . . . engenders all the vices, and by it, master and slave are mutually corrupted."[20] But if "all have something and none of them has anything superfluous," then no one will be "constrained to sell himself." Only in this condition, when no one is rich enough or powerful enough to corrupt the ideal of equality under law, can people be autonomous, or morally free, for only then can they obey laws that they prescribe for themselves. And only then are they likely to see themselves as citizens, sharing a common will in a cooperative enterprise.

Rousseau's devotion to the small community and his hatred of big cities also play a part here. More than mere nostalgia for the Geneva of his youth or for the city-states of antiquity, this concern for scale reflects his underlying conception of the political order as a cooperative practice. As the size of a cooperative practice grows, each person's contribution seems less and less significant, just as "the share of each member of the State" in "the sovereign authority" decreases (III, 1:79). It also becomes more likely, to return to the "forced-to-be-free" argument, that the members will consider "the moral person of the State as an imaginary being" and "wish to enjoy the rights of the citizen without wanting to fulfill the duties of a subject" (I, 7:55). To avoid this and other "abuses of large States," we must recognize that "it is always an evil to unite several towns in a single City" (III, 13:100). Indeed, "a town, like a nation, cannot legitimately be the subject of another, because the essence of the body politic lies in the harmony of obedience and freedom; and the words *subject* and *sovereign* are identical correlatives, whose meaning is combined in the single word citizen" (III, 13:100; emphasis in original). If we want to promote citizenship, then, we must establish and preserve the conditions that lead to the harmony of obedience and freedom. We must keep the polity small enough, that is, for its people to be able to see how important their cooperation, in the form of obedience to the laws, is to maintaining the freedom the cooperative enterprise makes possible.[21]

Rousseau's discussion of education in *Emile* and elsewhere also aims at cultivating the cooperative attitude of the citizen-subject, as do his supposedly totalitarian remarks on "the legislator" and civil religion in the *Social Contract*. However unappealing it may seem, the civil religion is "a purely civil profession of faith, the articles of which are for the sovereign to establish, not exactly as religious dogmas, *but as sentiments of sociability without which it is impossible to be a good citizen or a faithful subject*" (IV, 8:130; emphasis added). Indeed, the doctrine of the civil religion exemplifies Rousseau's attempt to combine the republican emphasis on civic devotion with a concern, subsequently associated with liberalism, for tolerance and freedom of thought:

> Now it matters greatly to the State that each citizen have a religion that causes him to love his duties; but the dogmas of that religion are of no interest either to the State or to its members; except insofar as these dogmas relate to morality, and to the duties that anyone who professes it is obliged to fulfill toward others. Everyone can have whatever opinions he pleases beyond that, without the sovereign having to know what they are. For since the sovereign has no competence in the other world, whatever the fate of subjects in the life hereafter, it is none of its business, as long as they are good citizens in this one. (IV, 8:130)

The civil religion consists, accordingly, of several "positive" dogmas—"[t]he existence of a powerful, intelligent, beneficent, foresighted, and providential divinity; the afterlife; the happiness of the just; the punishment of the wicked; the sanctity of the social contract and the laws"—and one "negative" dogma, or proscription—"intolerance. It belongs with the cults we have excluded" (IV, 8:131).

The de jure state must tolerate everyone, in other words, except for two categories of people. The first comprises those who lack the belief in divine retribution that discourages people from harming or exploiting others whenever it is to their earthly advantage to do so; the second comprises those whose "theological intolerance" sets people against each other and stands in the way of *civic* virtue. Against this latter group, and with Roman Catholicism clearly in mind, Rousseau's civil religion would ensure "that there is no longer and can never be again an exclusive national religion" (IV, 8:131).

In these respects, of course, Rousseau's position is quite similar to the one John Locke advocates in his *Letter Concerning Toleration*. Where he and Locke part company with subsequent liberals is in their conviction that it is necessary, for purely civil reasons, to require the profession of some kind of belief in a God who rewards and punishes in an afterlife. Rousseau adds fuel to Locke's fire, moreover, by proposing rather stringent measures to secure the civil religion and, through it, "the sanctity of the social contract and the laws":

Without being able to obligate anyone to believe [these dogmas], the Sovereign can *banish* from the State anyone who does not believe them. . . . If someone who has publicly acknowledged these same dogmas behaves as though he does not believe them, *he should be punished with death.* (IV, 8:130–31; emphasis added)

Whether they betray his totalitarian instincts or his pessimism about the possibility of finding less draconian ways to induce men to act as citizens, the penalties Rousseau prescribes here certainly seem harsh for someone whose aim is to promote religious tolerance.[22]

As for the legislator, this extraordinary person who drafts the fundamental laws and establishes the basic institutions

should feel that he is capable of changing human nature, so to speak; of transforming each individual, who by himself is a perfect and solitary whole, into a part of a larger whole from which this individual receives, in a sense, his life and his being; . . . of substituting a partial and moral existence for the physical and independent existence we have all received from nature. (II, 7:68)

Although he cannot himself enact the legislation he recommends, the legislator should feel capable of transforming human nature because such a transformation is necessary to replace the *natural* life of men with the *moral* life of the citizen. The legislator's task, in a sense, is to complete the passage from the state of nature to the civil state that Rousseau describes in the first book of the *Social Contract:*

This passage from the state of nature to the civil state produces a remarkable change in man, by substituting justice for instinct in his behavior and giving his actions the morality they previously lacked. Only then, when the voice of duty replaces physical impulse and right replaces appetite, does man, who until that time only considered himself, find himself forced to act upon other principles and to consult his reason before heeding his inclinations. Although in this state he deprives himself of several advantages given by nature, he gains such great ones, his faculties are exercised and developed, his ideas broadened, his feelings ennobled, and his whole soul elevated to such a point *that if the abuses of this new condition did not often degrade him beneath the condition he left,* he ought ceaselessly to bless the happy moment that tore him away from it forever, and that changed him from a stupid, limited animal into an intelligent being and a man. (I, 8:55–56; emphasis added)

The legislator's task, then, is to provide the legal and institutional foundation that will prevent the abuses of the civil state that degrade people below their natural condition. By doing this—by directing people toward the general will—the legislator will complete the transformation of human nature begun when people first left the state of nature.[23]

Remaining Problems

Through these and other measures, Rousseau sought to encourage men to act as citizens—to seek and follow the general will. If some of the measures seem excessive, it is probably because Rousseau regarded the challenge—reconciling "what right permits with what interest prescribes," as he said at the beginning of Book I—as extraordinarily difficult. Some of these measures may now seem out of place or anachronistic—the invocation of the legislator, for instance—and others, such as the call for a civil religion, may fit better with a strong form of classical republicanism than with republican *liberalism.* There are other problems with Rousseau's theory as well, notably his exclusion of women from the public realm. This exclusion is objectionable not only for what seems to be his condescending attitude but also for the way it condemns women to the personal dependence he so frequently abhors. As one of Rousseau's admirers was soon to complain, the fare of women has too often been "the bitter bread of dependence." [24]

In addition, some problems associated with Rousseau's formulation of the general will persist even when we understand it as a principle that requires us to act as citizens rather than as men. First is the question of how the general will is to be applied. What does it mean to say that public policy must attend to the common interest of citizens and ignore the private interests of men? Is the viewpoint of the citizen always readily apparent? Consider the case of a city, akin to the one depicted in Henrik Ibsen's *An Enemy of the People,* that finds its fortunes tied to a single industry. Cities of this sort often find themselves on the horns of a dilemma. There may be reliable evidence that pollution from the industry is hazardous to the health of those in the community, but eliminating that hazard may involve the loss of the industry with all of the money and jobs it directly and indirectly provides. Everyone in the community will suffer if the hazard is not eliminated, yet it is also conceivable that everyone will suffer if the industry leaves. In this case, is there a single viewpoint that is distinctly the citizen's? What would the general will have those in this predicament do?

By altering the example slightly, we can produce yet another problem for Rousseau. Suppose that many people in this city will suffer severe economic hardship if the industry leaves and that a few, for one reason or another, will not suffer at all. In this case *all* of the members of the community share an interest in eliminating the hazard, but all do not share an interest in keeping the industry in town. The general will, presumably, would require the elimination of the hazard because that would be in the interest of the *citizens,* even though it might spell disaster for most of the *men* in the city. Given possibilities of this kind, is it clear that we should always ignore the private interests of men when deciding matters of public policy?

A second set of difficulties arises in connection with Rousseau's remarks on the majoritarian decision rule. If we grant the three assumptions mentioned earlier—that (1) political questions have uniquely right answers; (2) everyone has an equal, better-than-even chance of discovering these answers; and (3) everyone wants the right answers to prevail—then the majority is more likely than the minority to hit upon the right answer. But these are strong assumptions, and it is not at all obvious that we ought to accept them. If these three conditions are not met, moreover, then a person who voted with the minority may actually be *less* free when or if he or she acquiesces to the will of the majority.

It is true that Rousseau is talking about the de jure state when he argues that those in the minority are mistaken about what the general will requires, and perhaps in the de jure state everyone will want the right answers to prevail. Even if we grant this and the other assumptions, however, the problem of civil disobedience remains. Should a person go along with the majority on a matter of conscience simply because he or she knows that they are more likely to be right? Are matters changed if we add, with Rousseau, that "the more important and serious the deliberations, the closer the winning opinion should be to unanimity" (IV, 2:111)? The size of the vote against the conscientious individual will give him or her pause, no doubt; but so long as there is a possibility that the winning side has failed to discover *a* general will that conforms to *the* general will, there is a case to be made for civil disobedience. Rousseau fails to make this case— not surprisingly, perhaps, in view of the political circumstances of the time. But should he have done so?

To answer these questions, we shall have to go beyond Rousseau. We may find it necessary to refine his analysis and concepts or even to abandon some of them. But the simple fact that it leads to such potentially rewarding exploration may well be the most fitting testimony to the richness of Rousseau's brand of republican liberalism. This richness will become more evident, I hope, in the following chapters.

CHAPTER 7

Encouraging Citizenship

In Part I of this book, I tried to show how a concern for individual rights is compatible with a commitment to the importance of community, duty, and virtue. Rousseau's contractarian republicanism reinforces this point. But Rousseau's outline of an association in which each man unites with all yet obeys only himself and remains as free as before also points up the difficulty of ensuring the civic virtue necessary to republican liberalism. That is, he leaves us with the question of whether republican liberalism is *practically* possible.

The question arises because republican liberalism ties individual rights to civic duties by way of reciprocity and fair play. Those who enjoy the benefits of a cooperative enterprise, such as the rights guaranteed by a political order, must also bear their share of the burdens of the enterprise. They must act as citizens, in Rousseau's terms, not as men. Yet if Rousseau is right, people are typically inclined to follow their particular wills rather than their general will. Even if he is wrong, the size, diversity, and complexity of the modern state make it difficult for us to see ourselves as members of a body politic that is also a cooperative enterprise. If we cannot see ourselves as citizens, in Rousseau's sense, we cannot act as citizens. For republican liberalism to work, it must be possible to overcome these difficulties by finding ways to foster citizenship. But is this possible?

The first step toward an answer is to explicate the conception of citizenship at work here and to explain why citizenship of this sort is worth encouraging. I take up these tasks in the first two sections of this chapter. In the third section I turn to the problem of identifying tactics for encouraging citizenship that are compatible with republican liberalism.

Republican-Liberal Citizenship

As Rousseau conceived of it, citizenship is intimately related to civic virtue—so intimately that he practically defined "citizen" as "one who acts with the good of the community in mind." In this respect, of course, he was following a tradition that goes back at least as far as Aristotle.[1] For Rousseau and other republicans, citizenship was not simply a matter of legal status that carried with it various privileges and immunities. Citizenship was a way of life that required commitment to the common good and active participation in public affairs. It was also a way of life that Rousseau believed to be in danger of extinction in the mid-eighteenth century: "We have physicists, geometricians, chemists, astronomers, poets, musicians, and painters in plenty; but we have no longer a citizen among us."[2]

With his implicit distinction between the legal and the ethical aspects of citizenship, Rousseau provides a useful starting point for the explication of a republican-liberal conception of the citizen. Such a conception must go beyond Rousseau, however, by giving greater weight to the legal and educative aspects of citizenship than he and other republicans usually have given. From the standpoint of republican liberalism, in fact, citizenship has four overlapping dimensions: the legal, the ethical, the integrative, and the educative.

For many people, citizenship simply *is* a matter of legal status. I believe this view to be inadequate for reasons I shall explain shortly. But it is important to note at the outset that the legal dimension is absolutely necessary to the concept of citizenship. To be a citizen is, at the least, to be a member of a body politic who enjoys certain rights—and is subject to certain duties—by virtue of one's citizenship. Holding this status does not require one to exercise the rights of citizenship, such as the right to participate in public affairs, nor does it require one to set aside one's private interests when participating. But it does make it possible to exercise those rights if one chooses, and it provides protection against those who would infringe upon one's rights. Citizenship as legal status is also something that can be invoked when a person thinks that others are treating him or her as a "second-class citizen." In these respects, legal status is as necessary to a republican-liberal conception of citizenship as to any other.

It is necessary, but not sufficient. If citizenship is nothing more than a matter of legal status, we face the kind of difficulties identified by those who complain of the excessive individualism and civic irresponsibility that "rights talk" has fostered. We also neglect the conviction, still widespread, that *real* or *true* citizenship entails a duty to work with one's fellow citizens to promote the public good.[3] Some who hold this conviction even argue that voting is not enough to satisfy the requirements of citizenship. According to the authors of a recent study of political participation in American cities, for example,

[r]ebuilding citizenship in America means that reform must move beyond getting more people into private voting booths to getting more people to public

forums where they can work with their neighbors to solve the problems of their community. Once America has real citizens, increased voting will be sure to follow. And once we have real citizens, campaigns will be held to higher standards and elections will be more concrete manifestations of the people's will.[4]

"Real" citizenship thus requires us to go beyond legal status to the ethical dimension. A true citizen will take an active part in public life, and this activity must involve more than an occasional trip to the polling place. The character of one's participation also counts, for it is possible for a person to approach the public arena as simply another venue in which to advance his or her personal interests. One conception of citizenship, as we shall see, regards such conduct as perfectly proper. For a republican liberal, however, the real citizen is one who acts with the common good in mind.

That is not to say that citizens must constantly sacrifice their private interests to help achieve the public interest. Occasional sacrifices will be necessary, but there must be substantial agreement between personal and public interests if people are to be willing to act as ethical citizens. When conflicts do arise, individuals must be able to see that acting against their own short-term interests may promote their interests in the long term, all things considered. They must also be able to see themselves as citizens in Rousseau's abstract sense of the word. They must be able, that is, to recognize that they are members of the public who share an interest in producing public goods. Although they may prefer as individuals to drive to work alone, for instance, they may nevertheless see that they stand to gain as citizens from the cleaner air that will result from increased carpooling and use of public transportation. Their sacrifice produces some benefit for them, then, at least when enough other people act as responsible citizens by making similar sacrifices.

If others consistently fail to make these sacrifices, of course, one will have little incentive to continue making them oneself. It is foolish to sacrifice one's private interest when doing so will not contribute to the public good. That is why coercion is necessary to secure cooperation. Other means of promoting civic cooperation—of promoting ethical citizenship—are also necessary, as Rousseau knew and as I shall explain later in this chapter. But if people can see that their interests as individuals frequently coincide with the public interest, either in the short or the long term, then they will find it in their interest to act as responsible citizens who must occasionally make sacrifices in order to promote the common good. This is what Alexis de Tocqueville had in mind when he praised the doctrine of "self-interest properly understood," which requires only that a man has "the sense to sacrifice some of his private interests to save the rest." This doctrine is not likely to inspire extraordinary deeds or heroic sacrifices,

Tocqueville admitted, "but every day it prompts some small ones; by itself it cannot make a man virtuous, but its discipline shapes a lot of orderly, temperate, moderate, careful, and self-controlled citizens. If it does not lead the will directly to virtue, it establishes habits which unconsciously turn it that way."[5]

As Tocqueville's remarks suggest, there is another respect in which ethical citizenship may prove to benefit the individual. The person who acquires the habit of active citizenship is also likely to become a better person. To see how this can happen, we need to consider the two remaining dimensions of the republican-liberal conception of citizenship: the *integrative* and the *educative*.

From the republican-liberal perspective, citizenship is more than merely one of the many roles that people may occupy in modern societies. As Sheldon Wolin has observed, "[C]itizenship provides what other roles cannot, namely an integrative experience which brings together the multiple role activities of the contemporary person and demands that the separate roles be surveyed from a more general point of view."[6] Wolin may put the point a bit too strongly, since religious commitment surely provides many people with a similar integrative experience. Yet the point remains valid. Citizenship helps to integrate the various aspects of a person's life. When we act as citizens, we cannot simply speak or vote as parents or workers or consumers or members of this group or that sect. A policy that will work to my benefit as a consumer may work to my detriment as an employer or parent, for instance, so I must search for a more synoptic understanding of my interests. Citizenship thus requires that we think of ourselves as something more than the sum of the roles we play.

Such a view may seem to contradict Rousseau's vision of the citizen as someone who thinks and acts only as a member of the public. This view goes beyond Rousseau's, to be sure, but I do not believe that it contradicts his. As I indicated at the end of the last chapter, Rousseau's advice—follow your general will as a citizen, not your particular will as a man—is not always helpful, primarily because what thinking and acting only as a member of the public entails is not always clear. Does acting as members of the public mean that we should close the local factory so that everyone in town will benefit from cleaner air, or does it mean that we should keep the factory open in order to prevent the loss of jobs and the town's slow death? In cases such as this, we cannot truly act as members of the public unless we have some understanding of the personal interests of the people involved. The activity of citizenship—the exchange of viewpoints, the give-and-take of debate—helps to provide this understanding. Indeed, the activity of citizenship performs an integrative function in two respects: first, it enables the individual to integrate the various roles he or she plays; second, it integrates individuals into the community.

Assuming that citizenship does indeed provide this integrative experience, how does this benefit the individual? How does it help him or her to become a better person? It helps by instilling a more secure sense of the self, of one's identity and integrity as a person. One of the most common complaints about modern society is that our lives tend to be divided into a series of almost discrete compartments. We leave home to go to work, where the division of labor often confines us to a narrow and repetitive task; we leave work to go shopping, where we encounter people we know only as clerks and customers; we leave the store to drive or ride home, seldom seeing a familiar face along the way. Modern, urban society presents a far greater range of opportunities than earlier forms of society, but it also separates people from one another and splits their lives into fragments.[7] In such circumstances it is hardly surprising that many people suffer from an identity crisis that leaves them unsure of who they are and what they want. Nor is it surprising that so much time and effort are devoted to "getting in touch with oneself." To the extent that active citizenship requires the individual to see himself or herself as more than the sum of the various roles he or she plays, it will work to establish a secure sense of self. Anyone who finds this desirable will also have good reason to believe that the integrative aspect of citizenship will be, at least in the long run, of personal benefit.

There are, however, other ways to deal with the problems that follow from the multiplicity of roles and the fragmentation of identity characteristic of modern society. One way is to renounce modern life and withdraw into a cave or an all-embracing community of like-minded people. Another is to concentrate on a single role—parent, perhaps, or soldier or scholar—to the virtual exclusion of all others. Either way, one may overcome the role conflicts and identity crises of modern life. One may do this, anyhow, to the extent that one can truly evade the insistent demands of modern life. From the republican-liberal standpoint, active citizenship is a better alternative. It is better because it promises an educative as well as an integrative experience.

Perhaps the best way to make this point is in terms of a distinction Dennis Thompson draws between Rousseau's and John Stuart Mill's conceptions of citizenship.[8] According to Thompson, Rousseau's conception is "patriotic" and Mill's is "enlightened." For Rousseau, in other words, the principal duty of the citizen is to put the good of the community above all other considerations. Being a good citizen requires simplicity—a wholehearted devotion to duty—rather than sophistication. For Mill, however, the citizen is someone who develops his or her faculties through active engagement in public life. As Mill says in *Representative Government,*

> It is not sufficiently considered how little there is in most men's ordinary life
> to give any largeness either to their conceptions or to their sentiments. Their

work is a routine; not a labour of love, but of self-interest in the most elementary form, the satisfaction of daily wants; neither the thing done, nor the process of doing it, introduces the mind to thoughts or feelings extending beyond individuals; if instructive books are within their reach, there is no stimulus to read them; and in most cases the individual has no access to any person of cultivation much superior to his own. Giving him something to do for the public, supplies, in a measure, all these deficiencies. If circumstances allow the amount of public duty assigned him to be considerable, it makes him an educated man.[9]

In addition to the intellectual growth stimulated by civic activity, the citizen should also acquire "the practical discipline which the character obtains" from the occasional exercise of "some social function."[10] And "[s]till more salutary" than either intellectual or practical development is

the moral part of the instruction afforded by the participation of the private citizen, if even rarely, in public functions. He is called upon, while so engaged, to weigh interests not his own; to be guided, in case of conflicting claims, by another rule than his private partialities; to apply, at every turn, principles and maxims which have for their reason of existence the common good: and he usually finds associated with him in the same work minds more familiarized than his own with these ideas and operations, whose study it will be to supply reasons to his understanding, and stimulation to his feelings for the general interest. He is made to feel himself one of the public, and whatever is for their benefit to be for his benefit.[11]

On Mill's account, in short, the individual stands to gain in three ways—intellectually, practically, and morally—from the exercise and development of his or her capacities through engagement in public affairs. If Mill is right, active citizenship performs an educative function by drawing out abilities in individuals that might otherwise remain untapped. Because these abilities will prove valuable in other aspects of the citizens' lives as well, the educative dimension of citizenship clearly promises to work to their benefit.

Two other features of this educative dimension are also noteworthy. Both pertain to "the moral part of the instruction" afforded by participation in public affairs. The first is that this participation leads individuals to Tocqueville's doctrine of "self-interest properly understood." For reasons Mill set out, active citizenship promises to widen individuals' horizons and deepen their sense of how their lives are involved with others', including people who are unknown to them. By doing so, participation works to overcome *individualism* as Tocqueville understood it: "a calm and considered feeling which disposes each citizen to isolate himself from the mass of his fellows and withdraw into the circle of family and friends; with this little society formed to his taste, he gladly leaves the greater society to look after itself."[12] Active citizenship works to overcome this pernicious form of individualism by fostering the individual's sense of himself or herself as a part of, rather than apart from, the public.

It is also important to notice *how* participation encourages responsible citizenship. The legal dimension inclines us to think of citizenship in categorical terms: either one is a citizen of a certain country or one is not. From the perspective of ethical citizenship, however, one can be more or less of a citizen—a "real" citizen, a citizen "in name only," or somewhere in between. Mill's insight is that real citizenship can be cultivated by encouraging those who are citizens in name only to join in public life. From modest beginnings in occasional activities that require a man to "weigh interests not his own" and to look beyond "his private partialities," political participation can transform the nominal citizen into one who, "made to feel himself one of the public," is moved to act by the desire to promote the common good. Participation in public life thus seems to be a pathway to, as well as a defining feature of, ethical citizenship.

This conclusion is especially important because it suggests the possibility of fostering the kind of citizenship republican liberalism requires—and of doing so without resort to Rousseau's civil religion or to other tactics uncongenial to liberals. Indeed, the republican-liberal conception of citizenship I have sketched here has the virtue of generating its own support. In its legal and ethical dimensions, it combines a respect for the rights and liberties of the individual as a citizen (in the legal sense) with a recognition of the need for active, public-spirited citizenship (the ethical sense). In its integrative and educative dimensions, it also promises the individual a more secure sense of self and the opportunity to develop important capacities— and thus helps him or her to feel, in Tocquevillean fashion, the connection between his or her interests and the public interest. In strictly conceptual terms, then, there seems to be no reason to doubt the practical possibility of republican liberalism. If republican-liberal citizenship demanded singleminded, unstinting devotion to the public good, then republican liberalism would be practically impossible. But its conception of citizenship is more modest than that, and its prospect of encouraging citizenship more likely.

In politics, however, we cannot confine ourselves to strictly conceptual terms. In the third section of this chapter, therefore, I shall begin to explore various ways to overcome the obstacles that inhibit people from acting as (republican-liberal) citizens. But such an exploration will be worthwhile only if (republican-liberal) citizenship is itself worth encouraging. To show how it is, I shall now defend it against a rival conception of citizenship.

The Citizen as Consumer

This rival conception derives from the so-called economic theory of democracy. As developed by Joseph Schumpeter, Anthony Downs, and others, this theory attempts to explain politics in terms of economic competition.[13] Political parties compete for votes just as corporations compete for profits. To win elections, parties try to offer the most attractive candidates and the most popular programs. Citizens, following the analogy, are consumers whose votes the parties are trying to gain. If they are sensible consumers, the citizens will spend their votes—or, more precisely, the time and energy required to weigh the alternatives and cast their votes—so as to strike the best bargain for themselves. Or they may decide that the political marketplace offers nothing appealing or that their resources are better invested elsewhere; either way, they will maximize their expected utility by turning their attention away from politics.[14]

This way of thinking about citizenship and politics is far removed from the republican ideal of civic virtue. It is consistent with liberalism, however, or at least with that strand of liberalism, running from Hobbes through Bentham and James Mill, that regards the public as a loose collection of atomistic individuals and politics as simply another way to advance or defend one's personal interests.[15] It is this strand of liberalism that communitarians decry—and perhaps mistake for liberalism in general.

Thinking of the citizen as a consumer is also consistent with the legal dimension of citizenship, since the citizen-consumer enjoys rights and liberties protected by law, including the right to pursue his or her personal interests both in the private and public realms. But there is no room in this conception for the ethical, integrative, or educative dimensions of citizenship. That is an advantage of this conception of citizenship, according to its proponents. In their view, defining "citizen" so as to require active and public-spirited engagement in politics is to make excessive and unrealistic demands on people. It is also dangerous, for it inspires attempts to shape the views and preferences of people in the name of "enlightened" citizenship. It is both safer and more realistic to assume that people will always act to further their personal interests, that their preferences reveal these interests, and that they enter the political arena—if they enter it at all—with their preferences already formed. The job of the government is not to decide which preferences are right or good or worth promoting but merely to aggregate the preferences so as to reflect the citizens' will—a will, like Rousseau's "will of all," that is nothing more than the sum of their individual preferences. Therefore we ought to regard the citizen as a consumer and to reject any conception, such as that of the republican-liberal, that smuggles notions of civic virtue into citizenship.

The rivalry between these two conceptions of citizenship—the citizen as consumer and the citizen as republican liberal—stems from two different strands of liberal thought and, perhaps more broadly, two different ways of thinking about politics. Jon Elster captures the difference in his contrast between "the market" and "the forum." According to the first view, the purpose of politics is to coordinate or aggregate individual preferences;

hence the economic theory of democracy and the idea of the citizen as consumer. According to the second, the purpose of politics is to transform preferences, just as debate within a forum is supposed to lead the audience to reconsider and perhaps to change their positions.[16] To understand why the republican-liberal conception of citizenship is superior to that of the citizen as consumer, we shall have to examine some of the problems that beset the "market" view of politics. One of these is the apparent impossibility of finding an acceptable procedure for aggregating preferences.[17] This problem is also likely to trouble anyone who wants to include democratic voting procedures in a political system that aims at transforming preferences, however, so I shall set it aside and turn to four other difficulties with the market or interest-aggregation view.

First, it is a mistake to think that we face a fundamental choice between taking preferences as given or working to transform them. Preferences are not simply given, except perhaps in the vacuous sense that people typically prefer eating to starvation. That I prefer baseball to cricket, however, or bluegrass music to opera must have something to do with the time and place in which I was raised. Preferences are shaped by a variety of factors, from the influence of parents, teachers, and peer groups to that of the marketing experts and advertising agents who make their living by luring the rest of us into the marketplace. The question, then, is not *whether* we should subject our preferences to formation or transformation, but *how* we can best do this. Indeed, the point of the "forum" view of politics is to lead people to examine their preferences so that they may be better able to decide whether these preferences truly square with their interests. Among other things, the resulting enlightenment should include an understanding of how others are already trying to shape our preferences.

The second mistake of the interest-aggregation view is to think that we can or should want to remain absolutely neutral with regard to preferences. At the least, we need to discriminate between genuine statements of preference and those that are the result of manipulation or misinformation. We also need to rule out some preferences, such as those of the person who thinks that only his or her interests should count. If we could ignore or overcome these obstacles, moreover, we would still "need to be assured that all interests will be pressed with equal force." Yet this assurance is precisely what politics as interest-aggregation *cannot* provide, since it "favours those with the resources and the incentives to press their interests politically."[18]

A third problem is that market politics has little to offer with regard to the integrative dimension of citizenship. If the market view provides the individual with a secure sense of self, it does so less by integrating the roles one plays than by narrowing them until one sees oneself, in all aspects of life, as a consumer. And even this pinched sense of the self is unlikely to remain secure. When everything else becomes a commodity subject to exchange in the marketplace, people themselves become "human resources." When one's worth is fixed by the market value others set, as Hobbes thought it was, the result will be anxiety, not security.[19]

Finally, and most significant for my purposes here, politics as interest-aggregation is incapable of generating allegiance. If citizens are merely consumers and the political order nothing more than a mechanism for coordinating and aggregating the citizens' preferences, there is no satisfactory answer to the question, "What reason has anyone to accept the decision that emerges from the process of interest-aggregation?"[20] There is no appeal to solidarity or civic virtue, of course. In such a "resolutely individualistic" conception of politics, people "are essentially competitors—rivals for space, for resources, for power. . . . The only bonds between citizens are contractual in nature, formed by agreements based on the self-interest of the parties involved."[21] Where self-interest does not dictate obeying the law, there is simply no reason to obey.

Perhaps this is too hasty a conclusion. Someone who adheres to the market view can still point out that self-interest can provide two reasons for obeying the rules of the political order. The first rests in recognizing that it is in one's interests, in the long term, to have a system for aggregating preferences, especially when that system gives everyone's preferences equal weight. Some people may not take such a long view of their interests, to be sure, so it is necessary to employ the practice of punishment to secure their compliance. Avoiding punishment thus provides a second reason, rooted in self-interest, for obeying the law.

Neither of these reasons is satisfactory. The appeal to self-interest in the long term does not work because it leaves open the problem of free riders. As I argued in Part I, the political order is a public good, at least when we may reasonably regard it as a cooperative enterprise governed by the rule of law. But public goods are subject to free riders, and someone moved by self-interest—even self-interest over the long term—will look to escape the burdens of cooperation whenever possible. If we take citizens to be consumers looking for the best bargain, then we should expect everyone to disobey the law whenever he or she finds obedience burdensome. This being so, all of the weight must rest on coercion. Yet the more we rely on coercion to secure compliance, the more we shall have to rely on coercion. When obedience seems burdensome, the law and those who enforce it will be resented as obstacles, or even opponents, that block the satisfaction of one's desires. Government and law soon appear to be alien forces imposed on one—forces to be circumvented whenever possible. As lawbreaking increases, however, and our own interests suffer, we have no recourse but to call for more police, more jails, and more coercion. The only question is whether we can stop short of Hobbes's leviathan-state.

Even on the optimistic assumption that we can, there is still another reason to believe that other means of securing cooperation are superior to coercion: efficiency. As Diego Gambetta observes,

> [S]ocieties which rely heavily on the use of force are likely to be less efficient, more costly, and more unpleasant than those where trust is maintained by other means. In the former, resources tend to be diverted away from economic undertakings and spent in coercion, surveillance, and information gathering, and less incentive is found to engage in cooperative activities.[22]

Such inefficiency is both an embarrassing problem for and a telling argument against the market view of politics, for it demonstrates how that view subverts itself. Citizens who think of themselves as consumers will surely prize efficiency. Yet the more citizens think of themselves as consumers, as we have seen, the more likely they are to rely on the inefficient means of coercion to secure compliance with the laws. On its own grounds, then, the conception of the citizen as consumer is inferior to a conception, such as the republican-liberal, that does not rely exclusively on coercion to generate the necessary cooperation.

In short, politics as interest-aggregation simply cannot provide an adequate account of citizenship. It avoids the liberty-constricting features of stringent republicanism, but its narrow individualism deprives it of the capacity to inspire the loyalty of its citizen-consumers. For a conception of citizenship and political life that promises to generate its own support *and* protect individual liberty, we must turn to republican liberalism.

Republican Liberalism and the Assurance Game

Republican liberalism promises to generate its own support. But *can* it do so? Republican liberalism may be more promising than the market-based notion of the citizen as consumer, but whether that promise can be realized remains to be seen. We still face the question, in other words, of the practical possibility of republican liberalism.

Answering this question requires a return to the problem of collective action and a brief excursion into game theory. The excursion is necessary partly because game theory may indicate that there are certain conditions, *not* involving coercion, in which self-interested individuals will find cooperation to be in their interests. If so, those who take the market view of politics may yet escape the difficulties raised in the previous section. I shall argue, however, that escape is possible only because the relevant conditions encourage people to think of themselves as citizens, in the republican-liberal sense, rather than as consumers.

The starting point is those problems of collective action in which a pure public good is involved—those in which the good in question is indivisible, nonexcludable, and nonrival. In these situations, as in the classic examples of clean air and national defense, everyone in the group may either cooperate to help produce the good in question or defect (withhold cooperation) in hopes of enjoying the good without contributing to its provision. Except in special circumstances, in which one person or a small subset of the group can provide the good without the help of the others, each individual will find it rational to defect. As in the prisoners' dilemma, the outcome will be less desirable to all than the outcome that follows from everyone's choosing to cooperate.

How does all of this bear on citizenship? It provides an insight into the obstacles to republican-liberal citizenship today. The life of active, public-spirited citizenship is a demanding one, and under current conditions it is likely to be unrewarding as well. The person who plays the part of the republican-liberal citizen may also find that he or she is playing the part of the sucker, working futilely to help provide public goods while others try to enjoy these goods without bearing any of the costs of their production. There is simply no incentive to take an active, public-spirited part in public affairs when there is no reason to expect one's actions to make any difference in those affairs and little reason to expect more than a few to join in cooperative efforts. If such conditions do not always prevail, they do occur often enough to serve as significant obstacles to cooperation—including the cooperation manifested in obedience to the law.

Another instance is the problem of voting. Because a system of open elections is a pure public good, maintaining such a system presents a problem of collective action, an n-person prisoners' dilemma. In this case, a woman contributes to the provision of the good (cooperates) when she votes; she fails to contribute (defects) when she abstains from voting. Should she vote? The answer depends upon the circumstances and the voter's objectives. If her only reason for voting is to affect the outcome of the election, she will probably judge voting to be irrational, for in most elections there is little chance that one vote will swing the election. Nor is it rational to vote if her objective is to preserve the electoral system. One vote will not accomplish this goal, and if a sufficient number do vote, the woman may continue to receive the benefits of the system without enduring the burden, however slight, of going to the polls to vote. When these conditions obtain, the question may not be why so few people vote but why more than a mere handful do.

The same logic applies when those who live in a city or region are asked to make an effort or sacrifice of some kind to help provide a specific public good. Voluntary carpooling to reduce traffic congestion and air pollution is an example of this, as is voting for a bond issue to raise funds for the purchase of land for public parks. If most of the people in my city form carpools, I may enjoy uncrowded streets, clearer skies, and perhaps even lower fuel prices as I drive, alone, to work. But if too many people reason and act as I do, the carpooling program will fail—as such programs often seem to do. Given the nature of the problem, it is easy to see why local governments encounter such difficulty in persuading their citizens (in the legal sense of the term) to cooperate to achieve public purposes.

Yet we know that many people sometimes do support projects for public goods, just as we know that many eligible voters do take the trouble to go to the polls. There must be some possibility of republican-liberal citizenship, then. But how can we account for such ostensibly irrational behavior?

One answer particularly congenial to the market view of politics is that people respond to selective incentives, which encourage the members of a group to contribute to cooperative efforts by offering private rewards of some sort to those who contribute or by imposing penalties on those who do not.[23] For instance, one way to promote carpooling is to reserve desirable parking spaces or special traffic lanes for vehicles carrying three or more passengers.

Another answer is that people sometimes respond to moral considerations. People who vote or contribute in another way to a cooperative effort often say that they do so simply because it is their duty or because it is the right thing to do. Edna Ullmann-Margalit even argues that prisoners'-dilemma situations generate social norms that "solve" problems of collective action by the "bringing about of restraints on choices, or of changes in the preference-order among the outcomes which are reflected in pay-off changes."[24] If they are powerful enough, according to her analysis, such notions as "death before dishonor" help to keep soldiers from fleeing in the face of the enemy. In similar if less dramatic fashion, the notions of civic duty and fair play may move some people to take the part of the active, public-spirited citizen in civic affairs.[25] Such notions, of course, are not available to the citizen-consumer.

In the case of civic virtue, neither private rewards nor penalties are promising methods of ensuring public-spirited action; certainly we may doubt that those who vote merely to avoid paying a fine, say, are practicing "real" citizenship. Moral incentives may be more appropriate in this case, but they too have their limits. One of these is that we simply cannot expect moral incentives to lead to widespread (ethical) citizenship unless the norms defining civic duty are widely shared throughout the relevant group. In a diverse and pluralistic society, however, consensus on social norms is difficult to achieve. The tendency to think of the citizen as a consumer also undercuts the idea of civic duty. Whatever force norms of civic duty retain in these circumstances will be diminished even further by the size of the polity. The man or woman who acts as an (ethical) citizen out of a sense of duty or fair play will probably find that his or her actions go unnoticed and unremarked, which is bound to be disheartening—especially when he or she can take the part of the free rider with equal anonymity. Without social approbation to support those who display civic virtue, the moral incentive withers.

But we have yet to take *time* into account in these considerations. Time is important here because it requires us to distinguish between two versions of the prisoners' dilemma: the original version, in which the persons caught in the dilemma have only one choice to make, and the iterated or sequential prisoners' dilemma, in which the action continues over time and the persons in the dilemma face, and know that they face, a series of choices. In the single-shot dilemma, the rational course for each player, acting independently, is to defect. In the iterated dilemma, however, there is no dominant strategy—no strategy that is clearly best for a player regardless of what the others do. This difference is due in part to considerations of time. The individuals in the iterated dilemma must establish, however roughly or intuitively, a rate of discount for future goods so that they may decide whether to cooperate in one iteration, thereby running the risk of playing the sucker, in the hope that this cooperation will convey a message to the others that will lead them to cooperate—and thus produce a more desirable outcome for all—in subsequent iterations. The higher the rate of discount, the less likely the individual will run the risk of cooperating; the lower the rate, the more rational cooperation will become.

Michael Taylor draws on the logic of the iterated dilemma to argue that rational actors will gradually come to cooperate with one another to produce the collectively desirable outcome *if* certain conditions are met.[26] In addition to holding future goods at or near the same value as present goods, Taylor also requires that the individuals in the dilemma know that a sufficient number of others have cooperated in the past. This confidence in one another forms the basis for cooperative action. As Taylor notes, though, this condition is "more likely to be met in a small group of players than in a large group—and even more likely in the sort of small community in which people have contact with and can observe the behaviour of many of their fellows and which is fairly static, in the sense that there is little mobility in or out."[27]

When these circumstances prevail, people will find cooperation in a collective effort rational, even in the absence of selective incentives. This prospect appears to rescue the citizen-consumer, who is capable of making sacrifices in the short term in order to promote his or her long-term interest. But two problems block the rescue. First, the necessary circumstances simply do not prevail in modern states, in which large and mobile populations make it all but impossible for the individual to know his or her compatriots well enough to have confidence that they will (continue to) cooperate rather than defect. In such a state, in fact, it is unlikely that a single game is being played, over and over, with the same set of players. In the absence of a small, stable group, it matters little whether we regard the body politic as a single-play or an iterated prisoners' dilemma.

What if the necessary circumstances do prevail? In that case a second problem arises for the citizen-consumer conception of citizenship. This problem is that the conditions that generate cooperation are also the conditions that will transform the motives of the individual. The small and stable group of players who will find it rational to cooperate over time to produce pure public goods will also share at least two of the three attributes of a community, as Taylor defines it: "shared values and beliefs, direct and many-sided relations, and the practice of reciprocity."[28] They will come to know and care about one another because, in their "direct and many-sided relations," they will see themselves as something more than consumers. Instead of self-interested consumers locked in an *n*-person prisoners' dilemma, they will be *conditional altruists* playing *the assurance game.*[29]

The assurance game differs from the prisoners' dilemma in two key respects: motives and information. In the prisoners' dilemma, whether iterative or not, the assumption is that the parties involved are rational and narrowly self-interested. In the assurance game, the assumption is that the parties are rational and conditionally altruistic. They are altruistic because they take the interests of others into consideration; they are willing to forgo the opportunity to ride free on the efforts of others. But their altruism is qualified or conditional because they are not willing to cooperate when they believe that others will take advantage of their cooperation and play them for suckers.[30] If they are to act cooperatively, however, they must have the information, or the assurance, that the others will indeed cooperate. But if there is insufficient reason to believe that others are acting, have acted, or are likely to act cooperatively, the assurance game degenerates into the prisoners' dilemma.

From the perspective of republican-liberal citizenship, the assurance game is clearly more promising than the prisoners' dilemma. Because the difference between the two rests on motives and information, though, the question is whether we can encourage the motives and provide the information necessary to the assurance game. Can we assume that people are conditional altruists, or is it safer to conclude that human beings are irrevocably egoistic? On the basis of experience and the criticisms directed against Hobbes and other proponents of the egoistic or "economic" conception of human nature, I see no reason to believe that all people have been, are, and must be narrowly or strictly self-interested.[31] Yet all that needs to be said on this point is that people may be either egoists or (conditional) altruists, and perhaps both, at different times. If this is the case, then there is no reason to reject the possibility that conditional altruism may be cultivated, thus establishing the basis for the assurance game. If it is possible to establish this basis, furthermore, it is also possible to convert the political order into an assurance game. And if that is possible, then republican liberalism is a practical possibility as well.

That is a lengthy string of "ifs," however, and we cannot simply leap to the conclusion. First it is necessary to determine what cultivates conditional altruism. The answer seems to be prolonged interaction and interdependency, a sense of common condition, and the bonds that grow with familiarity. These are, as Elster notes, the same conditions that generate the information needed for the cooperative solution to the assurance game: "[A]ffection for others and information about them tend to grow *pari passu*."[32] Consequently, if we are to lay the groundwork for the assurance game, we must identify and establish the conditions that work toward prolonged interaction and mutual affection. Five factors should be considered in this light: size, stability, fairness, communication, and participation.

Montesquieu seems to have perceived the importance of *size* when he wrote, "In a large republic, the common good is sacrificed to a thousand considerations; it is subordinated to exceptions; it depends upon accidents. In a small one, the public good is better felt, better known, lies nearer to each citizen; abuses are less extensive there and consequently less protected."[33] In recent years both formal studies of collective action, such as Taylor's and Mancur Olson's, and the experiments of social psychologists have borne out the observation that size inhibits cooperation.[34] The larger the group, the less likely are its members to cooperate for the good of the group. Small groups encourage solidarity and reciprocity because the individual's contribution is more visible and more meaningful—not the mere "drop in the bucket" it is in a large group. For anyone who wishes to see the body politic resemble an assurance game rather than a prisoners' dilemma, the overwhelming size of the modern state, and even of many of its subordinate units, is a tremendous obstacle. That is why a number of analysts, wittingly or not, have followed the lead of Montesquieu or Tocqueville and suggested a greater and more creative use of federalism or local government, or both, to overcome the size problem.[35]

The *stability* of a group is the second factor related to its ability to encourage cooperation, although the relationship is positive rather than negative in this case. The more stable the group—the greater the continuity of its membership over time—the more likely it is to resemble an assurance game. One reason for this is that the members of a stable group know they are engaged in an ongoing enterprise, which should lead them to lower the rate of discount for future goods.[36] Social psychologists' experiments confirm this reasoning. According to a survey of experimental studies of the conditions that foster and inhibit cooperation, "one important consideration for subjects is whether or not they view the interchange from a short-term or a long-term perspective. In particular, if subjects believed that they would need to interact with each other after the study was concluded . . . , their behavior became considerably more cooperative."[37] Stability thus enables the actors to develop the ties of affection that promote conditional altruism: the desire to do one's part in a cooperative effort as long as others are doing theirs. Solidarity and stability go together, as Elinor Ostrom discovered in her study of groups that have avoided the overuse of a "common pool resource" such as a forest or fishing bank:

> [T]he populations in these locations have remained stable over long periods of time. Individuals have shared a past and expect to share a future. It is important for individuals to maintain their reputations as reliable members of the community. These individuals live side by side and farm the same plots year after year. They expect their children and grandchildren to inherit their land. In other words, their discount rates are low.[38]

As Ostrom's remarks about reputation suggest, considerations of *fairness* also play a part here. Those who believe they are being treated fairly will look upon their efforts in the cooperative enterprise as genuine contributions to the well-being of the group and hence to their own well-being. Even conditional altruists are not likely to work to produce a public good when they suspect that others are enjoying a disproportionate share of that good or simply failing to contribute to its production. This suspicion in turn generates claims of exploitation and, along with these claims, the selfish motives associated with the prisoners' dilemma. What counts as playing fair will vary with the circumstances, but it is always related to the idea of equality. As I argued in Chapter 5, underlying the notion of fairness is the conviction that every member of a cooperative practice deserves to be treated as an equal.

It is difficult, to be sure, to say exactly what is involved in treating people as equals. But it means at least that the interests of every member of a practice are to be taken into account and that no member's interests automatically count for more or less than any other's. In politics this translates into two familiar maxims: what touches all should be decided by all, and one person, one vote. Political equality in this sense is an essential ingredient in the "civic community" that Robert Putnam takes to be a successful democracy. According to his study of Italian politics, "the more that politics approximates the ideal of political equality among citizens following norms of reciprocity and engaged in self-government, the more civic that community may be said to be."[39]

Vital as it is, equality in this formal sense may not be enough to ensure conditional altruism. If there is reason to believe that formal equality merely masks an inequality of power or influence that gives some people's interests greater weight than others', then those with less influence may see themselves as locked in an exploitative relationship rather than a reciprocal one in which (almost) everyone is playing fair. When this happens, cooperation will collapse. To sustain an assurance game, people must perceive that they are being treated fairly, and their perceptions will follow in part from their sense of the distribution of resources among the members of the cooperative practice. Absolute equality of resources is not necessary, certainly, but something like a distribution according to Rawls's difference principle, which holds that social and economic inequalities are justified when and because they work to the benefit of the worst-off members of society, will probably promote solidarity.[40]

Communication, the fourth factor, is essential because no one will cooperate in the assurance game unless he or she has reason to believe that others will also cooperate. This information is easiest to gather in small, stable groups, where it grows naturally out of the "direct and many-sided relations" that Taylor takes to be an essential attribute of community. There is, again, experimental support for this conclusion: "[T]he greater the amount of communication there is between the players in a wide variety of games, the greater the likelihood of there being a mutually beneficial outcome."[41] Communication is inhibited as groups grow and become less stable, but some forms of signaling are available in larger groups as well. The knowledge that rules exist and are enforced, for instance, provides the individual with some basis for confidence in the cooperation of others. So do firmly rooted customs and traditions, the unwritten rules that enable the individual to develop reasonable expectations about the actions of his or her fellows. As societies become more fluid and more diverse, however, these unwritten rules lose much of their force. Then it becomes increasingly important for schools and other public institutions to convey some form of "common knowledge" that will provide the basis for communication among the citizenry.

Finally, the greater their *participation* in the affairs of the group, the more likely the members are to act cooperatively. Those who take an active part in the life of a group or community tend to develop an attachment to it and to identify their interests with the group's. This identification promotes solidarity, and it follows that one way to encourage solidarity in the body politic is to enable, or even to require, more people to participate in public affairs. In this way, as Mill recognized, those who are citizens in name only may transform themselves into active, public-spirited citizens.

It is important to note that participation need not occur in narrowly political settings to have this effect. Any kind of association that brings people together and facilitates communication among them will encourage conditional altruism, at least among the members of that association. As a network of associations develops that draws in more and more people, the sense of solidarity spreads and grows stronger. As Tocqueville put it in his celebrated analysis of the role of voluntary associations in American life, "Feelings and ideas are renewed, the heart enlarged, and the understanding developed only by the reciprocal action of men one upon another."[42] Participation in private associations thus generates reciprocity that spills over into the political arena. Putnam's study of Italy again provides support for this claim since his findings show that people in the "most civic" regions of the country were much more likely to participate in local associations than were those in the "least civic" areas. "In the civic community," he concludes, "associations proliferate, memberships overlap, and participation spills into multiple arenas of community life."[43]

Conclusion

If we want to encourage republican-liberal citizenship, we must keep these five considerations—size, stability, fairness, communication, and participation—clearly in mind. Together they suggest the difficulty of the task in a world in which states are growing larger, populations more mobile, and traditions less secure. But they also indicate that the task is not hopeless. With sufficient creativity, the marriage of republicanism and liberalism can be accomplished in practice as well as in theory.

In the next three chapters, I draw upon the analysis of this chapter to provide some prescriptions for political practice. I make no attempt to canvass all of the possibilities of republican liberalism or to define its limits and direction. My purpose instead is to provide examples of the kind of recommendations that republican liberalism is likely to inspire. My hope is that these prescriptions and arguments will be attractive enough to lead others to think that republican liberalism is worth pursuing and provocative enough to lead them to pursue it.

CHAPTER 8

Education, Autonomy, and Civic Virtue

Education is an obvious way to try to cultivate dispositions such as conditional altruism. As Shelley Burtt points out, classical republican theorists often argued that it is necessary to ground civic virtue in "the education of desire." For republicans such as Machiavelli, Algernon Sydney, and Rousseau, this meant that we should "seek to secure the priority of public over private goods not through extinguishing or subordinating personal desires but by carefully molding them."[1] If conditional altruism is a key ingredient in the republican-liberal conception of civic virtue, then it seems that republican liberals must also advocate "the education of desire."

But Burtt's words also indicate how the classical republican position may be, once again, too stringent for republican liberals to accept. From the republican liberal standpoint, it is neither possible nor desirable to take people's preferences simply as given, as I noted in the previous chapter. But that does not mean that republican liberalism prescribes "carefully molding" desires and passions. For republican liberals, part of the point of education is to help people live autonomously. Rather than "carefully molding" the desires and passions, then, a republican-liberal education will try to enable people to govern their desires and passions so that they may live as autonomous individuals in community with other autonomous individuals.

How might this be done? *Can* this be done? Is it even possible, that is, to educate people for autonomy and for civic virtue at the same time? In this chapter I shall try to show that it is. But there is another matter to settle first. My claim is that republican liberalism offers a compelling account of the purposes of education: to promote autonomy and civic virtue. This claim assumes that there must be some purpose or set of purposes that define education, and that assumption has recently been challenged. I begin, therefore, with a defense of that fundamental assumption.

The Purpose(s) of Education

Like other institutions, schools seem to need a sense of purpose, an idea of what they are supposed to be doing that guides their activities and sets standards for their appraisal. When there is no clear agreement on what this purpose is, public schools must struggle to meet the demands of all of those who are vocal enough to make themselves heard. The result, according to John Chubb and Terry Moe, is that public schools, at least in the United States, are

> directed to pursue academic excellence, but without making courses too difficult; . . . to teach history, but without making any value judgments; . . . to teach sex education, but without taking a stand on contraception or abortion. They must make everyone happy by being all things to all people—just as politicians do.[2]

The obvious solution to this problem is to find or forge a consensus on the proper purpose, or purposes, of education. This is the path that republican liberals must take, as I hope to make clear in this chapter. But there is another way of solving the problem that shares the market orientation of those who conceive of citizens as consumers. This second approach comprises three steps: (1) abandon hope of achieving consensus on the purpose(s) of education; (2) allow each school to define its own purpose(s); and (3) encourage competition among a variety of schools pursuing a variety of goals. Such is the recommendation of the so-called *choice* approach, advocated perhaps most prominently by Chubb and Moe. As they see it, "schools have no immutable or transcendent purpose. What they are supposed to be doing depends on who controls them and what these controllers want them to do."[3] The core solution to educational problems thus is to free individual schools to pursue whatever goals they deem appropriate, thereby freeing parents and students to choose the schools that best suit their preferences. In other words, schools should have to compete for customers in the marketplace, and successful schools, like successful periodicals, will find "their niche—a specialized segment of the market to which they can appeal and attract support."[4]

This approach to education certainly has its merits, as Chubb and Moe demonstrate. It is only in its most extreme form, however, that educational "choice" truly escapes the need to arrive at some sort of agreement about the purpose(s) of education. In Chubb and Moe's proposal, for instance, schools will have to meet certain standards—for teacher certification, graduation requirements, and nondiscrimination, among others—before they can qualify for the public funds that follow students to the schools they and their parents choose.[5] In their scheme, apparently, a Nazi may not receive public funds for teaching the importance of racial purity in a school open only to "Aryans," not even if the Nazi can find a specialized segment of the market from which to attract support. At some point, some public decision will have to be reached about what schools must and must not do. Even "voucher" proposals encounter this problem, for without some standards to determine what counts as an honest-to-goodness school, anyone who teaches anything could have a claim on the public funds that underwrite the vouchers. The only way to escape this difficulty is to adopt an extreme libertarian position and call for either anarchy or some version of a night-watchman state—one in which there will be no public funding, no public schools, and no public requirement that anyone see to the education of children.

If we do not want to follow the market mentality that far, we shall have to face up to the task of forging an agreement on the purpose(s) of education—or, more narrowly, on what we want our schools to do. In a modern, pluralistic society, this is no easy task, but neither is it an intractable problem. There are educational goals, albeit quite general ones, that enjoy widespread support. This is evident in the implicit distinction that is commonly drawn between various specialized schools—business schools, dance schools, schools of broadcasting, and so on—and schools *simpliciter*. The purpose of the latter is not to prepare people for a specific career or activity but in some way to prepare them for life. There is a difference, in other words, between *training*, which is the business of the specialized school, and *education*, which is the business of the school as such.[6]

These distinctions suggest that the task of reaching a consensus on the goals of our schools is not hopeless. Unfortunately, they do not take us far toward accomplishing that task. One may doubt, for instance, that there is any great insight in the observation that the business of the school is to educate. Even if we add that the purpose of education is in some way to prepare people for life, we still have to reach agreement on what "preparing people for life" entails. Given the variety of views about how life should be lived, it is not easy to see how this can be done. My suggestion is that republican liberalism contains the answer. Without specifying a particular way of life as the one that everyone should follow, republican liberalism holds that people must be prepared to exercise autonomy and play the part of the active, public-spirited citizen. We should therefore think of the purposes of education, or preparation for life, as promoting autonomy and civic virtue.

The obvious objection to this suggestion is that autonomy and civic virtue are competing, or even incompatible, goods. To ask schools to promote both, therefore, is simply to ask the impossible. Or if these ideals are not competing, it is only because the concepts of autonomy and civic virtue are too vague to be useful. People may agree that schools should promote both autonomy and civic virtue, then fall immediately into bitter disputes concerning exactly how schools should try to realize these two goals.

I have already addressed in earlier chapters these complaints, first by showing in Chapter 2 that autonomy and civic virtue are complementary rather than contradictory goals, then by demonstrating in Chapter 3 that autonomy is not too vague a notion to serve as the basis for a fundamental right. Now I shall extend the argument of those chapters into the realm of education. My aim is to show how these two ideals underpin widely accepted educational practices and how they point the way to possible resolutions of various difficulties or controversies now facing public schools. The frame of reference for this chapter is the United States, but the topics I touch on here surely have a more wide-ranging significance.

Autonomy, Virtue, and Civic Education

With education, as with autonomy and virtue, etymology provides a helpful starting point. The word "education" derives from the Latin *educere,* which means to lead or draw out and from which we retain "educe." Originally, then, education involved drawing out or developing the potential within a person—or, for that matter, within other animals.[7] This could consist of the activity of drawing out a specific ability, such as the ability to perform some skill or craft. In the last two centuries, however, a distinction has emerged between education and training, with the understanding that education *as such* is concerned with cultivating the whole person, thereby developing those human attributes that make a worthwhile life possible.

Such a conception of education is obviously congenial to the view that autonomy is the ability or capacity to lead a self-governed life. Like other capacities and abilities, autonomy begins as a potential that must be *realized,* in both senses of the word, before a person can become autonomous. But this can happen only if the potential is drawn out through education of some sort. It is not surprising, then, to find some educators and philosophers insisting that the purpose of education—or at least one of its most important purposes—is the promotion of autonomy.[8]

Much the same can be said of the relationship between civic virtue and education. Like the other virtues, civic virtue is a character trait or disposition that is not likely to thrive without encouragement and cultivation. This cultivation can occur in a number of ways, but there is a widespread expectation, especially in the United States, that schools will be responsible for much of the civic education a person receives.[9]

So it is not uncommon for educators and others to regard personal autonomy or civic virtue as capacities or dispositions that schools ought to develop. There have even been some hints that the two ought to be combined. In 1918, the National Education Association's Commission on the Reorganization of Secondary Education issued a report, *Cardinal Principles of Secondary Education,* that called for a focus on the goals of specialization, "whereby individuals may become effective in the various vocations and other fields of human endeavor," and unification, "the attainment of those common ideas, common ideals, and common modes of thought, feeling, and action that make for cooperation, social cohesion, and social solidarity."[10] Although "specialization" does not correspond exactly with autonomy, the two ideas are close enough to suggest that the attempt to establish autonomy and civic virtue as the aims of education is not at all farfetched.

One can also explain or justify much of what takes place, or is supposed to take place, in public schools in terms of autonomy and civic virtue. In broad terms, the curriculum begins in primary school by stressing basic skills, then goes on to offer more options and individual choice in secondary school, then offers even more options in colleges and universities. The basic skills enable children to "function" in the world; anyone who fails to acquire them is almost certain to remain too dependent on others to have a chance of becoming autonomous.[11] By enhancing the capacity for self-expression, moreover, these skills help the child to overcome frustration and strengthen self-esteem. As the word "basic" suggests, these skills also provide a base from which students can go on to appreciate what options are open to them and what their choices entail.

Although the term itself is seldom used, the attempt to foster civic virtue, or citizenship (in the ethical sense), is also incorporated into the curriculum. Indeed, civic virtue seems to receive more explicit attention than autonomy, since state laws in the United States typically require students to study American history and government, to pass tests on the state and national constitutions, and to take courses in social studies and "civics." Even time devoted to the basic skills of reading, writing, and arithmetic contributes to civic virtue. Those who lack these skills are likely to remain dependent on others for information and political guidance as well as for a livelihood and other forms of assistance. By helping students acquire and develop these skills, the school promotes independence in the sense appropriate to both autonomy and civic virtue.

The desire to promote personal autonomy and civic virtue may also figure in the "hidden curriculum." That is, in addition to the explicit curriculum, schools also teach by example, especially the example of the organization and conduct of the school and classroom. Student governments are supposed to help students learn the value and procedures of democracy, for instance, and the conduct of teachers is supposed to exemplify some of the virtues, such as "empathy, trust, benevolence, and fairness," that make cooperation in general and democracy in particular possible.[12] Teachers who encourage students to raise questions and think for themselves presumably help to develop the autonomy of their charges.

Yet there is another side to this story. Because of the emphasis within most schools on order and organization—typically, hierarchical organization—the implicit curriculum often discourages critical thought and teaches only a passive conception of citizenship. According to Richard Battistoni,

> [t]he presence of a hidden curriculum in high schools is severely disruptive to the political education of future democrats. Not only does the "authoritarian atmosphere" of order and discipline promote attitudes of passivity, unhealthy dependency, submission, competition, and inequality that may be transferred to the polity, but it also prevents the actual teaching of values essential to democratic political behavior.[13]

Where autonomy and civic virtue are concerned, then, there seems to be considerable room for improvement. This is true of the explicit as well as the implicit or hidden curriculum.[14] But there is also reason to believe that school administrators and teachers recognize the promotion of something like personal autonomy and civic virtue to be among their chief responsibilities. That they already do this lends support to my claim that fostering autonomy and civic virtue ought to be, and can be, the acknowledged aims of public schools. It also gives us good reason to try to improve our schools in these respects. To add further plausibility to the case for autonomy and civic virtue, I want now to show how these ideals provide guidance in addressing some of the difficulties and controversies surrounding education these days. There are many more issues than I can address here, however, even in a cursory fashion. So I shall simply offer some comments on three areas of concern in the hope that these comments will suggest the power of autonomy and civic virtue—and thus of republican liberalism—as educational goals. The areas of concern are school size, the question of school choice, and cultural pluralism.

School Size

In the previous chapter I pointed out that a group's ability to secure its members' cooperation in the production of public goods is related to its size. A similar consideration figures in a controversy among educators over the issue of optimum school size, particularly for secondary schools, with the debate divided generally into one side favoring "small" and the other favoring "large" schools.[15] According to the latter, the large school, with several hundred students in each grade, should continue to provide the standard. Large-school defenders argue that, in addition to significant economies of scale, the large high school provides greater opportunities for students to pursue their particular interests while associating with other students with similar interests and abilities. Unless a school is large, there is little chance for it to be *comprehensive*—that is, to offer a wide range of subjects and activities for students with widely varying needs and interests. Those who champion smaller schools, however, insist that the large high school is too impersonal. Students tend to feel lost in large schools, critics claim, which allow most students to proceed to graduation with little supervision or encouragement—and little to challenge them—as long as they do not cause trouble. The small school can give every student more attention, even if it cannot give everyone the courses that appeal to his or her special interests.

There seems to be little hope of settling this dispute, especially if academic performance as measured on standardized tests is taken as the measure of success. As Chubb and Moe report, "high performance and low performance schools are about the same size on average."[16] If we turn to the considerations of autonomy and civic virtue, moreover, it appears that we are pulled in opposite directions. The large high school seems to promote autonomy by widening the range of choice for students, but the small school, with its ability to encourage cooperation, seems more likely to boost civic virtue. Perhaps it simply makes no difference whether schools are large or small, then, since there seem to be equally strong arguments for both sizes.

This conclusion would be correct if it were true that autonomy and civic virtue pull in opposite directions here. But there is reason to believe that the desire to promote autonomy should also favor the small school. Autonomy implies the ability to choose, but it also requires a strong sense of self. Such an identity, or sense of selfhood, is more likely to be nourished in small schools, where students have the chance to know and be known by other students and the school staff. In particular, students in small schools seem to have a better chance of participating in extracurricular activities—activities that are typically supposed to develop special talents, enhance self-esteem, and promote cooperation and responsibility. Students in large schools may have more activities to choose from, but students in small schools have more opportunities to participate in the activities available to them. Some studies indicate, furthermore, that students in small schools take advantage of these opportunities by participating in more activities than their peers in large schools.[17]

Small schools apparently encourage a sense of responsibility and reciprocity in their students. A particular student may take a part in a school play, for instance, not because she is interested in drama but because she knows that the play cannot be staged if only those few students who are actively interested agree to participate. Rather than see her friends disappointed, she will devote some time to the play—and perhaps discover something about herself along the way. In return for her participation, she is likely to expect her theatrically minded classmates to reciprocate on another occasion by participating in an activity of more interest to her. If they do, she and the other students will be practicing conditional altruism.

It is possible, of course, that some high school students who have a well-developed sense of self will find their autonomy enhanced by the opportunities for special classes and activities provided by the larger school. First things must come first, however, and in this case that means that if we want to promote autonomy, we should do what most students will find most beneficial. Following the line of argument developed in Chapter 3, we should give priority not to those who are already well on their way to being autonomous but to those whose ability to lead a self-governed life needs most encouragement.

Even if we conclude that the claims of autonomy lend as much support to the large school as to the small, the claims of civic virtue should still tip the balance toward the latter. The more extensive participation of students in small schools appears to promote a sense of competence, self-esteem, and effectiveness that is essential not only to personal autonomy but to responsible citizenship as well. If the sense of efficacy engendered by participation in school activities increases the chances of participating in public affairs, as seems likely, then the small school will prove a better breeding ground than the large for civic virtue. Taking personal autonomy and civic virtue as our goals, therefore, should lead us to prefer the smaller school to its larger, more impersonal counterpart.

Certainly there is reason to believe that the small school's *size* will provide a more personal atmosphere that improves *communication* among students and inspires their *participation* in school activities. If it does, then it has in its favor at least three of the five factors that promote conditional altruism. The large school cannot claim even one.

The Question of "Choice"

Although the proposals for introducing greater choice into the educational system of the United States are a diverse lot, they typically focus on two goals. The first is to allow students and parents a greater degree of choice in deciding where the students go to school. At present the choice is usually between attending the nearest public school or paying to attend a private one. "Choice" proposals, in contrast, devise various ways to give students and parents the option of determining which school to attend. The second goal also allows a greater degree of choice, although in this case it consists of providing the staffs with more control over the organization and operation of their schools. Some schools may thus feature "open" classrooms and emphasize cooperative learning, while others maintain strict discipline and stress competition; some may offer a curriculum strong in mathematics and science, while others devote themselves principally to arts and humanities; and so on.

Another characteristic of "choice" proposals is that they blur or obliterate the distinction between public and private schools. In Chubb and Moe's plan, for example, parents will be free to enroll their children in any school that meets standards "roughly corresponding to the criteria many states now employ in accrediting private schools—graduation requirements, health and safety requirements, and teacher certification requirements."[18] Schools that meet these standards will be eligible, under their plan, to receive the tax-generated funds that follow each student to the school he or she attends, including schools that are now considered private. All private schools could become public under this arrangement since they would have to do nothing more than meet the requirements they currently meet, yet the public school would resemble what we now regard in the United States as a private school.

"Choice" proposals have a number of attractive features, one of the most important of which, as Chubb and Moe point out, is their promise of reducing the bureaucracy that is widely regarded as one of the greatest obstacles to effective schools. In some forms, they also seem to offer a better chance of racial integration than current arrangements have provided. Furthermore, as Chubb and Moe suggest, a "choice" approach can address the concern that it will simply add to the educational opportunities of the affluent and subtract from those of the poor. Thus Chubb and Moe call for "an equalization approach that requires wealthier districts to contribute more per child [into the fund distributed by the state] than poor districts do and that guarantees students in all districts an adequate financial foundation."[19]

But how does "choice" look from the perspective of autonomy and civic virtue? At first glance it seems, like the large high school, to enhance the former at the expense of the latter. It does offer students and parents a wider range of choice, and a wider range of choice generally entails a greater degree of autonomy. But it appears to offer little to encourage civic virtue. Presumably the accreditation criteria will include some work in history, government, and other areas related to civic education. But if the requirements are loose or vague, many schools are likely to give scant attention to these topics. The stiffer and more explicit these requirements are made, however, the less choice students and parents—and school officials—will have.

A similar point holds with regard to Chubb and Moe's "equalization" proposal, which represents a deviation from a purely market-oriented approach. Two aspects of this proposal are consistent with republican liberalism. First, it promises to promote autonomy in the appropriate way: by widening the range of choice for those who have least autonomy—

the poor. Second, by making educational resources more nearly equal, it should foster the spirit of cooperation and conditional altruism by responding to the sense of *fairness.* "Choice" schemes that do not try to correct or mitigate inequalities of wealth offer no reason for the poor and disadvantaged to believe that they are important members of a cooperative enterprise and therefore no reason to believe that fairness requires them to contribute to that enterprise. Such schemes are more consistent applications of the market-oriented, citizen-as-consumer, registration-of-preferences approach to problems of education, however. Chubb and Moe's "equalization" proposal makes their scheme superior to other "choice" plans, but it does so by moving in the direction of republican liberalism.

And what about autonomy? There is probably no definite answer here, but the first glance that seemed to promise greater autonomy from "choice" schemes may prove deceiving. The advantage of a wider range of choice that follows from being able to choose which of several specialized schools to attend will be offset to some extent by the narrower range of people and interests with whom and with which the student associates. Such narrowing is especially likely if "choice" begins at an early age and a child is thus educated—perhaps "trained" is the appropriate word—from kindergarten on for a specific, constricted way of life. To a certain extent, neighborhood schools already do this, particularly in metropolitan areas where neighborhoods are highly homogeneous. If the specialized schools that spring up in response to the "choice" approach magnify this tendency, it surely should not count as a victory for autonomy.

These are not conclusive arguments against "choice," nor are they meant to be. They do suggest, however, that there are reaons to scrutinize these proposals with particular care, for something that is quite valuable and already in precarious condition—civic virtue—may be at stake. They also suggest the importance of looking about for alternatives. If the leading virtue of "choice" is that it will cut away bureaucracy and thus produce more effective schools, at least as effectiveness is measured by performance on achievement tests, then it may be worthwhile to look for a way of lessening school bureaucracy that does not threaten civic virtue. Rather than a decentralized, market-oriented system, perhaps we should look for a decentralized, territorially oriented system that will reduce state regulations and hierarchical control while vesting power in larger school boards consisting of teachers, parents, and other citizens. Proposals to allow for "charter" schools move in this direction. They offer the promise of more effective schools *and* the cultivation of civic virtue. "For politics," as Michael Walzer says,

> is always territorially based; and the neighborhood (or the borough, town, township, "end of town": the contiguous set of neighborhoods) is historically

the first, and still the most immediate and obvious, base for democratic politics. People are most likely to be knowledgeable and concerned, active and effective, when they are close to home, among friends and familiar enemies. The democratic school, then, should be an enclosure within a neighborhood: a special environment within a known world, where children are brought together as students exactly as they will one day come together as citizens.[20]

Cultural Pluralism

Although I shall return to the topic of cultural pluralism in Chapter 11, it is necessary here to ask what republican liberalism has to say about the problems cultural pluralism presents for education. These problems are especially difficult because the ties of diverse cultural traditions seem to be at odds with both personal autonomy and civic virtue. Yet there also seems to be something of value in every tradition and something of value, too, in diversity. The question, then, is whether it is possible to devise a system of education that respects traditions and diversity while promoting autonomy and civic virtue.

The answer depends upon what one is willing to count as "respecting" traditions and diversity. If this means that the members of every linguistic, national, cultural, religious, or irreligious group must be able to raise their children exactly as they please, without any exposure in the schools to ideas and beliefs that they consider threatening, then the answer must be no. If "respecting" traditions and diversity means that children must learn about ways of life and systems of belief different from their own, then the answer is yes. Autonomy, the capacity to lead a self-governed life, includes the ability to reflect upon one's beliefs, desires, and circumstances; to lead students to such reflection by exposing them, at the appropriate time and in appropriate ways, to different beliefs and practices is to cultivate autonomy. Civic virtue is the disposition to act for the good of the community as a whole; such a disposition can only develop in a culturally diverse society if students gain a realistic sense of how the members of their community differ from one another.

The problem, of course, is that some people do not believe that autonomy or civic virtue is worth cultivating. Two legal cases in the United States—cases that have attracted considerable attention from political philosophers of late—make this point quite clearly.[21] In the first case, *Wisconsin* v. *Yoder* (406 U.S. 205 [1972]), the State of Wisconsin sought to compel children of the Old Order Amish sect to attend school until their sixteenth birthday, as state law required. In the second, *Mozert* v. *Hawkins County Board of Education* (827 F.2d 1058 [6th Cir. 1987]), a group of fundamentalist Christians complained that the Board of Education violated their right to the free exercise of religion when it required their children to read a textbook that, in their view, denigrated their beliefs. In both cases, the claims of autonomy and citizenship seem to be in conflict with the claims of people whose fundamental commitment is to a life of religious devotion—a life that demands not that they seek the truth but that they adhere scrupulously to what their faith accepts as the truth.

Wisconsin v. *Yoder* poses the problem presented by this conflict in a particularly daunting form. The Amish resisted Wisconsin's attempts to compel their children to attend high school on the grounds that education beyond the fundamentals necessary for the simple life of the farm inspired a worldliness contrary to their religion. Compelling their children to attend school even for an additional two or three years beyond the eighth grade, they argued, posed a serious threat to the continued existence of the Amish community and the salvation of themselves and their children. In response, Wisconsin advanced (according to Chief Justice Warren Burger's opinion for the Supreme Court) two primary arguments: "[S]ome degree of education is necessary to prepare citizens to participate effectively and intelligently in our open political system if we are to preserve freedom and independence. Further, education prepares individuals to be self-reliant and self-sufficient participants in society."

Yet the Court ruled against Wisconsin's position. In doing so, the majority of the Court did not deny the validity of these two arguments, which proceed from a conception of education quite similar to the one I have advanced here. Instead, faced with two apparently legitimate and reasonable positions, the Court gave priority to the freedom of religion. Is this the proper answer?

There are two points to make in response to this question. The first is that the Court's ruling is not necessarily an improper answer. One may firmly believe that the purpose of education is to promote autonomy and civic virtue, that is, and also believe that other interests, concerns, or rights take precedence. The second point, however, is that those who take this position take the commitment to autonomy and civic virtue too lightly. If the mission of schools is to cultivate these qualities, it must be because these are qualities that adults ought to have. The commitment cannot begin and end with schools; it must be a commitment throughout the political order. This being so, I believe that the ruling in *Wisconsin* v. *Yoder* was wrong.[22]

I reach this conclusion reluctantly, for I am sure that the Amish religion and way of life are in many ways praiseworthy. I cannot see how they will become *less* praiseworthy, however, if Amish children gain a bit more knowledge and freedom to decide whether or not they want to remain part of the Amish community.

In this regard, the arguments of those who agree with the Court's verdict in *Wisconsin* v. *Yoder* are instructive. According to Jeff Spinner, for instance, Wisconsin was wrong to insist on further schooling because the eighth-grade education that the Amish want for their children is sufficient to meet the demands of autonomy.

> The Amish children probably do not have as many choices in their lives as do other children, but they do have a modicum of choice. The steady number of Amish that leave the Amish community shows that many believe that they have the ability to survive outside the Amish community. Furthermore, the Amish do not raise their children ill-equipped to live meaningful lives. The Amish prepare their children to live in the Amish community, just as other parents prepare their children to live in their communities. With most Amish children choosing to live in either Amish or Mennonite communities, their upbringing does in fact prepare them for their life plans and projects.[23]

Whether "a modicum of choice" is sufficient to meet the demands of autonomy, however, is doubtful. It is not even clear that "a modicum of choice" is consistent with Amish beliefs. As Spinner reports, "[t]he Amish stress the voluntary nature of their community. Indeed, there really are no Amish children, though there are children of the Amish. No one is baptized until adulthood, usually around the age of eighteen. At that time, each person must decide if he or she will become a part of the Amish community."[24] But this "stress on the voluntary nature of their community" leads to an obvious question: If it is so important that membership be the result of the *voluntary* acts of *adults,* how can it be wrong to insist that the children of the Amish attend school until the age of sixteen, as other children are required to do?

Even if we suppose that Spinner can find a satisfactory way of answering this question that supports the Amish position, it is important to note that his answer cannot reject the claims of autonomy. To do so would be inconsistent with his own belief that the "modicum of choice" available to the children of the Amish is sufficient. That is, Spinner and I disagree on the question of efficacy, not on a point of principle. We share the conviction that there is some educational threshold to which everyone ought to be brought—everyone whose capacity for learning allows it, at any rate—but we disagree on where that threshold is. At this point, the appeal to autonomy proves unhelpful.

Will the appeal to citizenship or civic virtue settle the issue? Spinner sees an important difference in this regard between the Amish and the fundamentalist Christian plaintiffs in *Mozert* v. *Hawkins:* "The parents [in the *Mozert* case] wanted their children to be part of mainstream society, but they also wanted their children to be taught Biblical Truth, as they understood it."[25] The Amish, however, have sought to withdraw from modern society, which leads Spinner to suggest that they deserve an exemption from the usual educational requirements. For the Amish "are *partial citizens,* and as such the state should intervene in their community only when they harm their members or when they harm the mainstream community."[26] Full citizens, such as the parents in the *Mozert* case, must expect their children to be educated to the extent and in the manner necessary to meet the demands of civic life, but the children of partial citizens should be held to a lower civic standard.

There are important differences, no doubt, between the Amish and the *Mozert* parents. Even so, there are at least three problems with Spinner's use of the distinction between partial and full citizenship to settle cases such as *Wisconsin* v. *Yoder* and *Mozert* v. *Hawkins*. The first is the familiar problem of determining what is to count as a harm. If "the state should intervene" in the affairs of a group of partial citizens "only when they harm their members or when they harm the mainstream community," we still have to decide whether the children of the Amish are harmed or not when their schooling is cut short. Second, creating a category of partial citizens who are exempt from various laws and civic obligations is troublesome in a number of ways. How will we decide what groups should and should not count as partial citizens? Will there be degrees of partial citizenship? Will different groups of partial citizens receive different exemptions? How will partial citizens differ from resident aliens?

Answering these questions and creating the category of partial citizenship may prove worthwile in other respects, but there is a third reason why the category will not resolve the problem in *Wisconsin* v. *Yoder*. Partial citizens must still meet some of the standards of citizenship. As Spinner acknowledges, the Amish "should follow the formal requirements of citizenship; they should pay taxes and provide service to the country in time of war (even if this is alternative service to fighting). The Amish do, after all, benefit from the protection of the state and use some of its services."[27] They should also, presumably, receive the education necessary to meet "the formal requirements of citizenship." But is an eighth-grade education enough for this purpose? Or does even *partial* citizenship require that children learn more about the political system and the legal order than an eighth-grade schooling usually provides? Might it even require public service of some sort? As with autonomy, the difference between Spinner's position and mine here is a matter of efficacy, not principle. We agree that educating children for citizenship is one of the purposes of schools, but we disagree about how much of that education is necessary.

This result may seem disappointing. Whether the consideration is autonomy or civic virtue, republican liberalism leaves room for disagreement in difficult cases like *Wisconsin* v. *Yoder*. But it would be utterly unrealistic to demand that republican liberalism or any theory yield precise and indisputable answers in cases of this sort. What republican liberalism does provide in these cases is guidance. By setting the educational goals as autonomy and civic virtue, that is, republican liberalism focuses disagreement on questions of *how much* and *how best:* How much education is necessary to promote autonomy and civic virtue? How best can we prepare children to live as autonomous citizens?

What is most necessary in cases like this, in which the desire to promote autonomy and civic virtue comes into conflict with people who find little of value in either, is sensitivity. We must be sensitive to the desires of those who do not want their children to be educated for autonomy and civic virtue but sensitive also to the possibilities that may be opened or closed to the children themselves.[28] What this means in practice will differ from case to case, of course, but in the Amish dispute with Wisconsin it could have led to a compromise—school until the age of sixteen for Amish children, perhaps, but schools that are alert to the interests of, and partly controlled by, the Amish community.[29] Such solutions are never entirely satisfactory, but they offer our best chance to reconcile autonomy and civic virtue with the tug of cultural pluralism.

A Republican-Liberal Education

Appealing to autonomy and civic virtue will not settle every question that arises with regard to education. Neither consideration will help us to choose between phonics and other methods of teaching reading, for instance, or determine when and how students should be introduced to various aspects of mathematics. Even so, autonomy and civic virtue can provide important points of orientation in dealing with educational questions—or so I have tried to show through the discussion of school size, "choice," and cultural pluralism. Those who take their bearings from republican liberalism will also want to investigate other ways to promote autonomy and civic virtue, such as the community or public service programs that some colleges, universities, and secondary schools have recently incorporated into their curricula.[30]

It should be clear, at any rate, that republican liberalism does not advocate "the education of desire" characteristic of a stringent form of republicanism. Its more modest aim is to promote autonomy and civic virtue. By emphasizing these goals, republican liberalism attempts to bring rights and responsibilities into balance. Among other things, this "would mean teaching citizens, first, their right to insist that their government maintain a basic level of security and prosperity for the individual and community and, second, their responsibility to defend these interests if and when government fails to provide for them."[31] Such an education is not a matter of "molding" citizens. It is, instead, a way of linking individual rights to public responsibilities.

CHAPTER 9

Political Participation and the Problem of Apathy

If we want the political order to resemble an assurance game rather than a prisoners' dilemma, we should encourage political participation.[1] That is one of the lessons drawn from the analysis in Chapter 7 of the conditions that foster conditional altruism and active, public-spirited citizenship. The lesson is clear. Participation brings the individual into contact with other members of a group, thus facilitating communication among them and strengthening his or her attachment to the group as a whole. How to put the lesson into practice, however, is not so obvious.

There are two problems here. One is that there are many different ways to expand opportunities for participation. As I pointed out in the previous chapter, small schools provide their students with better chances to participate than large schools. The social networks and the sense of competence that grow out of this kind of participation should spill over into the civic domain, thereby contributing to more political participation. One way to promote participation, then, is to convert large schools into smaller ones. But there are so many other ways to promote participation that determining where and how to start becomes a difficult problem.

The second problem is apathy. Participation may foster solidarity and active, public-spirited citizenship, but how can it do this when many or most people apparently prefer to play the part of the citizen-consumer? How do we inspire political participation among those who see little or no point to it?

In this chapter I shall examine two strategies for increasing participation and reducing apathy. These are not the only strategies worth considering, nor are they necessarily the best. Indeed, I shall argue that it would be a mistake to follow one of them. They do illustrate the variety of ways in which one can try to promote political participation, though, and the differences between them are striking. The first proposal would increase participation by installing a computer-assisted form of direct democracy; the second would preserve representative government, at least at the national level, while compelling citizens (in the legal sense) either to vote or to register to vote. The second proposal is consistent with republican liberalism; the first is not. Both seek to overcome apathy, however, so it seems best to begin by explaining why apathy is worrisome.

What's Wrong with Apathy?

"If it ain't broke," the saying goes, "don't fix it." In the case of political participation, this means that altering a political system that seems to be working poses a greater danger than the apathy exhibited by its electorate. Three arguments support this view.

The first is that apathy—as reflected in low rates of voting, for instance—may simply indicate that the members of the electorate are content with the situation in which they find their polity and themselves. Politics is not the whole of life, according to this argument; people generally turn their attention to campaigns and elections only when they think that some direct interest or concern of theirs is at stake. Therefore the failure to participate means only that many citizens do not find it necessary to go to the polling place to defend or advance their interests. Instead of thinking of low turnout as a disease to be cured, perhaps we should regard it as a sign of the robust health of a polity.[2]

A second argument against attempts to increase political participation is that no change is necessary as long as enough people are voting to maintain democratic electoral procedures. The value of democracy lies in competitive elections in which two or more parties sponsor candidates for office and voters choose among those candidates. If no one votes, no one wins—and the system collapses. If only a few vote, the outcome will be little better since the winners will be unable to claim the legitimacy conferred by the support of "the people." Even so, it is not necessary that every eligible voter participate, only that *enough* do so to maintain competitive elections. How many is enough is difficult to say, but in the absence of significant challenges to the legitimacy of candidates elected when turnout hovers around 50 percent—as it now does in presidential elections in the United States—there is no reason to believe that "enough" people are not voting. As W. H. Morris-Jones argues,

> [a]ll that is imperative for the health of parliamentary democracy is that the right to vote should be exercised to the extent necessary to ensure that the play of ideas and clash of interests can take place. If a symphony is scored for fifty instruments, there is little to be gained by trebling the number; massed bands are neither here nor there so far as the quality of the music is concerned. In a similar way, heavy polls are largely irrelevant to the healthy conduct of political business.[3]

Underlying both of these arguments is the belief that political participation has value for most people only in a purely instrumental sense: the market-oriented view of the citizen as consumer. According to the first argument, people will (and should) involve themselves in politics only when they think their participation will directly advance their personal interests. According to the second, people should turn out only if they believe their involvement will help to sustain an electoral system that works, on balance, to their benefit. In either case, relatively low levels of voting should not worry us because they simply indicate that people are engaged in activities they value more than voting.

The third argument goes further. Here the claim is that relatively high levels of indifference among an electorate are desirable and perhaps even necessary to ensure the health of a democracy. As survey data consistently show, most people possess little information about politics and public policy. The authors of *The American Voter,* for instance, described an electorate that is "almost wholly without detailed information about decision making in government," that lacks "coherent patterns of belief," and that probably finds most political matters "too difficult to comprehend."[4] When so many people are uninformed or misinformed about public affairs, encouraging more of them to vote may only dilute the quality of decisions rendered by the electorate. In view of other evidence indicating that many are not firmly committed to civil liberties and procedural rights, there is even reason to worry that a significant increase in voting may threaten "democratic viability" itself.[5]

Apathy mitigates this threat. It "plays an important role in making democracy function," according to John Mueller, by providing a buffer against demagoguery: "It is no easy task to persuade people to agree with one's point of view, but as any experienced demagogue is likely to point out with some exasperation, what is most difficult of all is to get them to listen in the first place."[6]

Such are the arguments available to those who believe that political apathy should not be a major concern. In every case, they follow from a particular view of democracy—one usually called "protective" or "economic" democracy because the vote is seen as a way of protecting or advancing one's interests, just as money is used in the marketplace. This is, of course, the familiar realm of the citizen as consumer. But there is also a rival conception of democracy that requires active and widespread political participation in the belief that such activity promotes the development of important human and civic capacities. According to this "developmental" or "educative" conception, democracy is more than a mechanism for aggregating interests. It is also a form of activity—perhaps even a way of life—that draws out the intellectual and moral capacities of the citizen.[7] Anyone who takes such a view, as republican liberals must, will therefore reject the three arguments in favor of apathy.

For that matter, even those who adhere to the "economic" conception of democracy have good reason to regard widespread apathy as worrisome. If elections are merely opportunities for voters to advance their interests or register their preferences, low levels of voting make it difficult to discern those interests or preferences. There is also the problem of the perceived legitimacy of victors in elections with low turnouts. Perhaps "enough" people are now voting, even in the United States, to prevent serious challenges to the legitimacy of elections. But what happens if turnout declines even further? Or if people begin to conclude that participation of only half the electorate—and often much less, in state and local elections in the United States—is not really "enough"? These problems are especially likely to arise as the "mandates" of winning candidates are called into question by commentators in the news media or members of the opposition. In his "landslide" victory of 1980, for instance, Ronald Reagan won just over 50 percent of the popular vote in a three-way election. Although many interpreted his victory as a "mandate," others noted that only about a quarter of the eligible electorate voted for Reagan.[8]

In short, whatever one's conception of democracy and citizenship, there is ample reason to regard political apathy as a problem to be overcome. With this point in mind, I now turn to two very different ways of promoting participation and overcoming apathy. The first is more congenial to the citizen-consumer, the second to the republican-liberal conception of citizenship.

Instant Direct Democracy

One oft-noted feature of Rousseau's political thought is his advocacy of direct democracy. Representation, he said in the *Social Contract,* is a form of slavery to be avoided in the truly just polity. Yet he also insisted that direct democracy is possible only in a community small enough for the people to be able to gather to conduct the public business (Book III, Chapter 15). As many commentators have since observed, this seems to preclude the possibility that direct democracy can play a significant role in modern politics. So it seemed, at any rate, until recent advances in communications technology made it possible to promote democracy by extending and enhancing opportunities for political participation.

Indeed, several writers have suggested that computers and coaxial cables now enable us to establish a new form of direct democracy, variously called "video democracy," "the electronic referendum," and "instant direct democracy."[9] With the aid of computers and cables, it seems, we can install electronic voting devices in the homes of all citizens, disband our legislative bodies, and proceed to set policy by the direct vote of the electorate. What had hitherto seemed suitable only for the Greek *polis*, the Swiss canton, and the New England town is now conceivable in the modern state.

To say that something is conceivable is not to say it is desirable, of course, and the latter point is my concern here. Is instant direct democracy a desirable form of government? It is an attractive prospect in some ways, as I shall indicate. But it also has serious drawbacks, the most important of which is its tendency to discourage people from acting as the active, public-spirited citizens that republican liberalism envisions. I must emphasize, however, that my criticism is aimed only at this particular form of direct democracy. For that reason, it seems best to begin with a sketch of instant direct democracy.

As a preface to this sketch, I want to enter the following qualifications. First, to avoid the charge that I have merely set up a straw man, I have tried to portray instant direct democracy in the most favorable light. Some readers may suspect that I overstate the case in its behalf. Second, I have based this sketch on the political system of the United States, the system with which I am most familiar. My criticisms should apply with equal force, though, to the conversion to instant direct democracy in other countries governed by a form of representative democracy. Third, some of the features of this sketch, such as the terms of office for president and judges, are somewhat arbitrary. Those who do not think that the president in such a system should serve a term of one year may shorten or extend the term as they see fit and make similar adjustments to other features of the scheme. Fourth, because I try to outline a form of instant direct democracy that is as direct and as democratic as possible, I have not considered the possibility of using computers and cables to create a mixture of representative and direct government. Some of the arguments against the pure case of instant direct democracy may tell against these mixed forms, but others may not. Finally, I simply have supposed in the following sketch that instant direct democracy is in operation. This may seem unfair, for I neglect the possibility that a gradual transformation may be necessary to prepare citizens to meet the demands of the new institutions and procedures.[10] But my purpose is to consider the claim advanced by some proponents that instant direct democracy will itself lead to a change in the habits and attitudes of the citizenry—especially the habit of political apathy.[11]

Instant Direct Democracy: A Sketch

Let us suppose, then, that the government of the United States has been converted somehow into an instant direct democracy. As with all forms of direct democracy, the basic premise of this regime is that the people, not their intermediaries, should themselves determine the policies that govern their lives. To make this possible, a computer device has been installed in the home of every member of the electorate. These devices, connected by interactive cable television to a computer in the capital, allow the citizen to cast a vote on an issue by touching one or more keys.[12] For some issues the voters may be asked to rank their preferences among a number of choices; for others they may be able to select from Approve Strongly, Approve, Don't Care, Disapprove, and Disapprove Strongly. This allows a voter to register intensity as well as support for or opposition to a proposal, although the range of intensity is quite limited. That is, the voter may cast no more than two votes for or against a proposal, so that someone who votes Disapprove Strongly (or Approve Strongly) will have cast the maximum number of votes on an issue, two, and someone who votes Approve (or Disapprove) will have cast one; Don't Care has no vote value. In every case, a proposal is adopted if it receives more positive than negative votes.

Each week the citizens vote on one or more issues, although they may simply vote to postpone a decision. The proposals of the week are broadcast over cable television, as are debates between their proponents and opponents. These debates are rebroadcast at various times throughout the week and made available through the Internet so that everyone may see, hear, or read them. At the end of the week, the referendum occurs. The polls are open, so to speak, at three different times during the day to give everyone a chance to participate. Those who cannot be at home at any of these times—and those who have no home—can arrange to vote at a post office, library, city hall, or public office of some sort.

The executive and judicial branches of government play important but diminished roles in this scheme. The executive branch is responsible not only for carrying out policies approved by the electorate but also for providing regular televised briefings on matters of public concern. The president is elected by direct popular vote to serve a term of one year in office. A president may be reelected, but not to consecutive terms, and the person who holds this office may be removed at any time by the vote of the majority of the electorate. Although the president exercises certain emergency powers, they do not include the authority to introduce or veto legislation.

The president appoints the members of the national judiciary, but nominees must be approved by a majority of those voting in special referenda, with the pool of eligible voters comprising the citizens who live in the jurisdiction in question. That is, every citizen may vote for or against a nominee to the Supreme Court, but only those who reside in the relevant jurisdiction may vote for or against a nominee to a lower court. Once admitted to the bench, judges remain subject to recall throughout their tenure. They apply and interpret the law, but they are not allowed to declare a policy approved by the citizens to be *ultra vires.*

These are the basic features of an instant direct democracy. I shall now add a bit more detail to the sketch by anticipating some practical objections that may be brought against a scheme of this sort.

The first objection is that it will prove too expensive. This claim cannot be refuted, strictly speaking, because no one (to my knowledge) has calculated the costs involved. Given the costs of maintaining 100 senators, 435 representatives, and their staffs, however, one may wonder whether instant direct democracy might not prove *less* expensive than the current form of government. One may also ask, What makes something *too* expensive? According to one advocate, the argument that instant direct democracy is "prohibitively expensive" is

> highly disreputable. . . . If we have any serious regard for the value of democracy, then we ought to be prepared to expend resources on it. A society which prefers to allocate resources to the pomp of Government, and to royalty, presidency or members of the inner caucus of the Party, has failed to take democracy seriously enough.[13]

Another objection is that instant direct democracy invites fraud. A number of safeguards can be employed, however, including steps to ensure that only the person(s) to whom it is assigned can operate a voting device. This could be accomplished by using cards and codes, as automatic cash machines at banks do, or the devices could be designed to require the thumbprint of the assigned person(s) before registering a vote.[14] The same measures could prevent voters from voting more than one time on any issue. Other precautions, such as security screening and fail-safe procedures, could protect against the possibility of someone tampering with the computer.

Perhaps the most serious practical objection is the charge that the electorate will be at the mercy of those who set the agenda. How issues are formulated, what proposals are put before the public, even the order in which alternatives are submitted to the vote—all of these are important problems that cannot be settled by the people's vote because they must be settled before the people vote. This means that one set of intermediaries is necessary even in an instant direct democracy. The problem is to ensure that the intermediaries are under the control of the people, not the other way around.

To meet this problem, we may suppose that once a year the citizens elect an Agenda Committee. This committee formulates proposals that its members present on television at the end of each week's referendum, and any proposal that draws at least a third of the votes cast is selected. When this is done, the Agenda Committee chooses speakers from its ranks to take part in the televised debate on the merits of the proposal(s) in question, then sets to work to formulate the proposals for the following week. Like the president and judges, members of this committee are subject to recall at any time to ensure that the Agenda Committee remains subject to the control of the citizenry.

The foregoing is only a sketch of instant direct democracy, of course, not a full portrait. Nevertheless, it should serve to show that a direct democracy of this sort is neither hopelessly farfetched nor a mere straw man. There are even reasons to find such a scheme attractive.

Advantages of Instant Direct Democracy

Instant direct democracy promises to be an attractive way to conduct a country's affairs in several respects. To begin with, the problems associated with representative government are problems no longer. There is no need to worry about whether representatives should act as delegates or trustees or in what proportion they should try to combine these roles. Nor will anyone be under- or overrepresented. As matters now stand in the United States, the Senate in one way and the House in another give more weight to some persons' preferences than to others'. In the Senate, the citizens of the less populous states enjoy an advantage because every state elects two senators. In the House, with its single-member districts, those who do not vote for the successful candidate—and this may be a majority of voters when there are more than two candidates—can be said, in a sense, to have no representative at all. Even proportional representation schemes cannot guarantee equal representation for every voter's views. Yet problems such as these simply vanish in a direct democracy.

A second attractive feature of instant direct democracy is that it reduces the influence of interest groups. In a representative government, the representatives of interest groups typically gather in the capital to try to influence the representatives of the people. In many cases interest groups even do what they can to determine who is elected to the legislature. Dispensing with the legislature might not bring a halt to the lobbying efforts of these groups, but it would certainly hinder them. Insofar as the Agenda Committee in the preceding sketch assumes some of the functions of a legislative body, of course, it will also afford some opportunities for lobbying. But insofar as these functions will be limited, lobbying opportunities will be limited as well.

Direct democracy also promises to end or minimize some of the legislative maneuvers that characterize representative government. There would be no filibuster in an instant direct democracy, for example, nor would there be committee chairs from "safe" districts to delay the passage of laws favored by a clear majority of the people. For better or worse, logrolling and pork-barrel politics in general would be nearly impossible in such a system. This is not a necessary consequence of direct democracy, to be sure, for direct democracy does not itself eliminate strategic voting. It is a consequence of *instant* direct democracy, however, because the large number of voters and their isolation from one another will prevent them from sending signals, "thus reducing the scope for strategic behavior to its bare minimum."[15]

We may note, too, that instant direct democracy will probably not suffer from what many consider to be a major defect of contemporary American politics—its emphasis on personalities and campaign strategies rather than issues. This tendency may be more pronounced in the United States than elsewhere, but it is likely to appear in all representative governments. When we have to choose a representative, after all, we usually want to know something about the character of the candidates. In a large polity in which access to television is widespread, this concern for character seems to degenerate into a concern for personality, image, or "charisma"—or perhaps the scandalous details of what once was considered private life. In an instant direct democracy, by contrast, the issues themselves are likely to be at the center of attention.

Finally, some may also find instant direct democracy attractive because it is free from the intolerance and pressure to conform that supposedly characterize other forms of direct democracy. In this view, direct democracy of the sort found in face-to-face societies purchases community and equality at the expense of more precious values—liberty and privacy. As one critic puts it, "direct democracy effaces boundaries and separations, while subjecting everything to the publicly political imperative. This imperative repels the exploration of possibilities in nonpublic life that the spirit of representative democracy fosters."[16] But instant direct democracy differs from the traditional forms in this respect largely because it is not confined to face-to-face societies. Given the size of the body politic and the isolation of citizens voting in the privacy of their homes, instant direct democracy seems to preserve the desirable features of other forms of direct democracy while reducing the prospect of smug or brutish intolerance to a minimum.[17]

In all of these respects, instant direct democracy appears to be an appealing system of government. But these are not the only respects that matter. More important considerations, I shall now argue, count against government by electronic referenda. For that matter, some people will not agree that all of the features mentioned above are to be counted in favor of instant direct democracy; indeed, I shall shortly try to turn the last feature—its ability to accommodate voting in the privacy of one's home—against it.

I hope, however, that I have said enough about the advantages of this novel form of direct democracy to forestall its outright rejection.

Disadvantages of Instant Direct Democracy

Any advocate of instant direct democracy must expect to face the challenge, Are the people of this (or any) country willing and able to govern themselves in this way? There is abundant evidence to suggest that they are not. According to *Participation in America*, 22 percent of the electorate of the United States takes no part in politics; another 67 percent participates only occasionally.[18] Furthermore, when researchers study levels of political awareness and information, the surveys almost always reveal that most people are uninformed, ill-informed, or misinformed. In these circumstances it is easy to understand how some might fear that the policies adopted by an instant direct democracy will prove to be shortsighted, ill-conceived, and ultimately disastrous.

This is the kind of argument that elitists, democratic and otherwise, usually advance: because the people lack the capacity to deal with the difficult issues of politics, they ought to entrust their governance to those who are wiser, more prudent, and more public-spirited. Yet even an advocate of participatory democracy may conclude that instant direct democracy goes too far. Thus C. B. Macpherson says that the most democratic government we can hope for at the level of the modern state, even with the aid of computers and cables, must still be a mixture of direct and indirect government. Some form of representation is necessary, as he sees it, if questions are to be formulated properly and inconsistent demands are to be reconciled. Otherwise, voters would

> very likely demand a reduction of unemployment at the same time as they are demanding a reduction of inflation, or an increase in government expenditures along with the decrease in taxes. . . . To avoid the need for a body to adjust such incompatible demands . . . the questions would have to be framed in a way that would require of each voter a degree of sophistication impossible to expect.[19]

One need not be an elitist, then, to believe that instant direct democracy requires too much of the average person. But some writers are not persuaded by this argument. Robert Paul Wolff, for one, is "a good deal more than half in earnest" about the proposal for instant direct democracy he advances in his *In Defense of Anarchism*. Wolff, anticipating the criticism just set out, offers the following rebuttal:

> The initial response to . . . instant direct democracy would be chaotic, to be sure. But very quickly, men would learn—what is now manifestly not true—

that their votes made a difference in the world, an immediate, visible difference. There is nothing which brings on a sense of responsibility so fast as that awareness. America would see an immediate and invigorating rise in interest in politics. It would hardly be necessary to launch expensive and frustrating campaigns to get out the vote. Politics would be on the lips of every man, woman, and child, day after day.[20]

Admirable as his faith in democracy may be, Wolff's position is nevertheless untenable. We need not believe that the average person is stupid, selfish, or irrational to believe that instant direct democracy is too taxing a method of government. What disqualifies most of us as policy makers may simply be the lack of time to become suitably informed about the complex problems we face at the national level. Perhaps instant direct democracy can increase our political sophistication, but it cannot itself give us the time to learn all we would need to know.

Time is not the only consideration, of course. People seem to "find" time for matters that are important to them, and it is possible that the number of those who take an interest in political questions might increase dramatically with a shift to instant direct democracy, as Wolff insists. In his view, the real source of most people's apathy is the realization that their voices are too faint to be heard in an elite-dominated political system. If they see that their votes really make a difference, then they may attach more significance to public matters and find the time to inform themselves about them.

Wolff's account of the cause of political apathy may be true, though it may not be the whole truth of the matter. If we grant this, however, it still does not follow that the creation of an instant direct democracy is the cure for this malady. It is far from apparent that the citizens of an instant direct democracy will see that their votes make "an immediate, visible difference" in the world. Their votes will certainly make a difference in this system, for their votes collectively determine policy. But the individual voter is not likely to find that his or her vote makes a difference. As one voter among millions, the individual voter may conclude that his or her vote is utterly insignificant, and this may lead to the further conclusion that time spent gathering information and forming judgments on the issues of the day is simply time wasted.

This conclusion is at least as likely as that which Wolff foresees. If the voters perceive that their individual votes are insignificant, we cannot expect them to develop the sense of responsibility that follows, according to Wolff, from the awareness that their votes matter. It seems, instead, that the sense of responsibility is what now brings many of those who vote to the polls in a national election, for it is nearly certain that any individual's vote will have no effect on the outcome.[21] What an advocate of instant direct democracy must show is that some other feature or features of this system would instill a heightened sense of responsibility in the citizens, thus encouraging them to take an active part in public affairs. The opportunity to cast a vote that may be only one of more than a hundred million will hardly provide this encouragement. The opportunity to vote directly on policy matters rather than for representatives is simply not sufficient. In those parts of the United States in which referenda regularly appear on the ballot, in fact, fewer people vote on the referenda items than for the election of representatives.[22]

So Wolff's claim is implausible. Yet we must be careful to note what this implies. Even if Wolff is wrong, it does not follow that the critics of instant direct democracy are right when they contend that the result of this system will be contradictory, imprudent, and disastrous policies. That *might* happen, just as it *might* happen that people will meet their responsibilities in sterling fashion. But there is a third possibility: that most people, aware of the insignificance of their individual votes, will simply ignore the referenda and leave the resolution of policy to that small group who find politics enjoyable or compelling. If this should happen, we would have no cause to worry—no more than we presently have, anyhow—about the soundness of policy in an instant direct democracy. But is the risk worth taking? It may be, if government by electronic referenda has something else to offer. Sound policy is not the only thing to be desired from political institutions and processes; we may also want institutions and procedures that enrich human life. This goal cannot be reached unless people are encouraged to act as citizens (in the ethical sense), however, and that is something instant direct democracy is unlikely to do.

Other criticisms aside, instant direct democracy is undesirable at the national level because it threatens to discourage active, public-spirited citizenship. This is not to say that it is unique in this respect. In many ways it threatens only to extend certain conditions that already prevail in modern states, such as their overwhelming size. As I noted in Chapter 7, size inhibits cooperation, including the cooperation necessary to maintain the public good of a democratic system of elections. It is also likely to increase reliance on coercion. The size of the state is not the result of direct democracy, instant or otherwise, of course. Unlike those forms of direct democracy that call for the decentralization of political authority, however, instant direct democracy offers nothing to reduce or counteract the effects of size. The ability to vote at home may make voting easier and thus more attractive for some. But when the individual casts a vote in a national referendum, he or she should soon become aware of the futility of this action. Evidence of the immensity of the polity and the insignificance of the individual's vote will be brought into voters' homes on cable television.

The size of the modern state also contributes to another condition hostile to (ethical) citizenship—the lack of community. If an individual is to take the part of the citizen, he or she usually needs to feel a part of a community whose concerns are his or her concerns. We cannot expect many people to act with the public good in mind if that public holds no meaning for them. What we should expect in these circumstances is that many will fail to participate in politics, while many of those who do take part will simply regard their participation as the public pursuit of private ends—thus acting, in Rousseau's terms, as men rather than citizens.

Again, it would be foolish to blame instant direct democracy for the lack of civic virtue in a polity. This is a problem that the electronic referendum is likely to aggravate, however. By enabling us to vote in the privacy of our homes, instant direct democracy would isolate us still further from public contact. In such a system, we may lose even the slight contact now involved in going to the polls, standing in line, and casting a ballot. Little as it is, this public effort should remind us that voting is a public act that carries with it public responsibility.[23] In an instant direct democracy, this reminder may well disappear. Certainly it will be difficult to stir people to act on behalf of the public when the public is only a vague notion referring to something beyond one's walls.

Finally, we should note that instant direct democracy will probably accelerate the tendency for politics to become a spectator sport, or perhaps a television game show. The elements of politics that contribute to the integrative and educative aspects of citizenship—for instance, debate, compromise, and deliberation—are likely to vanish as the mechanical act of voting in the privacy of one's home, where one is free of the frustration of confronting others with different views, becomes almost the only connection between most citizens (in the legal sense) and public life. Judgment will not be sharpened by this process, deliberation will not be fostered, and the capacity of citizenship to enrich the life of the individual and the community will not be realized.

Whether one takes these to be telling criticisms of instant direct democracy will depend, in the end, on one's conception of citizenship. If one believes that citizenship is merely a matter of legal status and that political participation is primarily a means of expressing personal preferences, then the prospect of marrying computers and cables to democratic government may prove quite attractive, for it promises to be an efficient way to register the preferences of the populace. Democracy, in this view, is desirable because it affords everyone an equal opportunity to protect or promote his or her interests. This is, again, the familiar vision of the citizen as consumer. But, as I argued in Chapter 7, such a vision is narrow, cramped, and ultimately self-subverting. Political participation can and should be a way of transforming and enlightening preferences, not merely of registering them. For the republican liberal, who believes that political activity should promote both autonomy and conditional altruism, the prospect of instant direct democracy should be disquieting indeed.

All of this is to say that instant direct democracy threatens to discourage republican-liberal citizenship. These criticisms apply only to *instant* direct democracy, however, and not to other forms. There may be more to be said for more decentralized versions of direct democracy or even for more localized forms of instant direct democracy.[24] Proposals to introduce elements of the instant referendum into representative government may also prove quite attractive.[25] The opportunities exist; it remains to explore them.

Compulsory Voting and Voter Registration

Another method of increasing electoral participation and combatting apathy is considerably more modest than the political overhaul that would be necessary to install instant direct democracy. This approach leaves representative government intact and focuses instead on the rules that govern voting and registration to vote. The justification for this approach is found in the difference between turnout rates in the United States, in which both voting and registering to vote are voluntary, and those in other advanced democracies. In the United States, the highest turnout for a presidential election in this century was the 63 percent of the eligible voters who actually voted in 1960—a figure that would be remarkably low in most other advanced democracies, in which turnout ranges from about 70 to 90 percent.[26] There are undoubtedly many reasons for this difference, but the difference in rules regarding registration and voting is certainly among them.

Some states ensure high rates of voting by compelling their citizens (in the legal sense) to vote. Italy, Belgium, and Australia do this, as did the Netherlands from 1917 to 1970, and turnout in those countries approaches, and sometimes exceeds, 90 percent. Others place the burden of voter registration on the government rather than the individual. In these countries, turnout averages about 75 percent—roughly 25 percentage points higher than in recent U.S. presidential elections—with voting rates of just below 70 percent in Canada and 75 percent in Great Britain.[27] One scheme boosts turnout by making voting mandatory, another by removing the obstacle of registration, thus making it easier to vote. Adoption of either system would surely increase turnout in countries such as the United States. But is one better than the other from the standpoint of republican liberalism? The answer is clearly yes, in favor of a compulsory scheme.

Automatic Registration

Placing the burden of registration on the government rather than the individual does not generate quite as high a level of turnout as compulsory voting, but the experience of countries that employ such a system suggests that the increase in low-turnout states such as the United States would be dramatic. Even better, some might say, voters in these countries go to the polls not because of coercion but because they choose to exercise the right to vote. Yet there are problems with this scheme, from the perspective of both the market and the forum conceptions of politics.

In most respects, automatic registration of voters by the government fits neatly with the market view. Indeed, the argument for automatic registration follows directly from cost-benefit analysis. By reducing the costs of voting, automatic registration increases the likelihood that people will find it rational to vote. Even so, automatic registration is not likely to reduce the costs enough—not on the definition of rationality invoked by those who view politics in economic terms, anyhow. No matter how easy it becomes to register, other costs will still attach to voting. Some of these—the time spent waiting in line to vote, for example—will even increase if automatic registration brings more voters to the polls. But the key point is that the costs of voting will almost always outweigh the benefits. Whether one defines "benefit" as the individual's gain from the election of his or her preferred candidates or the preservation of the competitive electoral system itself, the chances of the individual receiving the benefit are almost entirely independent of his or her vote.

This leaves automatic registration subject to a familiar problem—that of the free rider. A system of free and open elections is a public good. Everyone in the polity presumably enjoys the benefits of the system, yet anyone can escape its costs—that is, the time and energy consumed by voting—by not going to the polls. That being so, why should one bother to vote? From the perspective of the economic conception of democracy, it is far from clear that one should.

To be sure, one attempt to demonstrate that it is rational to vote tries to join a sense of civic duty to the calculation of costs and benefits. As it is set out by William Riker and Peter Ordeshook, this attempt rests on the claim that it may be rational to vote when the individual derives satisfaction from the belief that by voting he or she has fulfilled a civic duty.[28] In this way the benefits of voting are more likely to outweigh the costs. The problem, as others have been quick to point out, is that this move succeeds in rescuing the rationality of voting only by abandoning some of the key assumptions of the economic approach.[29] What is more to the point is that Riker and Ordeshook's argument seems to work at cross-purposes to the argument for automatic registration. If they are right, civic duty is an important part of the decision to vote. Yet automatic registration, which takes the responsibility for registration away from the individual, is more likely to diminish than to enhance the sense of civic duty among the electorate. Automatic registration simply does nothing to awaken potential voters to their public responsibilities.

Because it requires no effort on the individual's part, automatic registration faces a related problem—namely, that many people may fail to vote simply because they are not aware that they can. As long as politics is not an important concern of theirs, many may never notice that the government has registered them to vote. In the United States, registered voters currently participate at rates higher than in countries that use automatic registration. One explanation for this pattern is that those who take the trouble to register themselves are interested enough in political matters or have a strong enough sense of civic duty to take the time to vote.[30] But it may also be that people who register themselves *know* that they can vote. Moreover, once people have bothered to register, they may feel that they have an investment in voting, which may lead them to examine the candidates, study the issues, and ultimately go to the polls. This process could feed on itself and generate an even more informed and interested electorate. Yet none of this happens when governments automatically register people to vote. Automatic registration surely makes it easier to vote, but it may also let sleeping would-be voters lie.

Compulsory Voting

Compulsory voting has found few advocates in the United States, but it has apparently worked well elsewhere. In Australia, for instance, turnout has ranged from about 85 to 95 percent since the introduction of mandatory voting in 1925. Although the nature of the compulsion varies, compulsory voting laws typically require all eligible voters to cast a ballot at election time or face a penalty. The unhappy voter may register a protest by defacing the ballot or leaving it blank, but he or she must either cast a ballot or be prepared to pay the price for his or her failure to vote.[31]

Because it produces very high rates of voting, compulsory voting accomplishes a number of worthwhile goals. First, with almost all the eligible voters turning out, the results of the election present a clearer picture of the electorate's preferences. No election will produce a perfectly clear picture, of course. There are well-known problems with using voting as a system of registering preferences, such as the problem of cyclical majorities demonstrated by Kenneth Arrow.[32] These problems are compounded when the elections do not decide matters of policy but elect representatives who will.[33] Such problems, however, can plague elections with small as well as large turnouts. Elections that draw a high percentage of eligible voters to the polls at least register the preferences of more people than elections that do not. This advantage takes on even more importance when one considers that voters are typically more affluent and better educated than nonvoters.[34] Compelling people to vote should therefore bring people whose voices are seldom heard to the ballot box and lead to election results more representative of the population. A larger turnout should also, as a side effect, lend victorious candidates a stronger sense of legitimacy as they take office.

To some extent, compulsory voting may also promote participation in more demanding forms of political activity. There is evidence that voting leads to other forms of political participation, such as writing to representatives, contributing money to campaigns, and discussing politics with others.[35] Indeed, nonvoters are much less likely than voters to engage in political activity of any sort. Anyone who values political participation as a way of developing mental and moral capacities and fostering conditional altruism should therefore find something appealing in compulsory voting.

In addition to these advantages, which stem from larger turnout, compulsory voting is also a straightforward means of overcoming the free-rider problem associated with democratic elections.[36] Compulsory voting neatly solves the problem by making it more rational for people to vote, at least when voting is less costly for them than the penalty for not casting a ballot. All members of the electorate are thus required to play fair—or to pay a penalty if they do not.

In all of these respects compulsory voting accords well with republican liberalism. Those who think that a liberal society is one in which people should be left to do as they please so long as they do not harm or violate the rights of others, however, may not be happy with the idea that citizens (in the legal sense) may be required to vote. But that requirement is merely one way of recognizing, as those who worry about "rights talk" have recently reminded us, that the enjoyment of individual rights and liberties relies on civic responsibility. It would be better, to be sure, if every eligible voter would cheerfully and freely do his or her part to maintain a system of free and open elections, just as it would be better if everyone would cheerfully and freely serve on a jury when asked. A degree of coercion is necessary in these cases, though, just as coercion is necessary to secure individuals against rape, robbery, and other crimes. As long as it serves to stimulate participation and promote fair play in practices that themselves protect individual rights, such coercion is warranted.

For that matter, a republican liberal can argue that people who fail to do their part to keep their polity's electoral system in good working order really are violating the rights of their fellow citizens. If the electoral system is an integral part of a polity that may reasonably be regarded as a cooperative venture for mutual benefit, an individual then has an obligation, based on fair play, to the cooperating members to vote. Failure to discharge this obligation may therefore violate their rights to his or her cooperation. As a "man," in Rousseau's sense of the word, he or she will hope to conclude the "advantageous treaty" that Rousseau sketches in the *Letter to D'Alembert*—an agreement in which "everyone will faithfully render him what is due him, while he renders to no one what he owes."[37] Thinking as a citizen who is exercising moral liberty, however, the individual can prescribe and obey a law that treats every member of the public fairly. If a system of free and open elections is in the interests of the citizens, then every citizen must have both an obligation to do his or her part to maintain the system and a right to expect the others to do theirs. In that sense, compulsory voting may simply ensure that the person who wants not to vote—and not, therefore, to do his or her part—will be forced to be free.

Still, someone may agree that citizens have an obligation to vote yet believe that the problem with compulsory voting is the degree of its reliance on coercion. As I argued in Chapter 7, the more we rely on coercion, the more we shall have to rely on coercion. Too much coercion begets resentment, and compulsory voting may thus lead to the kind of reluctant, grudging voting that hardly bespeaks active, public-spirited citizenship. As with jury duty, unfortunately, compelling people to vote could easily encourage them to regard voting as an onerous duty to be shirked or avoided whenever possible.

Such an argument is not, I think, convincing. The compulsory aspect of compulsory voting serves more to impress upon people the importance of voting as a civic duty than to frighten them to the polls with the threat of punishment. Those who think that a lighter degree of coercion would be better, however, should consider a third electoral scheme for combating apathy.

Compulsory Voter Registration

This third scheme is compulsory self-registration of the electorate. Such a scheme requires every citizen to register to vote upon reaching the legal voting age. Anyone who neglects to register within a specified period of time is subject to a penalty. Once registered, however, the individual is free to decide whether to vote or not in any election for which he or she is eligible. The citizen will have a *duty* to register, in other words, but a *right* to vote.

Like compulsory voting, then, compulsory self-registration should enhance the sense of civic duty by impressing upon the citizen the importance of voting. Like compulsory voting and automatic registration, it should also stimulate greater turnout in polities in which both registration and voting are left entirely to the discretion of the individual citizen (in the legal sense).

The experience of New Zealand, which has employed such a system for more than half a century, provides evidence that compulsory voting registration works quite well. Before the adoption of compulsory self-registration, turnout in New Zealand was about 79 percent. Since adoption, it has been nearly 90 percent. Given the high rate of participation prior to reform, a gain of ten percentage points is quite impressive. It is even more impressive in light of the modest penalty for those who fail to register.[38]

Like compulsory voting, compulsory self-registration is superior to automatic registration in a number of respects. The first is that compulsory self-registration is likely to generate a higher level of turnout than automatic registration. As I indicated earlier, the evidence suggests that many people who are automatically registered may not be aware that they can vote. One study in particular suggests that those who register themselves are more likely to vote than those registered by the government. This study examined the effectiveness of registration drives by comparing the rate of turnout of people who registered themselves with the rate of those who were registered by an organized group of private individuals.[39] Among self-registered individuals, 56 percent went on to vote in the 1982 elections in Los Angeles; among the group-registered people, turnout was only 41 percent. To be sure, being "group-registered" is not the same as being registered automatically by the government. But if there is a fifteen-point gap here, there should be an even larger one when the government does the registering, since registration then requires no effort at all from the individual—hence the expectation that compulsory self-registration will lead to greater electoral participation than automatic registration by the government.

Compulsory self-registration of voters is also more satisfying from the standpoint of republican liberalism. If voting is a step toward other, more demanding forms of political participation, as I noted earlier, then requiring people to register should stimulate not only voting but other kinds of political activity as well. These activities should help to generate a stronger sense of community and civic duty. They should also cultivate the mental and moral capacities of the citizenry—their discipline, intelligence, and virtue, as Mill says in *Representative Government*—in the process. Compulsory voting registration cannot guarantee these gains, of course, but automatic registration cannot even promise them.

Despite the merits of compulsory voting and compulsory self-registration, critics may yet object that these schemes merely treat the symptoms and ignore the disease. What we need, they might say, is to discover why people are staying away from the polling place so that we can match our prescription to the diagnosis. Otherwise, compulsory schemes will simply allow the causes of electoral apathy to continue their pernicious work.

This is not a compelling objection. In the first place, it is possible that the disease, if that is the right word, simply *is* the tendency of more and more people to conclude that voting is a waste of time, especially when the trouble of registering is taken into account. But if this attitude is the problem—that is, if it is the principal reason for low (or declining) turnout—then all that is necessary is to lower the costs of voting or to raise those of nonvoting. That, in various ways, is exactly what automatic registration and the compulsory schemes do. By altering the calculations of potential (non)voters, then, these schemes may well address the disease itself, not merely its symptoms.

But let us assume that there is some deeper reason—some sense of alienation or dissatisfaction, perhaps—that lies behind the decline in turnout. In this case compulsory voting or compulsory self-registration are still good ideas. By contributing to a higher rate of voting, each scheme does treat the symptoms, but it does so in a way that helps to uncover the disease itself. That is, by bringing people to the polling place, the compulsory schemes enable them to make a statement about their preferences and desires. The choices available on the ballot will constrain the statements they can make, for better or worse, but at least the outcome of the elections will provide some clue as to what people—in the United States, substantially more people than at present—want to see done. Treating the symptoms, in this case, is a way of treating the disease, too.

In the absence of a better alternative, finally, treating the symptoms is often better than doing nothing. When physicians do not know why someone has an extreme fever, they still try to bring the fever down. Using the same reasoning, we may conclude that anyone who regards a low level of turnout as politically unhealthy should try to promote voting, even if he or she is not sure what lies behind the widespread failure to vote.

Republican Liberalism and Deliberative Democracy

I do not mean to suggest that either compulsory voting or compulsory self-registration is a panacea that will dispel all of the difficulties that arise with regard to political participation. Cyclical majorities and various problems associated with representative government will remain. Where political participation is concerned, moreover, voting is hardly more than a beginning. Nevertheless, it *is* a beginning.

Compulsory voting and compulsory self-registration are promising ways to make this beginning because they capture, far more effectively than automatic registration or instant direct democracy, the belief that democracy and free government do not fall like rain from the sky. Yet the present levels of apathy in some polities, notably the United States, suggest that many people either have lost this belief or forgotten what it entails. If we compel people to vote or to register to vote, we will be reminding them of it in an especially forceful way. We will be reminding ourselves, really, that anyone who expects to enjoy the rights of a citizen should be prepared to bear the responsibilities as well.

Republican liberals, of course, will not want to stop at this point. They will look beyond compulsory voting and compulsory self-registration for other ways to encourage active, public-spirited citizenship. In particular, they will look for ways to convert the political marketplace into a forum in which preferences become enlightened in the course of argument and deliberation—ways associated with the ideal of *deliberative* democracy.[40]

According to this ideal, voting should take place *after* deliberation, at the end of the open exchange of views in the forum. Republican liberals therefore must endorse attempts to establish and support these forums in which people can come together and deliberate as citizens (in the ethical sense). One way to do this, following Tocqueville, is to look to the local community as a school of citizenship and to work for the creation or resuscitation of town meetings or neighborhood assemblies. In the next chapter, I will return to this point.

There may be a sense in which all politics is local, as a Speaker of the U.S. House of Representatives once said, but that is not, in the modern state, the whole truth of the matter. In addition to the local, there must also be higher level and perhaps wider ranging forums such as parliaments, senates, and diets. That means, in turn, that there probably must be a place within a deliberative democracy for political parties and partisan campaigning. Such institutions and practices are also compatible with the market conception of politics and the citizen-consumer, however. To move them in the deliberative direction favored by republican liberalism, it is necessary to make parties and campaigns less sensitive to the need to raise money—and therefore less amenable to those individuals and groups who are able to invest substantial sums in election campaigns. Limits on campaign expenditures and contributions should help in this regard, but republican liberalism will probably demand the more thoroughgoing step of public financing of parties and elections.[41]

A third way to move politics in a deliberative direction is through "deliberative opinion polling," devised by James Fishkin and recently tried in Great Britain and the United States.[42] A poll of this sort brings together a random sample of an electorate to listen to presentations and engage in discussions about the merits of candidates for office or issues of public concern. Then, after this opportunity for deliberation, the members of the sample are polled. The result "provides a statistical model of what the electorate *would* think if, hypothetically, all voters had the same opportunities that are offered to the sample in the deliberative opinion poll."[43] More important from the republican-liberal standpoint is the example of citizenship set by those who participate in such a poll. They do not have to reach a consensus or even settle a matter by the vote of the majority, but they do have to listen and speak to one another. They will try to convince others to see things their way, and they may end by seeing things another's way, for they will not be able simply to register their preferences and return home.

More could and should be said about each of these ways of enhancing political participation, but this is not the place to say it. For now, the key point is that republican liberalism will look for and endorse those measures—such as local forums, public financing of parties and elections, and deliberative opinion polls—that will enable and inspire people to exercise their rights and meet their responsibilities as citizens. If apathy stands in the way of this kind of participation, then the republican liberal must try to overcome it. Compulsory voting or compulsory self-registration of voters should help.

CHAPTER 10

Cities and Citizenship

Education and participation, the subjects of the preceding chapters, are of obvious importance to the attempt to promote republican-liberal citizenship. A less obvious but no less important subject is the city: the site or context in which citizenship historically has been thought to develop. Nor is the city important only for its historical connections to citizenship. For better or worse, urbanism is apparently becoming the way of life of more and more people around the world. If republican liberalism is to prove a plausible and persuasive theory of politics, it must attend to cities as well as citizenship.

My purpose in this chapter is to sketch the outlines of a republican-liberal conception of the city. Part of this sketch will focus on the obstacles that contemporary cities place in the way of conditional altruism and active, public-spirited citizenship; another part will suggest some steps that might be taken to remove or overcome these obstacles. But first I want to indicate what the republican-liberal conception of the city will *not* be.

To begin with, republican liberals cannot simply accept today's sprawling metropolis as the ideal city. In this respect they differ, once again, from those liberals who regard politics as merely another form of market activity. According to the market view, the metropolitan complex consisting of a central city surrounded by a profusion of suburbs is an efficient arrangement that responds to the preferences of "citizen-consumers." Much as a cafeteria provides a wide variety of foods to satisfy diverse tastes, so the proliferating municipalities of metropolis offer a wide variety of services and amenities from which mobile citizens (in the legal sense) may choose when they are deciding on a place of residence. As Charles Tiebout explains the point, "the consumer-voter moves to the community whose local government best satisfies his set of preferences. The greater the number of communities and the greater the variety among them, the closer the community will come to fully realizing his preference position."[1]

From the standpoint of republican liberalism, the problem with this cafeteria or shopping-mall conception of metropolis is that it undermines both community and citizenship. Mobile individuals who are perpetually shopping for a better return on their residential investment do not become citizens (in the ethical sense), nor do they together compose a community in anything but the most attenuated sense of the term. The shopping-mall metropolis may offer something to suit the tastes of most consumer-citizens, but it—and the municipalities it comprises—will not be able to hold their allegiance. There is no point in working to improve or maintain the city in which one lives, after all, when it is easier to pull up stakes and move.

So republican liberals cannot simply accept the sprawling, "polycentric" metropolis as a happy coincidence of what is and what ought to be. But this does not mean that they must reject the city altogether, as some republican writers appear to have done. Rousseau's preference for the country, for instance, led him to declare, "Cities are the abyss of the human species."[2] But other writers with respectable republican credentials, notably Aristotle, have held that the city is the breeding ground of citizenship. Their argument is that other forms of political association, such as province, nation-state, and empire, are too large and too remote from the everyday lives of their inhabitants to inspire the kind of interest and effort that citizenship (in the ethical sense) demands. The city is more accessible to its residents than these larger bodies, more closely tied to its residents' interests, and more likely to promote the sense of community usually associated with effective citizenship. Yet it is also large enough and sufficiently diverse in its composition to offer what the village cannot—a truly political environment. Hence the city is the true home of citizenship.

But what kind of city is this? If not the sprawling metropolis, then what form of city does republican liberalism prescribe? To answer this question, we must look first at the general condition of contemporary cities and the ways in which they discourage conditional altruism.

Three Obstacles

Citizenship is connected both etymologically and historically with the city-state—with the *polis* and the *civitas*. But the city-state was much more than a city; it was an independent, sovereign political unit. For all of the city-state's flaws—especially its reliance on slavery and its exclusion of women from public life—the autonomy the city-state enjoyed was a decided asset when it came to cultivating citizenship. Because of this autonomy, the attention and efforts of the citizens were concentrated on the affairs of the city-state, not divided among several centers of political authority. Autonomy also meant that there was no superior authority to overshadow the city-state and render its politics trivial by comparison.

Such is obviously not the case with our cities. Today one of the principal obstacles to the development of responsible citizenship appears to be the "sheer lack of significance at the local level."[3] Some might argue that this lack of significance is only apparent, not real. But the affairs of a city might not even *appear* to be insignificant were it not for the overwhelming presence of the modern state. Whatever the reason, it is clear that citizens (in the legal sense) of our cities are not acting as citizens (in the ethical sense) of their cities. According to one survey of metropolitan politics in the United States, usually no more than 30 percent of those eligible to vote bother to cast a ballot in local elections.[4]

Other differences between the city-state and contemporary cities are also pertinent to citizenship.[5] Three of these differences are especially important here, for they all contribute to the loss of civic memory and the decline of conditional altruism. I shall try to show how these three factors—the size of our cities, their political fragmentation, and the mobility of their people—discourage the inhabitants of our cities from taking the part of the active, public-spirited citizen.

Size

The population of political associations has long been regarded as a key to the quality of political life in general and to the character of citizenship in particular.[6] Plato stated in *The Laws* that the *polis* should comprise 5,040 families. Aristotle was less precise, but perhaps more helpful, when he maintained that a *polis* must be large enough to be self-sufficient but not so large that its citizens are unable to "know each other's characters; where they do not possess this knowledge, both the election to offices and the decision of lawsuits will go wrong. When the population is very large, they are manifestly settled at haphazard, which clearly ought not to be."[7] With Aristotle, then, concern with the size of the polity follows largely from his conception of citizenship. Because the self-governing citizen is one who rules and is ruled in turn, he must be capable of reaching informed judgments about those over whom he rules and who rule over him. Hence the population of the city could not grow indefinitely without diluting the quality of citizenship.

There is, of course, at least one significant difference between Aristotle's time and ours—the advent of the mass communications media. Given the benefits of radio, television, the printing press, and computer networks, we might expect that the size of a city's population would no longer prove an obstacle to responsible citizenship. But this does not seem to be the case. Modern means of communication do little to make us familiar with the other residents of our metropolis. They may enable us to know something about our cities' leading political figures, but they seldom put us in a position to "know what kind of people" the other residents of the city are. To make these judgments, we need to observe people in action, preferably in a variety of contexts and over a period of time. Such observation may still be possible for the residents of small cities and towns but not for most metropolitans.

Moreover, the sheer size of our cities is overwhelming. When there are so many people about—so many strange people who are almost certain to remain strangers—the individual finds it difficult to feel at home in a city that is familiar yet foreign. The inhabitants of the metropolis may look to their neighborhoods for a sense of place or comfort, but when there is no strong neighborhood tradition, or when that tradition has eroded, they are likely to feel isolated and alone in an alien environment. When people lose touch with the city in this way, they lose interest in its affairs. They may retain an interest in those matters that seem to affect them directly or perceptibly, but these matters will probably grow fewer as the city grows larger. Thus the inhabitants of the metropolis are likely to believe both that their participation in civic affairs is insignificant, dwarfed as they are by the size of the city, and that these matters are of no real concern to them anyhow.[8] Such an attitude, as well as the environment that fosters it, does not produce active, public-spirited citizens. It is more likely to produce those who practice Tocqueville's "individualism" by withdrawing into a small circle of family and friends. Like A. John Simmons, such people will find it easier to think of themselves as "dropped into" a city with a government that is imposing taxes and other obligations on them than to regard themselves as citizens who have "grown into" membership in a cooperative enterprise.[9]

As the population of a city grows, then, its inhabitants often come to feel, and perhaps to be, increasingly remote from its political life. This is true in a mathematical as well as a psychological sense. When everyone in the metropolis knows that he or she is only one among hundreds of thousands or even millions, it is difficult to attach much significance to participation in civic affairs. This consideration apparently discourages people from engaging in even the less demanding varieties of political action, such as voting. In mathematical terms, as Rousseau pointed out in the *Social Contract* (Book III, chapter 1), the chance that one's vote will have any appreciable influence in an election decreases as the size of the body politic increases: the greater the number of voters, the less the weight of anyone's vote. The odds are more daunting in national than in municipal elections, of course, but they are certainly great enough in the metropolis to keep at home those people who will only go to the polls when they believe that their vote may well affect the outcome of the election.

As we saw in Chapter 7, the same reasoning applies to the cooperation needed to achieve other kinds of public goods. If a city suffers from traffic congestion and air pollution, city officials may ask the residents to drive their cars less often. Since universal cooperation is not necessary in cases of this sort, any resident of the metropolis may decide that it is in his or her interest not to join a carpool or take the bus but to continue to drive as he or she pleases. As long as the city is large enough to render his or her cooperation insignificant, and his or her failure to cooperate unnoticeable, the individual will have an incentive to be a free rider. Not everyone takes this point of view; many even appear to be willing to make the sacrifices cooperation requires when they believe that they can trust others to make similar sacrifices. But this basis of trust—the basis for conditional altruism—is often lacking in the metropolis, in which the anonymity that comes with size encourages people to pursue private interests rather than public concerns. The larger the city is, the more likely it is that this situation will prevail.

There is, however, a good deal of evidence that shows that those who live in large cities and their suburbs are more likely to vote, at least in national elections, than those living in rural areas, small towns, and even relatively small, nonsuburban cities. Such evidence suggests that the size of a city is positively associated with political participation, if not necessarily with active, public-spirited citizenship. But even this conclusion is not warranted. Studies of voting in the United States indicate that the comparatively high levels of voting among those who live in large metropolitan areas are produced not by the size of those areas but by such social and economic factors as income and education. The residents of the metropolis tend to have higher incomes and to be better educated than those who live elsewhere, and these two variables are positively associated with voting, as numerous studies have shown.[10] But when the authors of *Participation in America* controlled these factors statistically so that population could be compared more directly with levels of participation, they found that residents of rural areas and "isolated villages" have higher voting rates than residents of metropolitan areas. When other forms of political participation are included, moreover, the rate of overall participation is markedly lower in metropolitan areas—in core cities and their suburbs—than in rural areas and "isolated" communities in which the population is generally less than 25,000.[11] We can add empirical evidence, then, to the logical and psychological reasons for believing that the size of our overgrown cities is a barrier to republican-liberal citizenship.

Fragmentation

Another difference between the city-state and the contemporary metropolis that bears on citizenship is the fragmentation that characterizes the metropolis. By this I mean the complications created by the division of authority and the multiplication of boundaries and jurisdictions in urban areas. This fragmentation takes two main forms, the more obvious of which is geographical fragmentation of political authority. Geographical fragmentation occurs especially, if not exclusively, when suburbs spring up around a central city. In the large metropolises of the United States, there are scores, sometimes hundreds, of suburbs clustered around the central city, each with some government of its own. Added to these municipalities are counties, townships, and the various regional coordinating councils that have been established in an attempt to prevent the chaos this geographical fragmentation sometimes seems to threaten.

The second form of fragmentation is functional.[12] Partly as a result of the distrust of urban political machines, many of the functions of city governments have been transferred to special districts or placed in the care of supposedly apolitical professionals. This transfer has led to the creation of numerous "functional fiefdoms" that are virtually independent of city governments—and virtually invisible to the residents of the metropolis. Furthermore, with the growth of state and federal programs to deal with economic security, welfare, and urban redevelopment, new sets of these fiefdoms have compounded the fragmentation of authority in the metropolis.

The consequences of this twofold fragmentation are readily apparent. Superimposed on the layer of municipal governments in the metropolis are a number of other jurisdictions—school districts, police and fire protection districts, sewer districts, cultural districts, transit districts, port authorities, metropolitan councils, and so on. According to the 1977 *Census of Governments,* the 272 Standard Metropolitan Statistical Areas (SMSAs) in the United States had a total of 25,869 "local governments," or an average of 95.1 each. In the 35 SMSAs with populations of a million or more, the average was 293.3. Metropolitan Chicago led the way with 1,214 local governments, including school districts, counties, municipalities, townships, and special districts. Metropolitan Philadelphia followed, with 864 governmental units, and then Pittsburgh, with 744.[13]

For the inhabitants of the metropolis, the consequences of the fragmentation are often confusion, disorientation, and a sense of impotence. It is easy to lose one's bearings, and one's interest, when there is no central political authority to provide a focal point. As jurisdictions proliferate, overlap, and cut across each other in an increasingly confusing manner, people may come to believe that charting a course through the maze that confronts them is neither within their capacities nor worth their efforts. Nor will they have much reason to discuss local politics or school board elections with coworkers when they know that they and their fellow employees reside in several different municipalities and send their children to school in several different districts. Fragmentation thus inhibits both participation and the communication necessary to the development of conditional altruism. Instead, it fosters isolation and apathy, an attitude that is especially prevalent where the effects of the fragmentation of authority are most severe—in the suburbs.

Here again *Participation in America* supplies supporting evidence. The data mentioned in the discussion of community size are also helpful with regard to fragmentation, for the highest rate of overall political participation is found in what Verba and Nie call the "isolated city"—the city that enjoys its own distinct boundaries and identity—rather than in the core city or suburbs. With its relative freedom from fragmentation, the isolated or independent city apparently affords a more hospitable environment for citizenship than the metropolis. Comparisons between the participation rates of those who live in core cities and those who live in those cities' suburbs provide even more telling evidence of the negative effects of metropolitan fragmentation. These comparisons reveal that when the socioeconomic characteristics of the population are separated from community characteristics, overall political participation is lower in the suburbs—the municipalities most troubled by the fragmentation of political authority.[14] It is hardly surprising, consequently, that Verba and Nie conclude:

> As communities grow in size and, more important, as they lose those characteristics of boundedness that distinguish the independent city from the suburb, participation declines. And it does so most strikingly for communal participation, a kind of participation particularly well attuned to deal with the variety of specific problems faced by groups of citizens. One last obvious point must be made here, for it has important implications. The communities that appear to foster participation—the small and relatively independent communities—are becoming rarer and rarer.[15]

There is also a third form of fragmentation that compounds the problems that geographical and functional fragmentation create. Like the other forms, this third form of fragmentation inhibits the development of conditional altruism by hampering communication among the residents of the metropolis. This third form, however, has a direct connection to the consideration of *fairness*. As I argued in Chapter 7, those who believe that they are being treated fairly will look upon their efforts in a cooperative enterprise as genuine contributions to the well-being of the group, and hence to their own well-being. Perceptions of fairness rest, in turn, on equality, at least in the sense that every member's interests are taken into account and no member's interests automatically count for more or less than any other's. If people believe that they are not being treated as equals, however, they will be more likely to regard themselves as the victims of coercion and exploitation than as contributing members in a cooperative practice governed by the principle of fair play.

In the sprawling metropolis, with its ghettoes, barrios, and privately guarded enclaves of wealth, the sense of equality and the perception of fairness are almost impossible to sustain. The geographical fragmentation of the suburbs from the central city and from one another make it clear that the residents of the metropolis do not see themselves as being "all in the same boat." On the contrary, these municipalities frequently engage in a kind of civil war, with some battling for survival while others defend their privileges. Some of the problem is beyond the control of municipal or metropolitan government, of course. Even if a central city and all of its suburbs were consolidated into a single municipality, poor people would still not be able to afford to move into wealthy areas and wealthy people would not choose to move into poor ones. But the consolidated city would be able to act in various ways—through land-use policies and distribution of its revenues, for instance—to ameliorate the problem. It might even join with other cities to work for changes at the national level that would reduce the gap between the richest and the poorest people.

Mobility

If the size and fragmentation that characterize the metropolis are hostile to conditional altruism and republican-liberal citizenship, so too is residential mobility. According to the argument of Chapter 7, *stability* is one of the factors that encourages conditional altruism. When the population of a group changes rapidly or frequently, it is difficult for its members to learn who other members are and whether they can be trusted to cooperate. Individuals may also face the question of whether to invest their time and risk their cooperation in an enterprise that they may be part of for only a short time. There is a time-horizon problem in these cases since people are not likely to make the sacrifices required by cooperation in the production of public goods (or common pool resources) if they do not take the long-term view.[16]

This tendency to move from place to place is not confined to those who live in metropolitan areas, but it does seem to be a feature of predominantly urban societies. And there is no doubt that residential mobility plays a significant part in the social and political life of the United States. "It is the norm to move," according to one scholar.[17] "High mobility is at the heart of American culture," according to another, who reports that the average American moves 11 to 13 times during his or her life.[18] Since 1950, one-sixth to one-fifth of Americans have changed residence every year; in 1990–91, "17 of every 100 Americans moved to a different home."[19] Nor are such rates of mobility confined to the United States. Residential mobility is typically more than 17 percent per year in Canada, Australia, and New Zealand; the rate ranges from 9 to 15 percent in France, Sweden,

Great Britain, Switzerland, Israel, and Japan; and it falls to less than 9 percent in the Netherlands, Austria, Belgium, and Ireland.[20]

The unsettling effects of such widespread mobility on citizenship should be apparent. Some of the obstacles to political participation, such as the legal barrier of having to reregister to vote in the new location and the sheer lack of familiarity with political issues and figures in the new location, are obvious. What may be even more important, however, is the tendency of residential mobility to loosen the ties that bind individuals into a community. Citizenship grows out of attachment to a place and its people—out of a sense of community—that only forms over time. Those who move about frequently are not likely to acquire this attachment. Even those who seem rooted to a place are affected, for they are likely to feel abandoned as the faces about them become less familiar and their neighborhoods less neighborly.

High rates of mobility *within* the boundaries of a city can be disruptive, too, largely because whatever sense of community the residents of metropolis have is often the product of a tie to a particular district or neighborhood. In large urban areas, these districts and neighborhoods provide the arenas most accessible to the ordinary citizen and closest to his or her concerns. But these arenas cannot survive when the established patterns of communication and interaction that hold a neighborhood together are destroyed by the constant shifting of the population. The implications for citizenship, as Jane Jacobs notes, are clear:

> If self-government in the place is to work, underlying any float of population must be a continuity of people who have forged neighborhood networks. These networks are a city's irreplaceable social capital. Whenever the capital is lost . . . the income from it disappears, never to return until and unless new capital is slowly and chancily accumulated.[21]

If "self-government in the place is to work," moreover, there must be a sense of place that people share. Daniel Kemmis, whose experience as mayor of Missoula, Montana, supplies a valuable perspective, observes that

> people who find themselves held together (perhaps against their will) in a shared place discover as well that their best possibility for realizing the potential of the place is to learn to work together. In this way places breed cooperation, and out of this ancient relationship of place to human willing, that specific activity which is rightly called "politics" is born.[22]

Professional concerns play an important role, too, since those whose careers encourage or require them to move are less likely to acquire an attachment to and invest time and energy in civic concerns. Their civic time horizon shortens as they gauge their expected length of residence in a city by the speed with which they can take the next step up the career ladder.

Stephen Elkin puts the point well in his study of changes in the politics of Dallas, Texas:

> [A]s Dallas has evolved into a major city with its businessmen and banks conducting business nationally and internationally, the question that increasingly presses on them concerns what incentive they have to remain or take an active interest in city affairs. The businessmen who founded and ran the CCA [Citizen Charter Association] and DCC [Dallas City Council] . . . had strong material and civic reasons for devoting themselves to city affairs. They were engaged in making a city that would make them rich and proud and provide a style of living that suited their tastes. The present generation of business executives are as likely as not to have other interests. Their city is already attractive, its government not corrupt. Moreover, they are as likely as not to seek to advance their careers in the national business arena and to seek entertainment outside the city.[23]

As Elkin indicates, upward mobility that requires geographical mobility complicates the problem of securing civic leadership. Well-educated people typically provide leadership, but they are also the ones most likely to move. In the United States in the early 1990s, for instance, a college graduate "was about three times more likely to move to another state than an individual who never completed elementary school."[24]

Whether the movement is within, between, or simply into cities, the effects are much the same: the sense of community is eroded, and so is the individual's willingness to participate in public affairs and cooperate for public purposes. In the case of cooperation, a fluid population acts, as does a large population, to discourage people from working together to achieve public goods. Michael Taylor's analysis of the conditions favoring cooperation are once again apt, for these conditions are "more likely to be met in a small group of players than in a large group—and even more likely in the sort of small community in which people have contact with and can observe the behaviour of many of their fellows and which is fairly static, in the sense that there is little mobility in or out."[25]

Several studies support the contention that unstable populations lead to low levels of political participation. In the earliest of these, a study of voting in England shortly after World War II, A. H. Birch found a "clear and positive relation between the stability of population of a town and the proportion of that population that exercises its right to vote."[26] Since then a number of studies have reported that length of residence and other signs of "community attachment" are positively associated with voting in national elections in the United States, while residential mobility "substantially decreases the probability that an individual will vote."[27]

Together with the size and fragmentation of contemporary metropolitan areas, then, residential mobility actively discourages active citizenship. It does this, as do size and fragmentation, by divorcing citizen from city.

When individuals see their city as something distant from their own lives and interests, as something that is not truly *theirs,* they will have little reason to take part in its affairs, to contribute to its well-being, or to make the least sacrifice on its behalf. This situation may be alarming, but it should not be surprising. We cannot expect citizens (in the legal sense) to act with the interests of the community in mind when they do not perceive themselves as members of a community. It is equally futile to expect them to perceive themselves in this way when there is no *civic memory* for them to draw upon—and to draw them together.

Civic Memory

Although the term may seem somewhat mysterious, the idea of civic memory is fairly straightforward. Civic memory is nothing more than the recollection of the events, characters, and developments that make up the history of one's city or town. As such, it has two dimensions. It is, first, something that individuals may possess *as* individuals, with some having better civic memories than others. But, more important, it is also a *shared* recollection of a city's past, of its accomplishments and failures, that both reflects and generates a sense of civic identity. When there is no widely shared recollection of this sort—when only a few of a city's inhabitants have more than a nodding acquaintance with its past—then we may say that civic memory has been lost.

Such a loss is devastating to citizenship because civic memory is related to citizenship in the same way that memory is related to personality: it is its foundation. Without memory there is no personality, no sense of self. Indeed, we can think and act as selves only because we can *re-collect* the experiences that constitute our selves. As Garry Wills says, "Memory is creative—we come to *be* what we can recognize as the self; and man is not an agent in history until he has acquired this intimate history, the working identity through which other things can be identified."[28]

What memory is to the self, civic memory is to the city. Civic memory is creative in the sense that it helps to constitute the city—to give it shape and meaning in the minds of its residents. It is through the recollections of its people, in other words, that a city comes to be something more than a bewildering agglomeration of streets and buildings and nameless faces. Their memories establish its working identity, and this identity enables them to take the part of the citizen.

Civic memory thus points both backward and forward, to the future as well as to the past, thereby providing the direction necessary for active, public-spirited citizenship. Like other forms of memory, as Christopher Lasch has noted, civic memory differs in this respect from nostalgia:

Nostalgia appeals to the feeling that the past offered delights no longer obtainable. . . . Memory too may idealize the past, but not in order to condemn the present. . . . It sees past, present, and future as continuous. It is less concerned with loss than with our continuing indebtedness to a past the formative influence of which lives on in our patterns of speech, our gestures, our standards of honor, our expectations, our basic disposition toward the world around us.[29]

In pointing to the past, as all memory does, civic memory is essentially conservative, for it preserves, as it creates, the identity and integrity of a city. When the people and events that formed the city are remembered, the city is seen not as a curious accident or an incomprehensible jumble but as something with a story—with a past that makes sense of the present. Those who know this story, even only some chapters of it, are likely to feel an attachment to the city, to see themselves as part of something enduring and worthwhile. By fostering these attachments, civic memory enables the people of a city to see it as *their* city—a perception that is essential if they are to regard participation in the government of the city as *self*-government.

That civic memory really works in this way is suggested by the common practice of commemorating the great events and leading figures in a city's history. To *commemorate* someone or something is to commit to a common memory—to remember together. Commemoration takes many forms, from the naming of cities after their founders to public holidays and the erection of statues and stadia in honor of civic leaders and heroes. Regardless of the form, however, these memorial tributes share a common set of purposes: to recognize those who have contributed to the well-being of the city, to preserve the identity of the city through a common memory, and to celebrate the vitality of the city itself.

By reminding us of the city's past, then, civic memory nourishes the sense of civic identity that is essential to citizenship. It does this by rendering the city familiar and comprehensible, by helping citizens to see that they are part of the city's life just as it is part of theirs. When this memory of the city's past is widely shared, it forges a bond of sympathy, a sense of common life. These circumstances inspire the individual to act as a responsible citizen, as a self-governing member of a self-governed community.

Here is where civic memory points to the future. It does this in two ways, each important to the development of citizenship. First, when the spirit of community is alive, the individual finds it difficult to regard his or her city, and the people who compose it, with detachment. He or she sees it, and them, not as something alien but as something closely connected to his or her own interests. This attitude is especially likely to arise when he or she can look back to generations of ancestors who have lived in and worked for the city. In this context, the individual is inclined to regard his or her contributions to the city's life as contributions to his or her own and his or her family's welfare. Civic memory thus promotes Tocqueville's "self-interest properly understood."

Civic memory also points to the future by demonstrating continuity, a continuity maintained by those who know and care for the city. The fact that the deeds of others have been remembered is a sign that one's own deeds may be remembered as well. Through the recognition it promises, then, civic memory provides both an incentive to civic action and a reward for those who contribute to the city's well-being. It inspires conditional altruism. This is perhaps obviously true of those whose contributions are heroic or in some way extraordinary, but it is also true of those whose contributions are not. Even those who only do their part may expect to be recognized as (good) citizens by others who know and care for the city. Tocqueville is again apposite: "Some brilliant achievement may win a people's favor at one stroke. But to gain the affection and respect of your immediate neighbors, a long succession of little services rendered and of obscure good deeds, a constant habit of kindness and an established reputation for disinterestedness, are required."[30]

All of this is to say that civic memory instills in its residents a concern for the health of their city and a willingness to act on that concern. But just as citizenship depends upon civic memory, so civic memory depends upon certain conditions for its preservation—conditions far from realized in the conurbations that dominate contemporary life. Certainly the three forces discussed in the previous section—the overwhelming size of the metropolis, the fragmentation of authority it fosters, and the mobility of our people—are hostile, each in its own way, to civic memory. They combine to detach us from our surroundings, from place and people, and lead us to think of ourselves as in the city but not of it. It is difficult to regard civic action as an investment in our future, or the future of our children, when it is likely that neither we nor they will long inhabit the city in which we now live. Nor can we expect to be recognized or remembered for our contributions to the city's well-being when the sheer size of the metropolis renders the contribution most of us can make all but invisible. When these three conditions—size, fragmentation, and mobility—prevail, civic memory fails.

The City as an Assurance Game

If the city is indeed the breeding ground of citizenship, it is the city as it can be, not the city as it too often is. Citizenship (in the ethical sense) is a responsibility that we cannot expect more than a few to assume in the contemporary metropolis. Although it needs a city large enough to pose problems of some significance, republican-liberal citizenship also requires a city that is more settled and in some ways simpler than the metropolis. If we want to encourage citizenship—if we are persuaded to follow republican liberalism—we must be prepared to reform and redirect our cities.

Another way to put the point is to say that we must convert the city from a prisoners' dilemma to an assurance game, to use the terms explained in Chapter 7. I shall now suggest, in an unabashedly prescriptive manner, how this might be done. I hasten to note, however, that these prescriptions provide neither a utopian vision of the good city nor a detailed blueprint for "practical" changes. They are instead a set of tentative, incomplete, and deliberately provocative suggestions that will serve, I hope, to focus and stimulate reflection on cities and citizenship.

Whether a city will resemble the assurance game more than the prisoners' dilemma will depend largely upon the factors discussed in the first part of this chapter: its size, the stability of its population, and its ability to overcome the problems of fragmentation. A city with a small and stable population within well-defined boundaries is a city in which the inhabitants may readily acquire the sense of community—and the assurance—that grows out of prolonged interaction and interdependence. These qualities are much more difficult to discover in the metropolis, in which people can easily travel miles from home to work every day and see only strangers along their journey. This difference immediately suggests two kinds of measures to be taken in the name of conditional altruism and republican-liberal citizenship—measures that will help preserve small, stable, and well-defined cities, on the one hand, and will redistribute some of the population of swollen metropolises into small cities, on the other.

First, we must determine what counts as a small, stable, and well-defined city. It is impossible to be precise and equally impossible not to be somewhat arbitrary on this point. What I have in mind is an "isolated" city in the range of 10,000 to 250,000 people, most of whom have lived in that city for twenty years or more. The upper end of this range may stretch our notion of a small city a bit, but the diversity and scope a population of this size brings to a city's politics should compensate for this. Suburbs do not qualify, of course, no matter how small and stable they are, because their boundaries are usually better defined on maps than in the minds of their residents. A small, stable, and well-defined city must be a recognizable municipality in a de facto as well as a de jure sense.

If that is what small, stable, and well-defined cities are, what measures will help to preserve them? To begin with, national and regional governments can provide incentives of various sorts that will bolster and diversify the economies and improve the services of these cities. Government funds for medical facilities, tax credits for businesses, and favorable rates on government-sponsored mortgage loans are measures of this sort. Other policies could aim at saving the small and stable cities that are in danger of being swallowed by sprawling suburbia. An example of such a policy is greenbelt legislation, whereby national or regional legislatures mark the outer bounds of suburban development in a metropolitan area and refuse to allow housing developments, industrial parks, airports, schools, shopping malls, and "outer belt" highways for, say, five miles beyond the boundary. A moratorium on the construction of expressways and turnpikes might complement this legislation, as would attempts to sustain or revive rail service that connects cities without blurring their boundaries.[31]

However successful programs of this sort may be, their success will be limited by the fact that so many people now live in giant urban agglomerations. These people cannot enjoy all of the civic advantages of a small, stable, and well-defined city while they live in the metropolis, so a wholehearted attempt to establish the foundation for civic virtue would also include plans for redistributing population. Part of this could be accomplished by policies, such as those sketched in the preceding paragraph, that would halt the spread of the suburbs. Incentives for settling in central cities and small, stable, well-defined cities might then attract more people to these areas. Relocation of government offices and attempts to redistribute opportunities in employment and education might also encourage people to move to such communities. Nor is there any reason to believe that these incentives and opportunities will face a sizable and intransigent predisposition for metropolitan life. In the United States, at least, there is some evidence that most people, including most of those who reside in large urban areas, would prefer to live in a rural, small-town, or small urban setting.[32]

If experience is any guide, however, we must conclude that the planned redistribution of population by noncoercive means promises only modest success, at least in the short run.[33] Voluntary redistribution may bring major shifts in the population, but if it does it apparently brings them very slowly. Many people will not want to leave the metropolis; many more probably will. The task is to make it easier for the latter to leave. In the meantime we may consider a number of measures that may help the metropolis to come a bit closer to the ideal of the assurance game. These measures fall under the headings of political structures, civic participation, and civic design.

If republican-liberal citizenship is the goal, then the *political structures* of metropolitan areas ought to be decentralized—not fragmented, but decentralized. The process of decentralization could begin, somewhat paradoxically, with the consolidation of a metropolis, suburbs and all, into a single city governed by a mayor and council. Beneath the city council would be two subordinate levels of government, the district and the ward. The number of these would vary with the population of the city, but we might imagine that a city of 1,000,000 would be divided into 20 districts of roughly 50,000 each, with each district subdivided into 10 wards. The wards and districts would have their own councils, elected by and from their residents. No one would be eligible to stand for the mayor's office unless he or she had served at least one term on the city council; council members would be chosen from among those who had served a term or more on a district council; and district representatives would be selected from those who had served as ward representatives. Each district would elect one representative to the city council, and a certain number—perhaps five, in a city of a million—would be elected from the city at large to provide a more synoptic view of the city's interests.

Decentralizing a city's political structure in this way would serve a number of purposes. One would be to provide something akin to small cities and towns within the metropolis, in which the urban resident may identify with a smaller piece of territory and a smaller group of people. If these district and ward councils serve several functions, furthermore, they should also help to overcome the fragmentation of authority that often frustrates the citizens (in either sense of the word) of the metropolis. Toward this end, each district council might be responsible to some extent for schools, parks, police, fire protection, and public health services within its district. This multifunctional approach should make government at the district level significant and straightforward enough to attract the interest and active participation of many of those who live in the district. Decentralization, then, is a way of cutting the metropolis down to a size more suitable for (ethical) citizenship. It should also enhance communication among district residents and encourage their participation in civic affairs—two more factors that promote conditional altruism.[34]

A decentralized political structure should also contribute to *civic participation* through the creation of more political offices. In our hypothetical city of a million people, for instance, there will be 2,226 elected representatives: one mayor, 25 council members, 200 district representatives, and 2,000 ward representatives. This increases the likelihood that the urban resident will either have held local office or have known someone who has, thus rendering city politics both more visible and more familiar. At the lower levels, party labels might prove unimportant, but in citywide elections partisan contests should also help to stimulate civic participation.

In addition to these measures, we might also invoke the selective incentive of coercion in order to encourage men and women to join in community affairs. There are a variety of ways to do this, including compulsory voting schemes. In keeping with the proposal I offered in the previous chapter, the law might require everyone to *register* to vote in national elections and to *cast a ballot* in city or district elections. Another possibility is to require community service of all suitable young people, either as a condition of graduation from school or for a period following the end of their schooling. Compulsory voting at the local level, community service, and similar schemes would draw people into public activity, thereby providing the basis for the prolonged interaction that is necessary to the assurance game. Community service programs in particular should also help the residents of a city to understand their rights and obligations as members of a cooperative practice.

Civic design can also be important in the attempt to transform the metropolis into a setting more hospitable to (ethical) citizenship. Much of the work of city planners today is concerned with the infrastructure of cities—streets, sewers, lights, and so on—and the decisions that are made in these areas are usually justified in terms of economy and efficiency. Economy and efficiency are desirable, to be sure, but they are not the only things that are desirable. If we want to promote responsible citizenship, we should count community spirit as more important than traffic flow. The physical arrangement and rearrangement of cities should be evaluated with civic virtue and civic memory, not simply economy and efficiency, in mind. It is particularly important in this regard to strengthen and preserve existing neighborhoods and to work to create a sense of neighborhood identity where none exists. Atlanta, Georgia, offers a useful illustration of how this may be done, for there the planning office has identified four tactics for fostering this neighborhood identity.

The first is to attach names to the neighborhoods. As the city planner explained,

> The requirement is for place recognition, so that a community can be referred to and endowed with pride and respect. In an otherwise large and anonymous urban region, the sense of belonging to some type of community grouping . . . is crucial. Also, a name often ties a person to a history, to a past, and, hence, to certain values and determinations of which way one is going.[35]

Neighborhood history projects help to strengthen these ties, as does the second tactic used in Atlanta: the creation, where they do not already exist, of distinct neighborhood boundaries that will "aid the task of sharply separating the familiar from the unfamiliar." Within these boundaries, according to the third tactic, there should be a central meeting place "where people naturally gather; a building where meetings can be held; a park where children can drift in and find companionship; or a plaza or village center where food can be purchased or people can sit, meet, read, or simply stare at one another." Finally, the planners in Atlanta have tried to identify and encourage neighborhood leaders and organizations, men and women who can mobilize and speak for the neighborhood.

Although he does not put it in these terms, the Atlanta city planner has set out four tactics for cultivating conditional altruism. These measures promote a sense of community, of belonging to a distinct group with common concerns, and they develop this through the interaction—through *communication* and *participation*—of the residents of the neighborhoods. In this fashion civic design can contribute to the attempt to remodel our cities as assurance games.

Civic design, civic participation, political structure—all of these are elements in the attempt to reform the metropolis so that it may approximate an assurance game rather than a prisoners' dilemma. Other elements might be mentioned, and more could certainly be said with regard to each of these three. But at this time it seems best to let these cursory remarks stand as suggestions that may stimulate the thinking of anyone who wants to reclaim the city for active, public-spirited citizenship.

The City and Autonomy

In offering these prescriptions for the transformation of our cities, I have ignored the many ways in which cities are constrained by other agents, some of them political only in a broad sense of the word. To a considerable extent, cities are at the mercy of national and regional governments, which means that any full-blooded attempt to reclaim the city for citizenship will have to take the city's relationship with these other levels of government into account.[36] Similarly, what happens in a city is often determined by economic circumstances and decisions beyond the city's control. One city planner put the point bluntly:

> Another characteristic of our Kansas City environment is that it is driven by the private sector. *We can help the private sector get things done, but the private sector is really making decisions that affect form, function, physical character, and life within the city.* With very few exceptions, the private sector is calling the tune within American cities.[37]

The implication of my argument is that this is not the way matters ought to be, even if it is the way they are. But implications are not enough; further attention to the city's economic role and powers, what they are and what they ought to be, is necessary. There is reason to believe that city governments are not so impotent as Kansas City's planner suggested, especially in view of their control over the use of their land.[38] And other steps could be taken to give cities greater power in their contests with private economic interests.[39]

My purpose, in any case, is not to suggest that each and every city can be absolute master of its own fate. That is no more possible for cities than it is for persons. Cities can achieve a large measure of autonomy, however, as people can, and autonomy does not require absolute mastery of one's fate. Indeed, I have argued that a proper understanding of autonomy requires us to recognize the extent to which we are dependent on—and interdependent with—others. Autonomy is the capacity for self-government, and this capacity can neither develop nor be exercised without the assistance of others. Education is necessary if this capacity is to develop; participation in public affairs is necessary if it is to be exercised. The city—the right kind of city—provides the location in which these activities can flourish.

PART III

REPUBLICAN LIBERALISM

CHAPTER 11

Difference, Excellence, and Republican Liberalism

In Part I of this book I tried to show how a concern for individual rights and autonomy, properly understood, is not inimical to the bonds of community and concern for the common good. In Part II I tried to show how a theory that marries these concerns—republican liberalism—is possible in practical as well as in conceptual terms. Chapters 8, 9, and 10, in particular, comprise an attempt to indicate the directions in which republican liberalism would take a body politic. Now that there is some practical flesh on the theoretical bones, I shall turn in this chapter to two final challenges to republican liberalism.

Although these challenges come from rather different directions, both arise from unhappiness with the fact that republican liberalism upholds an ideal of the good life—the life of autonomy and civic virtue, of republican-liberal citizenship—that seems to be at odds with cultural pluralism. According to the first challenge, this ideal itself is objectionable. In the name of autonomy and civic virtue, republican liberalism threatens to ignore the deep differences among groups of people and to impose an artificial homogeneity on them. Republican liberalism is therefore hostile to cultural pluralism, and anyone who values cultural pluralism must be hostile to it in return.

The second challenge comes from liberals who believe that cultural pluralism is a fact of life in modern societies that liberals must accommodate, even if they choose not to advocate it. The virtue of liberalism, in this view, is that it is neutral with regard to conceptions of the good. Republican liberalism, however, plainly is not neutral in this sense; on the contrary, it is a perfectionist doctrine that prescribes a certain conception of the good for everyone. Hence republican liberalism cannot be a satisfactory form of liberalism. If liberalism *must* be neutral or agnostic with regard to competing conceptions of the good life, republican liberalism truly is an oxymoron, despite the arguments of Chapter 2.

In a sense, the preceding ten chapters constitute an indirect response to these challenges, for I have tried in various ways to display the coherence and attractiveness of republican liberalism in those chapters. But a direct response is necessary here. Against the first challenge, then, I shall argue that republican liberalism promotes not homogeneity, artificial or otherwise, but autonomy and solidarity—two goods that any defensible version of cultural pluralism or "difference" must also endorse. Against the second, I shall argue that liberalism cannot escape the need to articulate and defend a conception of the good for liberalism necessarily contains its own standards of excellence—standards that comport well with a republican interest in civic virtue. In developing these responses, I shall concentrate respectively on the influential works of Iris Marion Young and John Rawls.

Autonomy, Solidarity, and the Politics of Difference

Although cultural pluralism figured in my discussion of education in Chapter 8, I confined that discussion to groups or sects that deny the value of autonomy. But there is clearly more to cultural pluralism, or multiculturalism, than that. There is so much more, indeed, that it is difficult to determine exactly what cultural pluralism is and what its advocates are advocating. In its most challenging form, however, cultural pluralism seeks to shift attention from individuals and individual rights to groups and group rights.

"Groups," according to Iris Marion Young, "constitute individuals. A person's particular sense of history, affinity, and separateness, even the person's mode of reasoning, evaluating, and expressing feeling, are constituted partly by his or her group affinities."[1] On this point, Young agrees with communitarians such as Michael Sandel. But Young does not equate groups with communities, at least not if "community" is taken to mean a political community or a society. In her view, societies consist of many groups that are largely defined by their differences from one another— hence the need for "the politics of difference" in the title of her book. Moreover, neither the definitions of these groups nor the identities of the individuals they constitute are fixed or stable. Instead, Young sees

> group differentiation as multiple, cross-cutting, fluid, and shifting. . . . The culture, perspective, and relations of privilege and oppression of these various groups, moreover, may not cohere. Thus individual persons, as constituted partly by their group affinities and relations, cannot be unified, themselves are heterogeneous and not necessarily coherent. (p. 48)

A politics of difference must therefore work to preserve and enhance heterogeneity or diversity.

But that, on Young's account, is precisely what liberalism and republicanism fail to do. Liberalism, with its emphasis on impartiality and equal respect for individuals, reduces plurality to unity and denies difference: "the ideal of impartiality generates" a "dichotomy, between a general will and particular interests. The plurality of subjects is not in fact eliminated, but only expelled from the moral realm; the concrete interests, needs, and desires of persons and the feelings that differentiate them from one another become merely private, subjective" (p. 103). As for republican theorists, their desire to establish a "civic public" leads to the same denial of difference:

> This ideal of the civic public . . . excludes women and other groups defined as different, because its rational and universal status derives only from its opposition to affectivity, particularity, and the body. . . . [I]nsofar as he is a citizen every man leaves behind his particularity and difference, to adopt a universal standpoint identical for all citizens, the standpoint of the common good or general will. In practice republican politicians enforced homogeneity by excluding from citizenship all those defined as different, and associated with the body, desire, or need influences that might veer citizens away from the standpoint of pure reason. (p. 117)[2]

Given these criticisms, there is no reason to believe that I can evade Young's objections by demonstrating how a republican-liberal hybrid is not susceptible to the charges she brings against liberalism and republicanism singly. Two other responses are available, however. One is to show that republican liberalism, despite Young's criticisms, is superior to her politics of difference. The second is to demonstrate that republican liberalism is more hospitable to difference and pluralism than her criticisms suggest.

The first response requires a closer look at Young's politics of difference. Such a politics directs us to preserve and enhance heterogeneity and diversity, but how is that to be done? Young's answer contains three parts. First, we must recognize two distinct sets of rights: "a general system of rights that are the same for all, and a more specific system of group-conscious policies and rights." The second level is necessary to ensure that "[g]roup-conscious policies cannot be used to justify exclusion or discrimination against members of a group in the exercise of general political and civil rights" (p. 174). Next, we must identify oppressed groups. In the case of the United States, Young includes in this category, "among others," the following: "women, Blacks, Chicanos, Puerto Ricans and other Spanish-speaking Americans, American Indians, Jews, lesbians, gay men, Arabs, Asians, old people, working-class people, and the physically and mentally disabled" (p. 40). The third part of the program is to accord group representation to these oppressed and disadvantaged groups.

> Such group representation implies institutional mechanisms and public resources supporting (1) self-organization of group members so that they achieve

collective empowerment and a reflective understanding of their collective experience and interests in the context of the society; (2) group analysis and group generation of policy proposals in institutionalized contexts where decisionmakers are obliged to show that their deliberations have taken group perspectives into consideration; and (3) group veto power regarding specific policies that affect a group directly, such as reproductive rights policy for women, or land use policy for Indian reservations. (p. 184)

This is clearly a program for radical change. It is also, as a number of more and less sympathetic critics have pointed out, troublesome in several ways. To begin with, there are a host of problems involved in deciding what counts as a social group, let alone an *oppressed* group that deserves special representation. Should the list of such groups include "Nazis, fundamentalists, or even the Amish, all of whom could claim to be victims of oppression . . . as Young describes it"?[3] Should Asian Americans, for example, count as a group, or should there be separate group representation for Japanese Americans, Korean Americans, and so on?[4] Could group representation even serve to entrench some forms of oppression? If working-class people receive special representation, for instance, their representatives could include men who, on Young's account, oppress women; if women receive special representation, their representatives could include white women who oppress blacks; if blacks receive special representation, their representatives could include heterosexuals who oppress lesbians and gay men; the representatives of all of the above could oppress old people; and so on.

In addition to these problems, another set of difficulties surrounds the idea of group *representation.* The most general of these is the problem of "what counts as 'representing' a group, for there are few mechanisms for establishing what each group wants."[5] Setting this aside, how do we decide *how much* representation each group should receive?[6] Is it fair to grant much more representation to some people—an elderly, disabled, working class, lesbian, Jewish woman, for instance—than to others? And assuming that these other problems are solved, how do we prevent the represented groups from using their power to block representation for other, newly emerging groups?[7]

A third set of difficulties arises when we ask how the politics of difference will generate decisions. Presumably all previously silenced voices will be heard in a "heterogeneous public . . . where participants discuss together the issues before them and come to a decision according to principles of justice. Group representation . . . nurtures such publicity by calling for claimants to justify their demands before others who explicitly stand in different social locations" (p. 190). But how will the representatives reach these decisions when their claims come into conflict? Unless we assume that all oppressed groups always agree with one another or will quickly see the justice of one another's position, there must be more to a politics of difference than granting groups representation as groups.[8] Young does say, of course, that some groups should have "veto power regarding specific policies" that affect them directly, but this is more likely to forestall than to generate decisions. Yet Young is willing to accept this result: "If . . . the alternative to stalled decisionmaking is a unified public that makes decisions ostensibly embodying the general interest which systematically ignore, suppress, or conflict with the interests of particular groups, then stalled decisionmaking may sometimes be just" (p. 189). Surely someone who presents herself as a champion of progressive causes cannot rest easy with the anti-democratic and conservative implications of "stalled decisionmaking." If ever there was a policy designed to frustrate the majority and enable a group to maintain the status quo, group veto power is it.

This last set of difficulties points to the superiority of republican liberalism to the politics of difference. Republican liberalism encourages people to search for common ground by acting as citizens; the politics of difference tells them to "stand in different social locations," which leads directly to "stalled decisionmaking." Young's point, to be sure, is that the search for common ground serves to justify the dominance of a particular group. But if there is no common ground or common good, how are *public* decisions, including those of the "heterogeneous public," to be justified?

Young obviously believes that some policies are better than others and can be justified as such. This belief, however, follows from two premises that provide the implicit underpinnings of her politics of difference. The first trades on an appeal to the ideal of autonomy. Why else should we care that "all oppressed people suffer some inhibition of their ability to develop and exercise their capacities and express their needs, thoughts, and feelings" (p. 40)? The point of acting to end oppression is precisely to enable people "to develop and exercise their capacities"—which is, at the least, closely akin to autonomy. Is the politics of difference an "emancipatory movement" because it aims at the "liberation" of groups as such or of the people within those groups (p. 163)? In the end, groups are important and deserve recognition and respect because they "constitute" or "are major constituents of individual identity" (p. 45). In the end, that is, it is the ability of individuals to develop and exercise their capacities that is important. To justify a policy, then, we shall need to show how it protects or promotes this ability.

The second implicit premise of Young's argument is an appeal to solidarity or civic virtue. For all her talk of particularity, diversity, and heterogeneity, Young also needs something "like a common good" to serve as a basis for agreement: "In a society differentiated by social groups, occupations, political positions, differences of privilege and oppression, regions, and so on, the perception of anything like a common good can only be an outcome of public interaction that expresses rather than submerges particularities" (p. 119). Expressions of particularity will be nothing more than expressions, however, unless there is some common element that emerges from them to lead to agreement and action. For all of her distrust of "a mythical 'common good' " (p. 119), Young's politics of difference no more escapes the need to find this good and to persuade people to act to realize it than any other theory.

Republican liberalism is superior to the politics of difference, therefore, because it explicitly recognizes a fundamental right of autonomy that requires a virtuous citizenry for its development and exercise. The politics of difference relies on an implicit appeal to autonomy and solidarity, then subverts itself by stressing difference and particularity rather than the sense of common ground—of sharing the benefits and burdens of a cooperative endeavor—that fosters solidarity. Young herself indicates the problem when she notes that "the only difference between myself and the wheelchair-bound person is my good luck. Encounter with the disabled person again produces the ambiguity of recognizing that the person I project as so different, so other, is nevertheless like me" (p. 147).[9] The sentiment is familiar: there but for the grace of God go I. The problem is that a theory that tells us to cherish our differences and protect our particularity with the veto is not likely to provoke that sentiment. Republican liberalism is.

But that is not to say that republican liberalism is more hospitable to cultural pluralism than Young's criticisms suggest. The weakness of her theory does not guarantee the strength of mine in this regard. So what can be said about the ability of republican liberalism to accommodate cultural pluralism?

Several things can, beginning with a point concerning autonomy I first made in Chapter 3. Autonomy does involve independence, but it is not the independence of the "lone rights-bearer," the person who is thoroughly self-sufficient. Instead, autonomy is something that we can develop and exercise only with the aid and cooperation of others, and these others will frequently be found in the groups and communities that do indeed partly constitute our individual identities. A proper regard for autonomy therefore demands that we recognize the extent of our *inter*dependence and our obligations to others who themselves have a right of autonomy.

What of citizenship and the supposedly false ideal of impartiality? Republican liberalism certainly does invoke this ideal, but, implicitly, so does the politics of difference, as I have shown. But the ideal is not false. Following Rousseau, we should indeed strive to think and act, when establishing laws and policies, simply as members of the public. As I pointed out in Chapter 6, though, this does not mean that we cannot take account of the particular needs and interests of the people who compose the polity.

We must try to prevent the particular will of any person or group from overruling the general will, but we still need to know what will work to the advantage or disadvantage of particular people before we can know what the general will is. In this sense, citizenship is *integrative,* as I argued in Chapter 7. It requires us to bring together the disparate elements of our individual lives as best we can. In working toward policies and laws that we can agree to despite our differences, citizenship also helps us to find unity in the midst of diversity. But it does not require that we surrender our particular identities or deny the value of diversity.

The importance of the principle of fair play to republican liberalism is also worth recalling in this context. If we have an obligation to obey the law, it is because we owe it to our fellow citizens. But this obligation holds only when we can reasonably regard the polity as a cooperative enterprise for mutual benefit. If respecting group differences helps to instill a sense of fair play and cooperation in people, then republican liberals will gladly respect difference.

The real issue, in sum, is not whether republican liberalism is hostile or hospitable to cultural pluralism but at what point the centrifugal tendency of pluralism ceases to add a healthy measure of diversity to the polity and begins to pull it apart. Some writers with republican sympathies have argued that we might sometimes go so far as to employ group representation as a temporary measure or a second-best solution for overcoming oppression or injustice.[10] Perhaps in complicated and difficult circumstances we should. But if we must, we must also find some way to ensure that "[p]ublic debate would not embrace the principle 'I am different from you,' but merely 'I have a difference with you.' "[11]

Liberalism, Political or Republican?

There is something odd about the second challenge to republican liberalism. How can anyone believe that liberalism is neutral in any significant sense of the word when we can and sometimes do refer to someone as "a good liberal"? That phrase seems clearly to imply that liberalism contains standards of excellence or perfection. A good liberal is someone who is strongly committed to the principles of liberalism; a good liberal does and believes what a liberal is supposed to do and believe. Thus one may be a better or worse, a stronger or weaker, a more or less excellent liberal. In this respect good liberals are like good surgeons and good bakers: they do well what people in their position are supposed to do.

It is possible, of course, that a good liberal is simply someone who is able to maintain his or her neutrality. In this respect, good liberals would resemble good judges and good umpires rather than surgeons and bakers.

Even in these cases, however, we must invoke standards of excellence that go beyond neutrality before we determine that someone is a good judge or umpire. Good judges and umpires must be fair and impartial, of course, but they must also be decisive and well versed in the laws or rules they are charged with applying. Someone who is merely good at being neutral will not make a good judge, a good umpire, or a good liberal.

It seems, then, that liberalism cannot be neutral—indeed, it must take a perfectionist stance—with regard to conceptions of the good life. To the liberal, that is, the good life must be the life of liberal excellence. Different liberals may not entirely agree about what constitutes such excellence, to be sure, but they must have some standards, more or less clear, of what a liberal must do and believe. They must also want to encourage others to meet those standards, for good liberals will want others to be good liberals, too. Why, then, are some liberal philosophers so eager to define and defend liberalism in terms of neutrality?[12]

The answer is that they apparently see this as the best way to justify liberalism. If liberalism is indeed neutral with regard to conceptions of the good, then it will be superior to rival theories in two ways. First, neutrality will give liberalism broader appeal. Because it will not presume any particular conception of the good, liberalism will be hospitable to people who hold many disparate views of the good or worthwhile life. Even if those who hold these views do not agree that liberalism is the most attractive theory of politics and government, they will be able to agree that it is at least acceptable as a modus vivendi in a pluralistic society in which there is little hope of converting everyone else to one's conception of the good. Neutrality also promises to justify liberalism in a second and perhaps more satisfying way. In this case, neutrality serves as a guarantee that liberalism is a reasonable doctrine, one that proceeds from noncontroversial standards of good argument, such as logical consistency and impartiality, and not from some arbitrary and ultimately indefensible vision of the good life. As a neutral theory, liberalism gives equal consideration to everyone's interests and all conceptions of the good. The political conclusions reached on the basis of these reasonable premises must therefore be sound.

These are unquestionably important considerations. But there are also two reasons to continue to regard the notion of liberal neutrality as problematic. First, the claim that liberalism is neutral with regard to conceptions of the good may simply be too implausible to accept, however attractive it may be. Second, liberals need to worry not only about justifying their theory but also about inspiring or motivating people to act on it. In a society that is widely acknowledged to be liberal, the task is to foster the dispositions and virtues necessary to preserve and strengthen the institutions and practices that embody liberalism. The appeal to neutrality, however, seems too weak to help here. At best it seems to encourage a hands-off, mind-one's-business spirit of tolerance; at worst it encourages an individualistic emphasis on personal rights and interests that makes it difficult to speak or act in terms of the common good. In either case neutrality seems to be self-defeating, for it lacks the motivational force necessary to inspire people to act as they need to act if liberal societies are to survive and prosper. Hence the justificatory force of neutrality seems to be at odds with the motivational needs of liberalism.[13]

In this section I shall consider these problems in the light of John Rawls's development of his theory of justice as fairness in *Political Liberalism*.[14] In this book Rawls suggests that it is possible for liberals to have the best of both worlds by combining the appeal to neutrality with an appeal to liberal excellence. My own view is that liberals cannot have it both ways. In the end, neutrality is implausible, and it is better to opt for liberal excellence all along. Rawls's own arguments tend toward this conclusion, I think, and the conception of liberal excellence they hint at is strongly suggestive of republican liberalism. But let us begin by seeing how Rawls makes the case for liberal neutrality.

In *Political Liberalism,* Rawls draws three sets of distinctions that are important for my purposes here. The first set distinguishes two forms of liberalism, political and comprehensive, from each other; the second defines three different conceptions of neutrality; and the third distinguishes classical republicanism from civic humanism. Because Rawls's argument turns on these distinctions, especially the first, it will be necessary to examine them with some care.

The distinction between the two forms of liberalism, political and comprehensive, follows from a more basic distinction between "a political conception of justice and a comprehensive religious, philosophical, or moral doctrine."[15] According to Rawls, a political conception of justice defines a reasonable moral conception of justice for the basic structure of a constitutional democracy, and it formulates this definition in terms of "certain fundamental ideas implicit in the public political culture of a democratic society" (p. 13), not in terms that presuppose or appeal to any comprehensive doctrine. These comprehensive doctrines, by contrast, are concerned with the whole of life and thus extend well beyond the scope of politics.

When applied to liberalism, Rawls's first set of distinctions require us to separate liberalism as a political doctrine from liberalism as a vision of the good or proper life. "The liberalisms of Kant and Mill," he suggests, fall into the latter category, for their versions of liberalism "may lead to requirements designed to foster the values of autonomy and individuality as ideals to govern much if not all of life" (p. 199).[16] But this is too ambitious for Rawls, who thinks it safer to defend liberalism as a strictly political conception of justice. Such a conception must draw upon various ideas of the good, but they will have to be political ideas compatible with constitutional democracy. In particular, these ideas will be the sort that "are, or can be, shared by citizens regarded as free and equal"; they will not be the kind that "presuppose any particular fully (or partially) comprehensive doctrine" (p. 176).

At first glance it may seem odd that Rawls prefers the narrower, more limited version of liberalism to the comprehensive version. As he acknowledges, the more fully articulated a theory is, the more that it explains or accounts for, the better or more satisfying it is often taken to be. Then why shy away from comprehensive liberalism, from liberalism regarded as a way of life? The answer lies in Rawls's desire to justify his theory of justice as fairness. If justice as fairness is part of a comprehensive liberalism, then it must rest on a particular (albeit comprehensive) conception of the good. Rawls wants to avoid this conclusion, apparently because he believes that it is impossible to demonstrate that any such conception is either the right or the best conception of the good. Instead, he defends justice as fairness in terms of political liberalism in order to gain the advantages of an appeal to neutrality.

This brings us to Rawls's second set of distinctions. In this case Rawls distinguishes three kinds of neutrality from one another. The first kind is neutrality of procedure. In the strict sense, procedural neutrality would obtain when a procedure that itself appeals to no moral values or beliefs is employed to settle questions of justice. In a weaker and more realistic sense, procedural neutrality appeals to "neutral values, . . . such as impartiality, consistency in application of general principles to all reasonably related cases, . . . and equal opportunity for the contending parties to present their claims" (p. 191). Justice as fairness is not neutral in this sense of procedural neutrality, according to Rawls, because "its principles of justice are substantive and express far more than procedural values, and so do its political conceptions of society and person, which are represented in the original position" (p. 192). He wavers on this point, however, when he states that justice as fairness "seeks common ground—or if one prefers, neutral ground—given the fact of pluralism. This common ground is the political conception itself as the focus of an overlapping consensus. But common ground, so defined, is not procedurally neutral ground" (p. 192).[17]

Justice as fairness is definitely neutral, Rawls tells us, in the second sense of "neutrality" that he distinguishes—neutrality of aim. Rawls notes that this kind of neutrality may itself be understood or interpreted in various ways, but the key is neutrality with regard to the aims of individuals. As he puts it, justice as fairness "hopes to satisfy neutrality of aim in the sense that basic institutions and public policy are not to be designed to favor any comprehensive doctrine" (p. 194). Comprehensive liberalism cannot be neutral in this way, of course, because it champions a particular conception of the good. It is, then, a perfectionist doctrine. As a form of political liberalism, however, justice as fairness makes no claim about the nature of the good except insofar as it is necessary to define the good in political terms. For Rawls, this means that it is necessary only to define the "primary goods," those goods citizens will need if we think of them only as free and equal persons (p. 180).

Although Rawls believes his political liberalism is compatible with neutrality of aim, he makes no such claim for neutrality in the third sense, which he calls neutrality of effect. On the contrary, justice as fairness expects to generate some highly desirable effects among the people who live in a society that follows its principles. Even if "political liberalism seeks common ground and is neutral in aim," Rawls says, "it is important to emphasize that it may still affirm the superiority of certain forms of moral character and encourage certain moral virtues. Thus, justice as fairness includes an account of certain political virtues—the virtues of fair cooperation such as civility and tolerance, of reasonableness and the sense of fairness." But "admitting these virtues into a political conception does not lead to the perfectionist state of a comprehensive doctrine" (p. 194).

Here we may begin to see how Rawls employs the notion of a strictly political liberalism to enjoy the justificatory advantages of an appeal to neutrality while avoiding its problems with motivation and implausibility. On the one hand, justice as fairness, understood as political liberalism, can claim neutrality in at least one of the two senses of neutrality that pertain to justification—that is, neutrality of procedure and of aim. If political liberalism is not exactly neutral with regard to procedure, it nevertheless looks for "common ground" that is the focus of an overlapping consensus among reasonable conceptions of the good. Once justified, on the other hand, justice as fairness will work to promote the virtues that will inspire people to act in the ways that will maintain the institutions and practices of political liberalism. All of this will be done, furthermore, without appealing to a particular, and therefore disputable, conception of the good.

Rawls can also use the distinction among three kinds of neutrality to defend himself against the charge that neutrality is simply implausible where political and governmental action are concerned. Such charges are raised, for instance, with regard to abortion. In one sense a government proclaims its neutrality when it allows, but neither requires nor endorses, abortions. As William Galston points out, however, the opponents of abortion are not likely to find such a proclamation persuasive.

> To permit a certain class of actions, they argue, is to make the public judgment that those actions are not wrong. No one denies that the state should prohibit

murder. To permit abortion is therefore to determine (at least implicitly) that abortion is not murder. But this is precisely the issue between proponents and opponents of abortion. Permitting abortion cannot be construed as neutrality, because it rests on a substantive moral judgment that is anything but neutral.[18]

Against such views, Rawls can invoke the distinction between neutrality of aim and neutrality of effect. In the case of abortion and other matters of public policy, there is no doubt that political liberalism will not be neutral in its effects. But this is not to say that liberalism must be a comprehensive rather than a political conception, nor is it to say that the claim to neutrality is implausible. As long as political liberalism can claim neutrality in at least one of the first two senses that Rawls distinguishes, it is neutral in the way that counts for purposes of justifying a conception of justice.

We can see, then, how Rawls tries to overcome the two objections to the claim that liberalism is a neutral doctrine. I shall shortly argue that he has not succeeded. For the moment, however, we should note that Rawls's account of the moral and political virtues his political liberalism will promote is rather thin. But he has more to say on this point, as we can see by turning to his third set of distinctions.

In this case Rawls distinguishes classical republicanism from civic humanism. According to Rawls, the former is compatible with his political liberalism; the latter is not. As he sees it, civic humanism is a comprehensive doctrine, "a form of Aristotelianism" in which "taking part in democratic politics is viewed as the privileged locus of the good life" (p. 206). Classical republicanism is the more modest view that the citizens of a democratic society must exhibit "to a sufficient degree" the political virtues, as Rawls has defined them, and "be willing to take part in political life." Classical republicanism thus encourages "widespread participation in democratic politics by a vigorous and informed citizen body" and deplores "a general retreat into private life" (p. 206). But it does not elevate participation into the essential ingredient in a comprehensive doctrine about the best way of life. So described, Rawls's "classical republicanism" closely resembles republican liberalism.

By invoking classical republicanism, Rawls seems to be responding to the complaint that liberalism, with its emphasis on the rights and liberties of the individual, is too individualistic or privatistic a theory to inspire people to place the common good above their own. These same charges cannot be brought against the classical republican theorists—the Machiavelli of the *Discourses* and Tocqueville are Rawls's examples here (p. 205, n. 37). So if classical republicanism and political liberalism are compatible—if there is "no fundamental opposition" between them (p. 205)—then political liberalism will be able to draw on the motivational force of republican arguments. Once again, political liberalism seems to enjoy the best of both worlds. It is a neutral doctrine, that is, in at least one of the respects in which neutrality carries justificatory force, but it also contains a conception of moral and political virtues robust enough to provide motivational force as well. In this way political liberalism appears to be self-sustaining, not self-defeating.

With the aid of these three sets of distinctions, in sum, Rawls has provided a powerful response to those who charge that liberalism cannot be a neutral or antiperfectionist theory of politics and government, any more than its rivals can. But is he right? For reasons related to his distinctions, I do not believe that he is. Because I have no quarrel with the way he distinguishes among neutrality of procedure, aim, and effect, I shall focus on the first and third sets of distinctions.

The first point to notice with regard to the distinction between classical republicanism and civic humanism is that Rawls is attempting to borrow from—and forge an alliance with—a school of thought that is often portrayed as a rival of liberalism. In the work of J. G. A. Pocock and Quentin Skinner, for instance, the "renaissance," "classical," or "Atlantic republican" tradition appears as a way of thinking about politics quite different from the liberal or contractarian tradition from which Rawls claims to follow.[19] Even William Galston, who embraces a form of perfectionist or comprehensive liberalism, is careful to avoid conflation in this regard. "The liberal citizen is not the same as the civic-republican citizen," he states. "In a liberal polity there is no duty to participate actively in politics, no requirement to place the public above the private and to subordinate personal interest to the common good systematically, no commitment to accept collective determination of personal choices."[20] Rawls is pursuing a risky strategy, then, in his attempt to ally classical republicanism with his political liberalism. If he succeeds, he will strengthen liberalism in an area where it seems—especially to those attracted to republicanism—to be weak. In order to succeed, however, he must show that there is some reasonable way of connecting the two doctrines, of forging an alliance between republican and liberal views. This he has not done. The two *may* be compatible in the sense that there is "no fundamental opposition" between them, but this possibility is not enough to demonstrate that republican ideas will fit neatly and harmoniously into Rawls's political liberalism only at precisely the point at which political liberalism needs help. Another possibility is that republicanism and liberalism *are* compatible—as I have been arguing throughout this book—but only if one is willing to surrender the belief that liberalism is a neutral doctrine.

A second point to consider is that the distinction between classical republicanism and civic humanism is itself questionable. It is easy to see why Rawls draws this distinction, but it is far from clear that it has any historical or exegetical warrant. Rawls gives Machiavelli as an example of a classical republican, for instance, but one could as easily say that Machiavelli was a civic humanist, a civic republican, or a republican humanist. There is, to be sure, a distinction between an Aristotelian or scholastic tradition, on the one hand, and the renaissance republican tradition, on the other, that Skinner draws in his article, "The Republican Ideal of Political Liberty."[21] This bears some correspondence to Rawls's distinction, especially since Skinner connects the republican view to a defense of personal or negative liberty, while the Aristotelian view, in his account, defends a positive conception of liberty rooted in the belief that human beings are naturally social and political animals. The latter is clearly what Rawls would call a comprehensive doctrine, in other words. It is not so clear, however, that the republican view that Skinner defines fits Rawls's notion of a more modest, strictly political conception. Indeed, Skinner summarizes the republican position in this way:

> In a manner that contrasts sharply with modern liberal individualism, [the republicans] not only connect social freedom with self-government, but also link the idea of personal liberty with that of virtuous public service. Moreover, they are no less emphatic that we may have to be forced to cultivate the civic virtues, and in consequence insist that the enjoyment of our personal liberty may often have to be the product of coercion and constraint.[22]

Defined in this way, classical republicanism looks too much like a comprehensive doctrine to fit comfortably within Rawls's political liberalism. Of course, Rawls may want to relax the definition of classical republicanism for his own purposes, and perhaps we should set aside worries about historical and conceptual accuracy to allow him to do so. But then the problem will be that a relaxed version of classical republicanism is not likely to retain the inspirational force—the insistence on civic virtue—that Rawls needs in order to overcome the complaints about the weakness of liberal neutralism. Not, that is, unless he is willing to forgo the claim of neutralism.

At the least, then, we must conclude that Rawls has more work to do before his distinction between classical republicanism and civic humanism will bear the weight he rests upon it. The same is true of his more fundamental distinction between political and comprehensive liberalism. Here, again, it is easy to see the value of the distinction for Rawls for it allows him to maintain that justice as fairness requires no commitment to a particular vision of the good. That the distinction is reasonable, however, is not so easy to see. The question is whether liberalism can be merely political, in Rawls's sense, or whether it must be, implicitly if not explicitly, comprehensive.[23]

To begin with, Rawls's political liberalism proceeds from the assumption that citizens are free and equal persons.[24] This immediately casts suspicion on the claim to neutrality, for there is no attempt to establish the value of freedom or equality. Indeed, Rawls restricts himself to arguing that justice as fairness articulates a theory of justice for constitutional democracies—for societies, that is, in which most of the people take for granted the worth of freedom and equality. Yet it seems that those who regard freedom and equality as valuable do so because they see freedom and equality as vital elements of a comprehensive, if perhaps rather vague, doctrine about the good life.

Thus the question arises of whether political liberalism is arbitrarily or unjustly biased in favor of certain comprehensive conceptions of the good—those that are individualistic and egalitarian, to be precise. Rawls responds to this concern with an example that is instructive for our purposes here. As he notes, "various religious sects oppose the culture of the modern world and wish to lead their common life apart from its unwanted influences. A problem now arises about their children's education and the requirements the state can impose" (p. 199). Comprehensive forms of liberalism, such as those of Kant and Mill, will come down on the side of state requirements, Rawls suggests, at least when those requirements foster autonomy and individuality.

> But political liberalism has a different aim and requires far less. It will ask that children's education include such things as knowledge of their constitutional and civic rights, so that, for example, they know that liberty of conscience exists in their society and that apostasy is not a legal crime, all this to ensure that their continued membership in a religious sect when they come of age is not based simply on ignorance of their basic rights or fear of punishment for offenses that do not exist. Moreover, their education should also prepare them to be fully cooperating members of a society and enable them to be self-supporting; it should also encourage the political virtues so that they want to honor the fair terms of social cooperation in their relations with the rest of society. (p. 199)

At this point, one begins to wonder whether there is any substantial difference between comprehensive and political liberalism. Rawls acknowledges this concern when he says that "it may be objected that requiring children to understand the political conception in these ways is in effect, though not in intention, to educate them to a comprehensive liberal conception" (p. 199). After admitting that "there is some resemblance between the values of political liberalism and the values of the comprehensive liberalisms of Kant and Mill," Rawls responds to the objection by referring to "the great differences in both scope and generality between political and comprehensive liberalism" (p. 200). Political liberalism, in other words, is confined to the political realm in which free and equal persons meet as citizens; it is not meant to be a "fully comprehensive" doctrine that "covers all recognized values and virtues within one rather precisely articulated scheme of thought," or even to be a "partially comprehensive" doctrine that "comprises certain (but not all) nonpolitical values and virtues and is rather loosely articulated" (p. 175). But this does not explain where "non-political values and virtues" stop and political ones begin.

The upshot, then, is that political liberalism may do inadvertently what comprehensive liberalism fully intends to do—educate children in the light of a particular conception of the good. When we consider that Rawls's political liberalism is now supposed to include classical republicanism, encouraging "widespread participation in democratic politics by a vigorous and informed citizen body" and discouraging "a general retreat into private life," we should probably remove the "may" from the previous sentence. It looks, that is, as if the republican brand of political liberalism will certainly educate children to a comprehensive liberal conception. This may not be its intent, but it is bound to be its effect. That means, in turn, that political liberalism begins to look very much like its comprehensive counterpart.

Within Rawls's remarks on education, in fact, we may discern a commitment to autonomy and civic virtue. Education is to prepare children to be "self-supporting" and "fully cooperating" members of society. Insofar as the purpose of education is to draw out and cultivate the potential within a person, then Rawls must assume that most children have it within them to become the kinds of self-supporting and fully cooperating people he envisions. He therefore seems to rely, however implicitly, on a conception of the good life that is tied to a conception of human capacities.

To this Rawls might respond that the virtues he outlines in his brief discussion of education are too modest or thin to count as autonomy or civic virtue. Such a response seems to me mistaken in two respects. The first is that it seems inaccurate. In Rawls's appeal to classical republicanism, he surely invokes civic virtue or at least something closely akin to it. In *A Theory of Justice*, moreover, his attachment to autonomy is plain.[25] It continues to be so, I think, when he states that children's education should "ensure that their continued membership in a religious sect when they come of age is not based simply on ignorance of their basic rights or fear of punishment for offenses that do not exist." The underlying idea is that children should become adults who are free to choose how to live. If it is wrong to slant a theory of justice or of political liberalism in favor of one conception of the good, then it must surely be wrong to deny children the opportunity to see more than one such conception as they grow into adulthood. How could it be otherwise when Rawls insists that "the exercise of the two moral powers is experienced as a good" (pp. 202–3)? The two moral powers are a capacity for a sense of justice and a capacity for a conception of the good. These powers cannot be exercised if children are simply taught what is right and wrong, good and bad, acceptable and unacceptable, without any opportunity to develop the capacity of judging for themselves.[26]

The second reason it would be a mistake to deny that Rawls's political liberalism takes autonomy and civic virtue to be of great importance is that it would rob liberalism of a potentially great resource. As I have tried to show in this book, a theory that effectively joins the liberal emphasis on autonomy to the republican devotion to civic virtue should be a theory of remarkably wide appeal. The appeal will not be universal, to be sure, but neither is the appeal of Rawls's political liberalism, which rules out of the "overlapping consensus" those conceptions of the good that Rawls deems unreasonable.

A republican-liberal polity would encourage people to become autonomous or, perhaps better, to realize their autonomy. Autonomy is the capacity to lead a self-governed life, so the educational and other practices of a republican-liberal polity would foster the development of this capacity. Through political activity, furthermore, the citizens of this polity would exercise and continue to develop this capacity as they participate as members of a self-governed community (or communities). They would do this in part out of a sense of fair play, an obligation to share the burdens of cooperation with their fellow citizens. They would develop, in short, the conviction that the well-being of the individual is closely tied to the well-being of the polity as a whole.

As I noted in Chapter 2, I do not mean to suggest that autonomy and civic virtue can be either conceived or put into practice in such a way that they are never in tension with each other. That is neither possible nor desirable. Autonomy and civic virtue both require a certain amount of tension or opposition, I suspect, so we should hope to find or create a situation in which the demands of one meet in healthy tension with the other. What I do want to suggest is that Rawls's theory, as developed in *Political Liberalism,* seems to offer a promising basis for bringing autonomy and civic virtue together. For this promise to be realized, however, the theory will need to be recast as a form of comprehensive—perhaps partially comprehensive—rather than political liberalism. As I have tried to show, Rawls implicitly trades upon a comprehensive conception of liberalism when he proceeds from the assumption that political liberalism concerns citizens regarded as free and equal persons. If the connection is made explicit, there is a better chance of joining liberal excellence, understood as autonomy, to civic virtue.[27]

It is easy to understand why Rawls and others want to avoid the charge that liberalism rests on or expresses a particular conception of the good. To say that it does seems to put it on the same footing with its rivals, and liberals would then have to argue about which theory expresses the best conception of the good or which conception of the good really is *the* conception of the good. Those who think that there is no way to establish the superiority of any one comprehensive conception will not find this a challenge they want to meet.

But this is to take too skeptical a view of the prospects of liberalism, especially a form of liberalism that has the potential of uniting autonomy with civic virtue. Such a view would be attractive in many ways to a great many people. But the attraction would derive largely from the conception of the good it expresses. Liberals may say, of course, that their theory does not appeal to a particular conception of the good. But what is the point of "particular" here? Liberalism is hospitable to more particular conceptions of the good than its rivals, apparently. But no one suggests that it is hospitable to any and all conceptions of what counts as a good life. Moreover, liberalism itself suggests that there is something especially worthwhile in the reflective activity of the person who draws upon his or her capacities to determine which of the competing conceptions of the good he or she finds most compelling. As Will Kymlicka observes, Rawls "believes that the capacity to examine and revise our plans and projects is important in pursuing our essential interest in leading a good life."[28] Kymlicka also defines the liberal individualism he and Rawls advocate as "an insistence on respect for each individual's capacity to understand and evaluate her own actions, to make judgments about the value of the communal and cultural circumstances she finds herself in."[29] Capacities must be developed, however, so we must assume that one of the tasks of a liberal society will be to foster the capacity to examine and revise, to understand and evaluate. Thus liberalism must contain a distinctive, if not necessarily a particular, conception of the good. Liberalism, we may say, holds that the good lies largely in the individual's ability to judge what is good. A good liberal, in turn, is someone who acts on that capacity in his or her own life and nourishes its growth in the lives of others.

Whether liberalism so conceived is or is not a *particular* conception of the good seems to me to be an insignificant matter. The point is that it appeals to a conception of the good that is powerful in two important respects. The first is that it is more inclusive, more hospitable to diversity and a wide range of views, than other conceptions of the good. It must be a comprehensive theory, then, at least in the sense that it comprehends, or finds room for, more particular conceptions of the good than other theories do. The second respect in which liberalism is powerful is that it draws on recognizable human capacities and suggests that they may be cultivated in ways that enrich the life of both the individual and the society of which he or she is part. Given these virtues, the appeal to liberal neutrality seems to offer less than the appeal to liberal excellence.

Liberal Excellence and Republican Virtue

If I am right about this—if liberalism need not, should not, and truly cannot be a neutral doctrine—then there is no reason to believe that it is fundamentally at odds with republicanism. They are, instead, quite complementary: liberal excellence can inform republican virtue and republican virtue can secure liberal excellence. Nor is there reason to reject, in the name of cultural pluralism, republican liberalism as a theory that would impose an artificial homogeneity on a polity. The two challenges posed at the beginning of this chapter have been met, and what remains are some concluding thoughts on the civic virtues of republican liberalism.

CHAPTER 12

Civic Virtues and Republican Liberalism

To classify republican liberalism as a perfectionist theory is in some ways misleading. Those who are not versed in the debate between liberal neutralists and perfectionists may take the term "perfectionist" to suggest that republican liberalism holds out a vision of a utopian society free from strife, struggle, and frustration. But that is not at all what republican liberalism aims to do. Nor is it the only way in which "perfectionist" may be misleading, for someone familiar with the neutrality-perfectionism debate may conceive of perfectionism as the attempt to maximize some form of human excellence or virtue—and republican liberalism certainly does not aim to do that.[1]

Conceiving of republican liberalism as a perfectionist theory in this maximizing sense would be mistaken in at least two ways. First, republican liberalism seeks to *promote* and *cultivate,* but not to *maximize,* certain virtues. According to the argument of Chapter 3, we ought to promote autonomy, which I defined there as the ability to lead a self-governed life. But I also noted that there is a threshold beyond which increasing someone's autonomy by widening the range of choices available to him or her—from the ability to purchase a Mercedes-Benz to the ability to purchase a Rolls-Royce, to use the earlier example—becomes less and less valuable. Rather than maximize autonomy, either in a select few individuals or in some abstract sense, as if we could pile up units of autonomy, we ought to be concerned with bringing as many people as possible up to that threshold. The idea is to promote autonomy by recognizing the right of autonomy, not to produce more and more autonomy for its own sake.

The second mistake is that this conception of perfectionism leads one to look for a single standard of human excellence or virtue—one yardstick against which every effort is to be measured. Republican liberalism supplies no such standard. Drawing as it does on the republican and liberal traditions, it aims to promote *both* autonomy and civic virtue. These are indeed complementary ideals, as I have argued, but they do not reduce to a single metric or index; the occasional tension between the two will not allow it.

Even civic virtue itself is a collection of various attitudes and attributes—of civic *virtues*—to be fostered.

If republican liberalism is a perfectionist doctrine, then, it is a perfectionism of a more modest and less single-minded sort. Without ever expecting perfection, a republican liberal will aim to promote the civic virtues that enhance the individual's ability to lead a self-governed life as a cooperating member of a political society. What these virtues are I shall now try to indicate as a way of summarizing the argument of this book.

Virtue and the Civic Virtues

Virtue, as I noted in Chapter 2, is a role-related concept, and the role appropriate to *civic* virtue is that of the citizen. Exactly what this role requires, however, is subject to dispute. According to the conception of the citizen as consumer, people ought to think of themselves as "private citizens" who give politics their time and attention only when it is to their individual benefit to do so. As I argued in Chapter 7, this market conception of "citizen" is self-defeating; people who think of themselves in this way will neither generate nor sustain the trust and cooperation—the conditional altruism—necessary to the civic life of any polity.

According to the republican-liberal view, "private citizen" is an oxymoron, for citizenship is a public office that requires the citizen to act with the common good in mind. The virtuous citizen, then, is one who acts from Tocqueville's sense of "self-interest properly understood" and will bear his or her share of the civic burdens when others are bearing theirs. Such a person is neither altogether apart from nor entirely absorbed into the community. Instead, the republican-liberal conception of citizenship "links our enduring concern for self to the public life of a deliberative citizen."[2]

What traits will such a citizen possess? It may be easier to say what these traits are not—the ties of race, blood, or religion, for instance. Homogeneity in any of these respects may help to promote some of the civic virtues, but it is certainly not necessary.[3] Nor do the civic virtues include the egoism celebrated by Ayn Rand or the kind of individualism that, according to Tocqueville, leads people to withdraw into the narrow circle of family and friends. But what, then, are the civic virtues of republican liberalism?

It is tempting to suggest that all virtues contribute to republican-liberal citizenship, from the classical virtues of wisdom, courage, temperance, and justice to the Christian virtues of faith, hope, and charity and the bourgeois virtues of thrift and deferring gratification. These and other qualities do indeed help to nourish personal autonomy or the sense of community—or both. For the purposes of this concluding chapter, however, it is best to leave them in the background in order to focus on those virtues that are most directly civic and most clearly vital to republican liberalism. There are six of these. They tend to overlap with one another, as virtues often do, so it may be best to begin simply by stating that the republican-liberal citizen is someone who respects individual rights, values autonomy, tolerates different opinions and beliefs, plays fair, cherishes civic memory, and takes an active part in the life of the community.[4]

To respect rights is to acknowledge that there is some sense in which all persons are equally worthy of consideration; thus it is wrong to treat others as mere objects to be used for one's own purposes. Nor does a person who respects rights allow himself or herself to be treated in that way. But that is not to say that rights are impenetrable barriers that surround and protect every person. Individuals do have rights, but, as I noted in Chapter 2, rights relate and connect people as much as they separate them. Indeed, respect for rights is a *civic* virtue because it recognizes that rights-holders have a claim upon others—a claim that cannot always be satisfied simply by leaving the rights-holder alone.

If all rights either derive from or are instances of the fundamental right of autonomy, as I argued in Chapter 3, then the person who respects rights must also value autonomy. The virtuous citizen will want to protect and promote the ability to lead a self-governed life, in himself or herself and others, not only as a matter of right but also as something that is intrinsically valuable. Although autonomy is not the only good, it is certainly essential to the republican liberal's conception of the good life. *How* people choose to live surely matters; but that they be *able* to choose is a prior concern. On this point, the virtuous citizen of republican liberalism will agree with Will Kymlicka's identification of "two preconditions" for leading a good life: "One is that we lead our life from the inside, in accordance with our beliefs about what gives value to life; the other is that we be free to question those beliefs, to examine them in the light of whatever information and examples and arguments our culture can provide."[5]

As with respect for rights, valuing autonomy requires more than merely leaving people alone—a point stressed in Chapter 3 and developed throughout this book. But it definitely does require a large measure of tolerance for those whose beliefs and convictions differ from one's own. The tolerant person recognizes that individuals must be free to think and decide for themselves—to lead their lives from the inside, in Kymlicka's terms—at least as long as they do not violate others' right of autonomy. In this respect, tolerance is the price one pays for valuing autonomy. But the tolerant person also believes that he or she will gain, in general if not in every instance, from the opportunity to hear or see diverse points of view expressed.

One reason to tolerate those with whom one disagrees, of course, is that one also expects to be tolerated by them. Turnabout is fair play in this case, as in many others, and playing fair is another of the civic virtues. The virtuous citizen has a strong sense of reciprocity—of the need to bear a fair share of the burdens of a cooperative enterprise *and* to insist that others bear their share as well. This virtue underpins the citizen's obligation to obey the laws of the polity, at least when that polity may reasonably be regarded as a cooperative practice, as I argued in Chapters 4 and 5. It also provides the basis of trust and cooperation—the conditional altruism—that sustains a cooperative enterprise producing collective goods. Fair play is a *civic* virtue, then, because it recognizes that other citizens are not merely potential obstacles to or allies in the accomplishment of one's personal projects but partners in a common enterprise who deserve *civil* treatment.

For this disposition to take root, it is necessary that the citizen truly see himself or herself as part of a common enterprise. But the conditions of contemporary life, especially urban life, make it difficult to gain this insight. In Chapter 5, I argued that it is a mistake to think of ourselves as individuals who are "dropped into" a political community; it is more accurate to think of ourselves as "growing into" membership. Yet it is easy to understand how the "dropped-into" view can seem to many people more plausible than mine. That is why the good republican-liberal citizen will need a strong civic memory. Without such a memory, it will be difficult to acquire and preserve a sense of attachment to place and to people; without that attachment, it will be difficult to see oneself as a citizen who has a responsibility to the other participants to bear a fair share of the burdens of the civic enterprise.

One of the obligations of fair play, at least in the political realm, is to take an active part in civic life. The republican liberal will be too much of a liberal to believe that politics is either the only or the highest good in life, but he or she must be enough of a republican to insist that the public business requires some attention and effort on the part of the citizen. The virtuous citizen will therefore be one who regards political participation as a necessary contribution—and perhaps even an enjoyable one—to the good of the community. If this participation often occurs close to home, in neighborhood associations, town meetings, district elections, and the like, it should prove especially effective strengthening the bonds of community.

How active must one be? How tolerant? How fair? How sharp a civic memory must one have? There is no precise answer to these questions, but that is true, I take it, of the virtues in general. Exactly how brave or martial must one be in order to be a good or virtuous soldier? How well must one be able to play before one is a good pianist, an excellent one, or a virtuoso? The important point is that these six virtues do not require a person to be an absolute paragon before he or she may be considered a good citizen on the republican-liberal conception. They are strict enough to exclude a great many citizens (in the legal sense of the word) of modern polities, to be sure. But they are not so strict as to make it impossible to cultivate these civic virtues on a wide scale.

Civic Virtues and Civil Society

How are these virtues to be cultivated? I have given some indication of how this question should be answered in earlier chapters, particularly Chapter 8, on education; Chapter 9, on political participation; and Chapter 10, on cities. Much remains to be said on each of those topics about the possibilities for cultivating civic virtues, however, as well as on several other topics that are surely worthy of exploration. Do state-sponsored lotteries encourage or inhibit the civic virtues?[6] Does republican liberalism require a civic or public service program of some sort?[7] What about the family and domestic life?[8] Or the arts and the mass media?[9] Can we foster civic virtues in the workplace, and should we try? In these and other areas the republican liberal is likely to find plenty of room for further thought.

As these examples suggest, it would be a mistake to think that cultivating civic virtues is the exclusive province of the state. The nature of these virtues indicates that much of the cultivation must take place in families, neighborhoods, churches, the workplace, and voluntary associations of various sorts—in what has come to be called "civil society." For that reason, republican liberals will want a thriving civil society. They will also welcome the protection that it provides against the possibility of an overbearing state. But they will hold that there neither can nor should be a wall of separation between the public and the private realm, the state and civil society. This conclusion follows from three observations.

First is the observation that we owe the distinction between state and civil society to Hegel. Before his *Philosophy of Right,* "civil society" was simply another term for political association.[10] In Hegel's hands, however, "civil society" designated an area between domestic life and the fully political order—an area in which commerce regulated by contracts and governed by the rule of law could take place. In this sense civil society was, and continues to be, civilized society. It is distinct from the state because the activities of civil society are private—that is, concerned with the personal interests of the participants—but it is nevertheless dependent upon the state. Without the state to guarantee the rule of law, there could be no civil society.

The second observation is that civil society presupposes a kind of equality. "Civil society overlaps with the concept of exchange," as Antony Black puts it, "which also connotes equality of status between parties."[11] This equality of status implies an equal right to pursue one's interests within civil society—including a right to join with others for mutual benefit. When these interests come into conflict, the citizens may defend their rights and pursue their interests by going to court, where they are supposed to enjoy equal favor in the eyes of the law.

These observations present a paradox. On the one hand, civil society is an intermediate realm, one that protects individuals against the overwhelming power of the state. On the other hand, civil society depends upon the state, the political order, for its existence. The third observation adds a complication to this paradox.

The complication is that civil society can, and often does, embrace forms of association that blur the boundaries between private and public activity. Churches, charities, and civic organizations such as the Kiwanis, Rotarians, and Soroptimists provide clear examples of such associations. But the best examples are neighborhood associations and parent-teacher organizations, which illustrate how the "private citizen" can work with agents of the state—municipal officials, school principals, teachers themselves—on matters of personal and public concern. And these examples are but a step short of jury duty, in which the "private citizen" becomes, for a time, a public official.

If civil society stands between domestic life and the state, then, it need not stand as a barrier between the two. On the contrary, civil society can best promote the public good when it serves as an intermediary between the official business of government and the personal affairs of the individual. There is, to be sure, the risk that civil society will degenerate into factionalism or interest-group liberalism as various groups compete to advance their interests by capturing or controlling some part of the government. The senses of community and of public purpose dwindle when this happens; cynicism sets in and apathy prevails as more and more people come to regard politics as the public pursuit of private interests. But republican-liberal citizens will resist these tendencies, and steps can be taken to avoid or overcome this danger.

One step is to increase the number and enhance the power of those groups, such as neighborhood associations, that connect the private and public aspects of life. Involvement in organizations of this sort can improve communication between individuals inside and outside of government while fostering a better understanding of public affairs and a sense of civic responsibility. Participation in these organizations should lead people to look upon the body politic as an assurance game requiring conditional altruism rather than a prisoners' dilemma, following the argument of Chapter 7. By cultivating a regard for the public good as they bring people into public life, in other words, organizations such as neighborhood associations can provide a safeguard against cynicism and apathy.

A second step is to prevent any group or groups from gaining enough power to become dominant. This is what Rousseau had in mind when, anticipating James Madison, he insisted that if there must be "partial societies" in the body politic, then they must be numerous and roughly equal in power (*Social Contract,* Book II, Chapter 3). To achieve or preserve this rough equality, entrepreneurial opportunities must remain open, especially for the formation of cooperatives and small businesses. Preventing the concentration of wealth is also necessary, as are measures that ensure that a society does not split into two categories: the rich and the poor. To stave off corruption, money must not be allowed to exercise too great an influence on campaigns and elections. Public financing of parties and elections may be the best solution, as I suggested at the end of Chapter 9, but strict limits on expenditures for campaign advertising or even on the length of campaigns are also helpful. By contributing to a roughly equal distribution of power in civil society, measures such as these will also support the equal status—equality as citizens in the eyes of the law—that civil society presupposes and republican liberalism prescribes.

Civil society can indeed promote the public good by serving as a buffer between the individual and the state. But this is not all that it can or should do. Civil society must also be civil in two senses of the word. First, it must promote civility in the sense of a decent regard for the rights and interests of others, including their right of and interest in autonomy. Second, civil society must promote civility in the sense of civic responsibility—of citizens working together for their common good. In both ways, civil society teaches the civic virtues. Through associations that join private life to public concerns, in particular, individuals can come to see how their interests depend upon and connect with those of others and thus develop a sense of community. In this way, and with programs such as civic education and compulsory voting or compulsory self-registration lending support, people can learn to see the state or government not as some remote and alien force but as a partner—something that they are *part of*—in a common enterprise. The irony is that civil society best protects us against the overwhelming power of the state by making the state familiar to us. The wall of separation may have its place, but it is not where state and civil society come together.

Conclusion

Republican liberalism contains a vision of the good society but not of a perfect one. In this society people will recognize and respect the right of autonomy, in themselves and in others. But they will not become perfectly autonomous; indeed, it is probably impossible even to conceive of perfect autonomy without venturing into the realm of theology. Republican liberalism neither guarantees nor seeks absolute freedom, the end of conflict, or total harmony. It offers, instead, the ideal of a political order as a cooperative practice that engages the affections and educes the abilities of autonomous individuals.

Such an ideal is far from utopian. It does not rule out despair and disappointment, anger and envy, and most of the other afflictions of human life. But it should enrich life through the promotion of autonomy, and it should enable people to deal better with pressing problems, such as the degradation of the physical environment, that require an appreciation of interdependence and far-sighted dedication to the public good. Republican liberalism shows, finally, that a concern for individual rights, properly understood, is indeed compatible with community, duty, and virtue.

In this way republican liberalism provides a reply to those who worry about the proliferation of "rights talk." Their worries are not unfounded. Too much talk of rights, and too little of responsibilities, can lead to short-sighted individualism and intransigence. Too much talk of a right to this and a right to that also threatens to rob the appeal to rights of its force. The solution, however, is to appreciate rights, not to abandon the appeal to them. To appreciate rights is to understand that they are as valuable for the way they connect us to as for the way they protect us from one another. That appreciation is at the heart of republican liberalism.

NOTES

CHAPTER ONE

1. Dworkin, *Taking Rights Seriously* (Cambridge, MA: Harvard University Press, 1977), p. xi: "Individual rights are political trumps held by individuals."
2. Ronald Beiner, "The Moral Vocabulary of Liberalism," in *NOMOS XXXIV: Virtue,* ed. John W. Chapman and William A. Galston (New York: New York University Press, 1992), p. 147.
3. For a vigorous statement of this complaint, see David Selbourne, *The Principle of Duty: An Essay on the Foundations of the Civic Order* (London: Sinclair-Stevenson, 1994), esp. p. 5: "Indeed, in corrupted liberal orders dominated by claims to dutiless right, demand-satisfaction and self-realization through unimpeded freedom of action, a politics of rights amounts, in conditions of civic disaggregation and disorder, to little more than a politics of individual claims *against* the civic order and of duties owed by the latter *to* the individual. Missing consistently is a third term: the duties of the individual to himself and to fellow-members of the civic order to which he belongs."
4. L. W. Sumner, *The Moral Foundation of Rights* (Oxford: Clarendon Press, 1987), p. 15.
5. See, e.g., Lance Banning, "Jeffersonian Ideology Revisited: Liberal and Classical Ideas in the New American Republic," *William and Mary Quarterly* 43 (1986): 3–19, and "Some Second Thoughts on Virtue and the Course of Revolutionary Thinking," in *Conceptual Change and the Constitution,* ed. Terence Ball and J. G. A. Pocock (Lawrence: University Press of Kansas, 1988), pp. 194–212; Jeffrey C. Isaac, "Republicanism vs. Liberalism?: A Reconsideration," *History of Political Thought* 9 (Summer 1988): 349–77; Thomas A. Spragens Jr., *Reason and Democracy* (Durham: Duke University Press, 1990), chap. 1; and Richard C. Sinopoli, *The Foundations of American Citizenship: Liberalism, the Constitution, and Civic Virtue* (New York: Oxford University Press, 1992).

CHAPTER TWO

1. Lance Banning, "Jeffersonian Ideology Revisited: Liberal and Classical Ideas in the New American Republic," *William and Mary Quarterly* 43 (January 1986): 12.

2. Ibid., 11–12; emphasis in original. Banning has Joyce Appleby and Isaac Kramnick in mind when he refers to those who take liberalism "to encompass capitalism or imply a bourgeois attitude and set of values," but others could easily be mentioned, as the next note indicates. For a different but related way of distinguishing republicanism from liberalism, see Michael J. Sandel, *Democracy's Discontent: America in Search of a Public Philosophy* (Cambridge, MA: Harvard University Press, 1996), pp. 4–7.

3. On this point, see Thomas A. Spragens Jr., *Reason and Democracy* (Durham: Duke University Press, 1990), p. 10: "The gap between [the liberal and republican traditions] has been depicted as greater than it is for two principal reasons. First, adherents of the civic republican viewpoint—perhaps because they have been unduly influenced by [C. B.] Macpherson's and [Leo] Strauss's identification of liberalism with possessive individualism—have chosen to emphasize their differences with liberalism as they interpret it. And second, there has been a near-exclusive focus on the issue that does separate republicanism from the more individualistic strands of liberalism: the question of the relationship between private commerce and public good. When we look more broadly at the two traditions, however, and especially when we look at those aspects of Locke, Mill, and other liberals that do not fit into the narrow confines of Spencerian or Nozickean libertarianism, the gap narrows considerably."

4. Alan Ryan begins his essay, "Liberalism" (in *A Companion to Contemporary Political Philosophy*, ed. Robert Goodin and Philip Pettit [Oxford: Basil Blackwell, 1993], pp. 291–311), by observing, "Anyone trying to give a brief account of liberalism is immediately faced with an embarrassing question: are we dealing with liberalism or with liberalisms?" See also p. 309 of that essay for a brief discussion of the relationship between republicanism and liberalism, as well as Knud Haakonssen's helpful essay, "Republicanism" (pp. 568–74 in the same volume).

5. Charles Taylor, "Cross-Purposes: The Liberal-Communitarian Debate," in *Liberalism and the Moral Life*, ed. Nancy Rosenblum (Cambridge, MA: Harvard University Press, 1989), p. 163. See also Alan Ryan, "The Liberal Community," in *NOMOS XXXV: Democratic Community*, ed. John W. Chapman and Ian Shapiro (New York: New York University Press, 1993), pp. 91–114. Both Taylor and Ryan acknowledge the doctoral dissertation of Mimi Bick, "The Liberal-Communitarian Debate: A Defense of Holistic Individualism" (University of Oxford, 1987).

6. Some scholars, such as Paul Rahe in *Republics Ancient and Modern: Classical Republicanism and the American Revolution* (Chapel Hill: University of North Carolina Press, 1992), have insisted on the need to distinguish classical from modern republicanism. Taking Sparta as his leading example, Rahe identifies the emphasis on martial valor as a distinctive feature of *classical,* but not of *modern,* republicanism. But too sharp a distinction distracts attention from the

respects in which thinkers as diverse as Aristotle, Polybius, Machiavelli, Harrington, and Rousseau, among others, share a common vocabulary and common concerns. For present purposes, I think it better to conceive of classical republicanism in the same broad sense that Zera Fink employed in *The Classical Republicans: An Essay in the Recovery of a Pattern of Thought in Seventeenth Century England* (Evanston, IL: Northwestern University Press, 1945) and that Banning and others continue to use.

7. Shelley Burtt, "The Good Citizen's Psyche: On the Psychology of Civic Virtue,"*Polity* 23 (Fall 1990): 24. In Montesquieu's terms, political virtue is "love of the laws and the homeland. This love, requiring a continuous preference of the public interest over one's own, produces all the individual virtues; they are only that preference." *The Spirit of the Laws*, Book IV, Chapter 5, ed. and trans. Anne Cohler, Basia Miller, and Harold Stone (Cambridge: Cambridge University Press, 1989), p. 36.

8. Aristotle, *The Politics*, ed. Stephen Everson (Cambridge: Cambridge University Press, 1988), 1283b42–1284a3 (Book III, Chapter 13).

9. See the note that ends Book I of Jean-Jacques Rousseau, *Du Contrat Social*, ed. Ronald Grimsley (Oxford: Clarendon Press, 1972), p. 123. For a recent republican's "Civic Case against Inequality," see Sandel, *Democracy's Discontent*, pp. 329–33.

10. See esp. Letter 13, in which Montesquieu's principal character, Usbek, describes how the Troglodytes defended themselves against invaders: "A new kind of ardour possessed their hearts: one wanted to die for his father, another for his wife and children; one for his brothers, another for his friends; and all of them for the Troglodyte nation. As soon as one died, his place was taken by another, who, besides the common cause, had in addition an individual's death to avenge." *The Persian Letters*, trans. C. J. Betts (Harmondsworth: Penguin, 1973), p. 59.

11. On this point, see Burtt, "The Good Citizen's Psyche."

12. Jean-Jacques Rousseau, *Emile*, trans. Allan Bloom (New York: Basic Books, 1979), p. 85.

13. Rousseau, *Du Contrat Social* (Book I, Chapter 8), pp. 119–20.

14. Ibid. (Book I, Chapter 6), p. 114. Here I follow the translation in *On the Social Contract*, ed. Roger D. Masters and trans. Judith R. Masters (New York: St. Martin's Press, 1978), p. 53.

15. Robert Young, *Personal Autonomy: Beyond Negative and Positive Liberty* (London: Croom Helm, 1986), p. 9; emphasis in original.

16. James Madison provides a useful example of the connection between interdependence, or "reciprocity of dependence," and "social rights" in his essay, "Fashion" (*National Gazette*, March 20, 1792), in which he draws a contrast between the "servile dependence" of those people whose livelihoods depend upon fashion or taste and those whose occupations grow out of a "*mutuality of wants.*" As reported by Rahe (*Republics Ancient and Modern*, pp. 732–33): "The story has a clear moral: occupations which depend on 'mere fashion' are extremely 'precarious'; they 'produce the most servile dependence of one class of citizens upon another class'; and they accord only too well with the spirit of monarchy. Such is not the case, however, where there is a '*mutuality* of

wants.' 'What a contrast is here,' [Madison] exclaimed, 'to the independent situation and manly sentiments of American citizens, who live on their own soil, or whose labour is necessary to its cultivation, or who were occupied in supplying wants, which being founded in solid utility, in comfortable accommodation, or in settled habits, produce a reciprocity of dependence, at once ensuring subsistence, and inspiring a dignified sense of social rights' " (Madison's emphasis). For a recent republican's stress on interdependence and mutuality, see William M. Sullivan, *Reconstructing Public Philosophy* (Berkeley: University of California Press, 1986), esp. pp. 166–67, 176–79.

17. Thomas Jefferson, Letter to Henry Lee, May 8, 1825, in *The Political Writings of Thomas Jefferson: Representative Selections,* ed. Edward Dumbauld (Indianapolis, IN: Bobbs-Merrill, 1955), p. 8.

18. Thomas Paine, *The Rights of Man* (1792), in *The Writings of Thomas Paine,* vol. 2, ed. Moncure D. Conway (New York: AMS Press, 1967), p. 404; emphasis in original.

19. Jeremy Bentham, "Anarchical Fallacies," in *Human Rights,* ed. A. I. Melden (Belmont, CA: Wadsworth, 1970), p. 32; emphasis in original.

20. Jeremy Bentham, *An Introduction to the Principles of Morals and Legislation* (New York: Hafner, 1961 [originally published 1789]), p. 1.

21. Edmund Burke, *Reflections on the Revolution in France,* ed. Conor Cruise O'Brien (Harmondsworth: Penguin, 1979 [originally published 1790]), p. 150.

22. Edmund Burke, "Appeal from the New to the Old Whigs" (1791), in *The Philosophy of Edmund Burke: A Selection from His Speeches and Writings,* ed. Louis Bredvold and Ralph Ross (Ann Arbor: University of Michigan Press, 1967), p. 54.

23. Karl Marx, "On the Jewish Question" (1844), in *The Portable Karl Marx,* ed. Eugene Kamenka (Harmondsworth: Penguin, 1983), p. 109.

24. Karl Marx, "Critique of the Gotha Programme" (1875), in ibid., p. 541. On Marx's views on rights, see John Dunn, *Western Political Theory in the Face of the Future* (Cambridge: Cambridge University Press, 1979), p. 38, and Jack Donnelly, *The Concept of Human Rights* (New York: St. Martin's Press, 1985), pp. 41–43.

25. T. H. Green, *Lectures on the Principles of Political Obligation* (Ann Arbor: University of Michigan Press, 1967), p. 45; emphasis added.

26. D. G. Ritchie, *Natural Rights* (London: George Allen and Unwin, 1952 [originally published 1894]), p. 102.

27. Wesley N. Hohfeld, *Fundamental Legal Conceptions* (New Haven: Yale University Press, 1964 [originally published 1919]), p. 36.

28. For helpful discussions of Hohfeld and other developments in the analysis of rights, see Joel Feinberg, *Social Philosophy* (Englewood Cliffs, NJ: Prentice-Hall, 1973), chap. 4, and the introduction to Jeremy Waldron, ed., *Theories of Rights* (Oxford: Oxford University Press, 1984).

29. As, for example, in A. I. Melden, *Rights in Moral Life* (Berkeley: University of California Press, 1988), p. 109: "[T]he rights that persons have as moral agents must not be narrowly conceived as pertaining to their property but broadly conceived as reflecting their status as members of the moral community. It is for this reason that the impoverished have rights against us, that we can meet

our obligations to them not by protecting them in the security of their right to property—for there is nothing there to be protected from trespass—but by providing them, as far as we are able, with what they need in order to live lives worth living."

30. Reprinted in Melden, *Human Rights,* pp. 143–49.

31. On the force of *dignitas* in the Roman Republic, see Ch. Wirszubski, *Libertas as a Political Idea at Rome during the Late Republic and Early Principate* (Cambridge: Cambridge University Press, 1960), pp. 12–13.

32. Joel Feinberg, "The Nature and Value of Rights," in Feinberg, *Rights, Justice, and the Bounds of Liberty* (Princeton, NJ: Princeton University Press, 1980), p. 151.

33. According to Iris Marion Young (*Justice and the Politics of Difference* [Princeton, NJ: Princeton University Press, 1990], p. 25), "[r]ights are not fruitfully conceived as possessions. Rights are relationships, not things; they are institutionally defined rules specifying what people can do in relation to one another. Rights refer to doing more than having, to social relationships that enable or constrain action."

34. Mary Ann Glendon, *Rights Talk: The Impoverishment of Political Discourse* (New York: Free Press, 1991), p. x.

35. The quoted phrase is from L. W. Sumner, *The Moral Foundations of Rights* (Oxford: Clarendon Press, 1987), p. 1. For the first view, see Martin Golding, "The Significance of Rights Language," *Philosophical Topics* 18 (Spring 1990): 60–64; for the second, see Sumner, *Moral Foundations,* esp. p. 15: "Inflation devalues a currency by eroding its purchasing power. The proliferation of rights claims has devalued rights by eroding their argumentative power."

CHAPTER THREE

1. Jeremy Bentham, "Anarchical Fallacies," in *Human Rights,* ed. A. I. Melden (Belmont, CA: Wadsworth, 1970), p. 32; Alasdair MacIntyre, *After Virtue,* 2d ed. (Notre Dame, IN: University of Notre Dame Press, 1984), p. 69.

2. Alasdair MacIntyre, *Whose Justice? Which Rationality?* (Notre Dame, IN: University of Notre Dame Press, 1988), p. 10.

3. Jeremy Bentham, *A Fragment on Government,* ed. Ross Harrison (Cambridge: Cambridge University Press, 1988), p. 108; emphasis in original.

4. *Teleological utilitarians,* to borrow Will Kymlicka's term, may escape this difficulty because their goal is simply to maximize utility, which means that every unit of pleasure or pain, utility or disutility, must be counted as equal to every other unit without any regard whatsoever to the entitlement of persons. On Kymlicka's account, however, Bentham's insistence that each count for one and no one for more than one places him in the camp of those utilitarians who want to grant equal consideration to everyone's interests. See Will Kymlicka, *Contemporary Political Philosophy: An Introduction* (Oxford: Clarendon Press, 1990), pp. 30–35.

5. H. L. A. Hart, "Are There Any Natural Rights?," *Philosophical Review* 64 (1955), reprinted in Melden, *Human Rights,* pp. 61–75.

6. See, e.g., William Galston, "Practical Philosophy and the Bill of Rights: Perspectives on Some Contemporary Issues," in *A Culture of Rights: The Bill of Rights in Philosophy, Politics, and Law—1791 and 1991,* ed. Michael J. Lacey and Knud Haakonssen (Cambridge: Cambridge University Press, 1991), p. 253: "A difficulty (and not the only one) with [Hart's] argument is that it comes perilously close to presupposing what was to be proved. Anyone who doubts that we have a particular social right (or any at all) will obviously be unimpressed by the regression to its necessary precondition."

7. See Joel Feinberg's "thought experiment" in "The Nature and Value of Rights," in Feinberg, *Rights, Justice, and the Bounds of Liberty* (Princeton, NJ: Princeton University Press, 1980), pp. 143–58.

8. I say "mere humanity, or personhood," to acknowledge a distinction Stanley Benn draws in "Human Rights—For Whom and for What?," in *Human Rights,* ed. Eugene Kamenka and Alice Ehr-Soon Tay (New York: St. Martin's Press, 1978), p. 66: "[I]t is not their humanity, a simple biological characteristic having no necessary moral implications, but their personality that makes the crucial difference between right-bearers and other objects." Since nothing important to my argument rests on this distinction, and since it seems odd to regard humanity as "a simple biological characteristic," I do not rely on it here.

9. Gregory Vlastos, "Justice and Equality," in *Social Justice,* ed. R. B. Brandt (Englewood Cliffs, NJ: Prentice-Hall, 1962), pp. 31–72; reprinted in part in Melden, *Human Rights,* pp. 76–95; see esp. pp. 86–95.

10. On the connection between autonomy and critical or self-reflection, see Jack Crittenden, "The Social Nature of Autonomy," *Review of Politics* 55 (Winter 1993): 35–65. For that connection, and for the distinction between autonomy and freedom, see also Gerald Dworkin, *The Theory and Practice of Autonomy* (Cambridge: Cambridge University Press, 1988), chap. 1.

11. For similar reasons I think that Ronald Dworkin's argument (*Taking Rights Seriously* [Cambridge, MA: Harvard University Press, 1977], chap. 12) against a fundamental right to liberty and for a fundamental right to equal concern and respect supports my argument for a fundamental right of autonomy. First, Dworkin specifically directs his criticism against *negative* liberty, which is the sort of liberty the lion and horse in my examples may enjoy. Even if his criticism is effective, then, it does not apply to positive liberty or to autonomy. Second, in defending the claim that there is a fundamental right to equal concern and respect, Dworkin takes treating people with respect to mean treating them "as human beings who are capable of forming and acting on intelligent conceptions of how their lives should be lived" (p. 272). To show equal respect for people thus seems to require us to respect their potential autonomy, from which it follows that a fundamental right to equal concern and respect must include a fundamental right of autonomy.

12. And we usually justify the deprivation of certain of their rights on the grounds that the insane lack the necessary capacity, at least temporarily, to exercise them.

13. Dworkin, *Taking Rights Seriously,* p. 227.

14. I say that men and women should *ordinarily* be left to decide what is in their own interests to leave open the possibility of paternalistic intervention to protect and promote the autonomy of an individual. As "ordinarily" suggests,

however, the burden of proof must fall on those who call for intervention. On this point, see Gerald Dworkin, "Paternalism," in *Morality and the Law*, ed. Richard Wasserstrom (Belmont, CA: Wadsworth, 1971), pp. 107–26, and Robert Goodin, *Political Theory and Public Policy* (Chicago: University of Chicago Press, 1982), esp. chap. 3.

15. According to Hart ("Are There Any Natural Rights?," p. 72), general rights are always negative: "In contrast with special rights . . . are general rights, which are asserted defensively, when some unjustified interference is anticipated or threatened, in order to point out that the interference is unjustified." As my argument indicates, I believe that some general rights may be positive rights as well. For a forceful challenge to the validity of the distinction between positive and negative rights, see Henry Shue, *Basic Rights: Subsistence, Affluence, and U.S. Foreign Policy* (Princeton, NJ: Princeton University Press, 1980), chap. 2.

16. John Rawls, *A Theory of Justice* (Cambridge, MA: Harvard University Press, 1971), esp. pp. 60–82.

17. On this point, see Richard Flathman, *The Practice of Rights* (Cambridge: Cambridge University Press, 1976), p. 75: "*[R]ights* is governed by a rule similar to that which states that *ought* implies *can* and *obligation* implies *ability*. An action or possession can be a right only if there is some *A* capable of serving as the holder of that right and only if there is some *B* capable of discharging the obligation(s) respecting the no-rights, disabilities, and so on, that *A*'s right to *X* imposes. Men and things being what they are, the notion of a right to jump fifty feet straight up is nonsensical."

18. Mary Ann Glendon, *Rights Talk: The Impoverishment of Political Discourse* (New York: The Free Press, 1991), p. 45. For a similar complaint from beyond the boundaries of the United States, see David Selbourne, *The Principle of Duty: An Essay on the Foundations of the Civic Order* (London: Sinclair-Stevenson, 1994), esp. p. 47.

19. Glendon, *Rights Talk,* p. 73.

20. Ibid., p. 48.

21. Isaiah Berlin, "Two Concepts of Liberty," in his *Four Essays on Liberty* (Oxford: Oxford University Press, 1969), pp. 135–36.

22. Ibid., p. 140.

23. Although I do not want to identify autonomy with self-realization, I do believe that they are more closely related than Joseph Raz allows. In *The Morality of Freedom* (Oxford: Clarendon Press, 1986), Raz argues that "[s]elf-realization consists in the development to their full extent of all, or all the valuable capacities a person possesses. The autonomous person is the one who makes his own life and he may choose the path of self-realization or reject it. Nor is autonomy a precondition of self-realization, for one can stumble into a life of self-realization or be manipulated into it or reach it in some other way which is inconsistent with autonomy." Anticipating the objection that the capacity for choosing one's own life is among the capacities one must develop in order to achieve self-realization, Raz goes on to say that "this and any other capacity can be developed by simulation and deceit, i.e., by misleading the person to believe that he controls his destiny" (pp. 375–76).

The problem with Raz's argument is that he mistakes *full realization* for *self-realization.* A show dog or a race horse may realize its full potential, for instance, without achieving self-realization. Self-realization requires an active self that makes some, although not all, of the choices that result in its realization. Others may manipulate or deceive us in ways that help us to realize a certain talent or capacity, such as physical strength; they may even manipulate or deceive us into beginning to develop the capacity for reflection and choice. At some point, however, the individual must make real or genuine choices—must exercise autonomy—if he or she is to achieve or approach self-realization. Someone who does not know that he is really responding to the directions of a scientist who has gained control of his brain may develop his strength, his intelligence, his compassion and generosity, and other valuable capacities to their full extent. In that sense, his life may be fully realized. He will not be autonomous, however, nor will he be *self*-realized.

24. Thus I disagree with Albert Weale's claim (*Political Theory and Social Policy* [New York: St. Martin's Press, 1983], p. 76) that autonomy is a "categorical concept." Others who regard autonomy as "a matter of degree" rather than a "categorical concept" are Richard Lindley (*Autonomy* [London: Macmillan, 1986], esp. pp. 69–70, 106–7); Stanley I. Benn (*A Theory of Freedom* [Cambridge: Cambridge University Press, 1988], p. 176); and Robert Young (*Personal Autonomy: Beyond Negative and Positive Liberty* [London: Croom Helm, 1986], esp. p. 8). Note also Lawrence Haworth, *Autonomy: An Essay in Philosophical Psychology and Ethics* (New Haven: Yale University Press, 1986), p. 83: "There is a pervasive tendency to think of autonomy as an on/off condition: you either have it or you don't. It is more accurate, however, to say that although most humans past a certain age are autonomous, some are more autonomous than others." Raz's comments in "The Adequacy of Options" (in *The Morality of Freedom*, pp. 373–75) are also helpful in this regard.

25. In "Mothers, Citizenship, and Independence: A Critique of Pure Family Values" (*Ethics* 105 [April 1995]: 535–56), Iris Marion Young argues that "the tradition of modern political theory" could hold independence and autonomy as civic ideals only because the writers in this tradition depended upon a "sexual division of labor . . . between noncitizen women who are emotionally attached to men and children whose autonomy they foster by nurturing their particular individuality, and citizen men who have become autonomous and independent thinkers thanks to the loving care of mothers" (546–47). Although I think Young's claim is too sweeping, her underlying appeal to a connection between autonomy, independence, and interdependence agrees with the conception of autonomy I have been developing.

26. See Crittenden, "The Social Nature of Autonomy," esp. 43–56.

CHAPTER FOUR

1. Henry Shue, *Basic Rights: Subsistence, Affluence, and U.S. Foreign Policy* (Princeton, NJ: Princeton University Press, 1980), pp. 131–32.

2. For the sake of convenience, I shall use "fellow citizens" in this chapter to refer to resident aliens as well as to those who enjoy the privileges and immunities

of citizenship. My point, for reasons relating to the argument from reciprocity developed later in the chapter, is that one need not be a citizen, in the legal sense of the word, to play a part in a political order that qualifies one for membership—if not, perhaps, for *full* membership—in that order.

3. Samuel Gorovitz, "Bigotry, Loyalty, and Malnutrition," in *Food Policy: The Responsibility of the United States in Life and Death Choices,* ed. Peter Brown and Henry Shue (New York: Free Press, 1977), p. 140. I should note that Gorovitz is referring only to individual responsibility and actions here; he goes on to say that the situation "appears quite different" at the level of the national government.

4. For the argument that efficiency is a "tie-breaker," see Charles Anderson, "The Place of Principles in Policy Analysis," *American Political Science Review* 73 (September 1979): 711–23, esp. 719–21.

5. Harry Beran provides a thorough and sophisticated defense of consent theory in *The Consent Theory of Political Obligation* (London: Croom Helm, 1987), but see the criticisms in George Klosko, "Reformist Consent and Political Obligation," *Political Studies* 39 (December 1991): 676–90, esp. 678–82, and John Horton, *Political Obligation* (Atlantic Highlands, NJ: Humanities Press, 1992), pp. 35–36.

6. H. L. A. Hart, "Are There Any Natural Rights?," in *Human Rights,* ed. A. I. Melden (Belmont, CA: Wadsworth, 1970), p. 70.

7. William Galston, "In Pursuit of Shared Purposes," *Responsive Community* 2 (Summer 1992): 59.

8. Michael Sandel, *Liberalism and the Limits of Justice* (Cambridge: Cambridge University Press, 1982), p. 148. The phrase quoted by Sandel is from John Rawls, *A Theory of Justice* (Cambridge, MA: Harvard University Press, 1971), p. 522.

9. Sandel, *Liberalism and the Limits of Justice,* p. 150; emphasis in original.

10. Ibid., p. 143.

11. Montesquieu, *The Persian Letters,* trans. C. J. Betts (Harmondsworth: Penguin, 1973), Letters 11–14, pp. 53–61.

12. For this and other criticisms of communitarianism, see, inter alia, Amy Gutmann, "Communitarian Critics of Liberalism," *Philosophy and Public Affairs* 14 (Summer 1985): 308–22; Don Herzog, "Some Questions for Republicans," *Political Theory* 14 (August 1986): 473–93; H. N. Hirsch, "The Threnody of Liberalism," *Political Theory* 14 (August 1986): 423–49; Will Kymlicka, *Liberalism, Community, and Culture* (Oxford: Clarendon Press, 1989), chap. 4; and Allen Buchanan, "Assessing the Communitarian Critique of Liberalism," *Ethics* 99 (July 1989): 852–82.

13. Michael Sandel, ed., *Liberalism and Its Critics* (Oxford: Basil Blackwell, 1984), p. 6.

14. For an excellent account of these and other aspects of the civil rights movement, see Taylor Branch, *Parting the Waters: America in the King Years, 1954–1963* (New York: Simon and Schuster, 1988).

15. Charles Taylor, "Cross-Purposes: The Liberal-Communitarian Debate," in *Liberalism and the Moral Life,* ed. Nancy L. Rosenblum (Cambridge, MA: Harvard University Press, 1989), pp. 159–82. See also Alan Ryan, "The Liberal

Community," in *NOMOS XXXV: Democratic Community,* ed. John W. Chapman and Ian Shapiro (New York: New York University Press, 1993), esp. pp. 98–105.

16. Charles Taylor, *Philosophy and the Human Sciences: Philosophical Papers,* vol. 2 (Cambridge: Cambridge University Press, 1985), pp. 197–98.

17. Ibid., p. 209.

18. Ibid., p. 197.

19. Ibid., p. 206; emphasis added. In his recent *Democracy's Discontent: America in Search of a Public Philosophy* (Cambridge, MA: Harvard University Press, 1996), Michael Sandel also stressses the importance of "obligations of solidarity" and "obligations of membership" (esp. pp. 13–17).

20. Taylor, *Philosophical Papers,* p. 310.

21. Raymond Plant, "Community," in *The Blackwell Encyclopedia of Political Thought,* ed. David Miller, Janet Coleman, William Connolly, and Alan Ryan (Oxford: Basil Blackwell, 1987).

22. Here, to put the quotation in context, is the relevant passage from Marx's and Engels's *The German Ideology:* "Only in community with others has each individual the means of cultivating his gifts in all directions; only in community, therefore, is personal freedom possible. In the previous substitutes for the community, in the state, etc., personal freedom has existed only for the individuals who developed within the relationships of the ruling class, and only in so far as they were individuals of this class. The illusory community, in which individuals have up till now combined, always took on an independent existence in relation to them, and was at the same time, since it was the combination of one class over against another, not only a completely illusory community, but a new fetter as well. In the real community the individuals obtain their freedom in and through their association." *The Portable Karl Marx,* ed. Eugene Kamenka (Harmondsworth: Penguin, 1983), p. 193.

23. Michael Taylor, *Community, Anarchy, and Liberty* (Cambridge: Cambridge University Press, 1982), pp. 26, 32. I should note that Taylor (pp. 160–65) doubts that autonomy and community are compatible outside the limited confines of the "secular family commune."

24. Ibid., pp. 27–28.

25. Ibid., p. 32; emphasis in original.

26. I owe this point to David Miller.

27. This is not to say that churches, professions, and political movements are necessarily cooperative enterprises but to note that such enterprises certainly arise within them.

CHAPTER FIVE

1. See Robert Paul Wolff, *In Defense of Anarchism* (New York: Harper and Row, 1970); M. B. E. Smith, "Is There a Prima Facie Obligation to Obey the Law?," *Yale Law Journal* 82 (1973): 950–76, reprinted in *Law in Philosophical Perspective,* ed. Joel Feinberg and Hyman Gross (Encino, CA: Dickenson, 1977); A. John Simmons, *Moral Principles and Political Obligations* (Princeton, NJ:

Princeton University Press, 1979); Joseph Raz, "The Obligation to Obey the Law," in Raz, *The Authority of Law* (New York: Oxford University Press, 1979); Rolf Sartorius, "Political Authority and Political Obligation," *Virginia Law Review* 67 (1981): 3–17; and Leslie Green, *The Authority of the State* (Oxford: Clarendon Press, 1988), pp. 220–47.

2. Wolff, *In Defense of Anarchism,* p. 18. Further citations to this book will appear within parentheses in the text.

3. For the distinction between *an* authority and *in* authority, see R. S. Peters, "Authority," in *Political Philosophy,* ed. Anthony Quinton (Oxford: Oxford University Press, 1967), esp. pp. 87–92.

4. Robert Nozick, *Anarchy, State, and Utopia* (New York: Basic Books, 1974), p. 95.

5. Ibid., p. 93.

6. Ibid., p. 90.

7. On this point, see Nora K. Bell, "Nozick and the Principle of Fairness," *Social Theory and Practice* 5 (1978): 65–73; and Simmons, *Moral Principles and Political Obligations,* pp. 118–36.

8. Smith, "Is There a Prima Facie Obligation to Obey the Law?," p. 111. All quotations from Smith are from this page of this article.

9. Consider another example, one that probably does not involve a cooperative practice. Suppose that I assign all but one of the students in one of my classes a term paper. I have no good reason for exempting this student—perhaps she too is a fan of the St. Louis Cardinals—so I ask her not to tell the others. Have I harmed the other students? Not if this exemption will not affect the way I grade their papers, since in the normal course of affairs I would have assigned them a term paper anyhow. And not if they do not learn of the exemption, for then they cannot feel anger or distress at their treatment. For that matter, they may even benefit from the mental stimulation and enlightenment they gain from writing the paper. Still, I would act unfairly in this case, for I would not be treating all of the students with equal concern and respect.

10. For the distinction between wronging and harming, see Richard Dagger, "Harm, Utility, and the Obligation to Obey the Law," *Archiv für Rechts- und Sozialphilosophie* 68 (1982): 102–8.

11. For similar views of fairness, see Daniel Sullivan, "Rules, Fairness, and Formal Justice," *Ethics* 85 (1975): 328, and David Lyons, *Forms and Limits of Utilitarianism* (Oxford: Clarendon Press, 1965), p. 177.

12. George Klosko, *The Principle of Fairness and Political Obligation* (Lanham, MD: Rowman and Littlefield, 1992), p. 37.

13. Simmons, *Moral Principles and Political Obligations,* p. 129.

14. Richard Arneson, "The Principle of Fairness and Free-Rider Problems," *Ethics* 92 (July 1982): 616–33; Klosko, *The Principle of Fairness and Political Obligation,* esp. chap. 2. See also Lawrence C. Becker, *Reciprocity* (Chicago: University of Chicago Press, 1986), pp. 252–62, 410–18, although Becker argues for a *disposition* rather than an *obligation* to obey the law.

15. Arneson, "The Principle of Fairness and Free-Rider Problems," 621.

16. Klosko, *The Principle of Fairness and Political Obligation,* p. 39.

17. Thomas Senor, "What If There Are No Political Obligations?: A Reply to

A. J. Simmons," *Philosophy and Public Affairs* 16 (Summer 1987): 260–68. See also A. John Simmons, "The Anarchist Position: A Reply to Klosko and Senor," *Philosophy and Public Affairs* 16 (Summer 1987): 269–79.

18. Simmons, *Moral Principles and Political Obligations,* p. 140.

19. Ibid., p. 131.

20. J. L. Austin, "A Plea for Excuses," in Austin, *Philosophical Papers,* ed. J. O. Urmson and G. J. Warnock (Oxford: Oxford University Press, 1970), esp. p. 191.

21. For a helpful attempt to distinguish cases of true duress from cases in which people simply face hard choices, see Jeffrie Murphy, "Consent, Coercion, and Hard Choices," *Virginia Law Review* 67 (1981): 79–95.

22. Simmons, *Moral Principles and Political Obligations,* p. 137.

23. Ibid., p. 139. See also Simmons, "The Anarchist Position," p. 273. But see the evidence to the contrary that George Klosko presents in *The Principle of Fairness and Political Obligation,* Appendix 2. Among other things, Klosko notes that "[p]eople's willingness to pay [taxes] appears to be bound up with their awareness that payments go toward providing public goods" (p. 181). Also: "An adequate account of political obligation should explain why *A*'s feeling that he is obligated to assume various burdens will be strengthened by his belief that other individuals are bearing similar burdens and weakened by his perception that they are not. I believe that this aspect of political obligation is especially well explained by the principle of fairness" (p. 184).

24. Jean-Jacques Rousseau, *On the Social Contract,* ed. Roger D. Masters and trans. Judith R. Masters (New York: St. Martin's Press, 1978), Book I, Chapter 7, p. 55.

25. H. L. A. Hart, *The Concept of Law* (Oxford: Clarendon Press, 1961), p. 193. In "Playing Fair with Punishment" (*Ethics* 103 [April 1993]: 473–88), I provide a justification of legal punishment grounded in the principle of fair play.

CHAPTER SIX

1. See, e.g., Adrian Oldfield, *Citizenship and Community* (New York: Routledge, 1990), chap. 4; Maurizio Viroli, *Jean-Jacques Rousseau and the "Well-Ordered Society,"* trans. Derek Hanson (Cambridge: Cambridge University Press, 1988); and Zev M. Trachtenberg, *Making Citizens: Rousseau's Political Theory of Culture* (London: Routledge, 1993).

2. These quotations are taken from Rousseau's *On the Social Contract,* ed. Roger D. Masters and trans. Judith R. Masters (New York: St. Martin's Press, 1978), at pp. 68, 130, 55. Henceforth I shall cite passages from the *Social Contract* parenthetically in the text by referring to the book, chapter, and page number of the Masters edition. In this case, the citations are II, 7:68; IV, 8:130; and I, 7:55.

3. Quentin Skinner, "The Republican Ideal of Political Liberty," *Machiavelli and Republicanism,* ed. Gisela Bock, Quentin Skinner, and Maurizio Viroli (Cambridge: Cambridge University Press, 1990), p. 301.

4. Brian Barry, "The Public Interest," in *Political Philosophy,* ed. Anthony

Quinton (Oxford: Oxford University Press, 1967), esp. pp. 119–26. For similar interpretations, see Andrew Levine, *The Politics of Autonomy: A Kantian Reading of Rousseau's Social Contract* (Amherst: University of Massachusetts Press, 1976), pp. 40–43, and John Charvet, *The Social Problem in the Philosophy of Rousseau* (Cambridge: Cambridge University Press, 1974), chap. 4.

5. Jean-Jacques Rousseau, *Politics and the Arts: Letter to M. D'Alembert on the Theatre,* trans. Allan Bloom (Ithaca, NY: Cornell University Press, 1968), p. 24.

6. At the conclusion of his valuable account of earlier uses of "the general will," Patrick Riley observes: "[W]hat holds together the tradition of French moral and political thought from Pascal to Rousseau, unifies it, and distinguishes it from either English or German political thought, is the notion that *généralité* is good, *particularité* bad—that, if one is just, one will embrace the general good of the body, to which one will subordinate egoism and self-love." Riley, *The General Will before Rousseau: The Transformation of the Divine into the Civic* (Princeton, NJ: Princeton University Press, 1986), p. 251.

7. John Rawls, *A Theory of Justice* (Cambridge, MA: Harvard University Press, 1971), Section 24, "The Veil of Ignorance."

8. For a contrasting view, see Trachtenberg, *Making Citizens,* esp. pp. 7–29. According to Trachtenberg, "the 'ingredients' of the general will—the 'material' on which the procedure that defines the general will operates—are the individual members of society's conceptions of their own welfare. Thus . . . the general will *aggregates* individuals' wants" (p. 9; emphasis added).

9. Barry, "The Public Interest," p. 120.

10. See also the chapter "Law" (II, 6).

11. Rousseau goes on to add a recommendation more akin to the pluralist spirit of James Madison's *Federalist* 10: "If there are partial societies, their number must be multiplied and their inequality prevented, as was done by Solon, Numa, and Servius. These precautions are the only valid means of ensuring that the general will is always enlightened and the people is not deceived" (II, 3:61–62).

12. On the similarities between Kant and Rousseau, especially with regard to autonomy, see Ernst Cassirer's essay, "Kant and Rousseau," in his *Rousseau, Kant, and Goethe,* trans. James Gutmann, P. O. Kristeller, and J. H. Randall Jr. (New York: Harper and Row, 1963), and Levine, *The Politics of Autonomy,* esp. pp. 57–58.

13. Cf. Brian Barry's explanation in *Political Argument* (London: Routledge and Kegan Paul, 1965), p. 198: "Rousseau does not deny that it may be in your interest to *break* a law which benefits you *qua* member of the community; all he says is that it is certainly in your interests to *vote* for it, and that if you have voted in favor of a certain punishment for a certain crime you have no business to complain if your wish for a certain policy is applied to you in a particular case."

14. I develop and defend this distinction in Richard Dagger, "Understanding the General Will," *Western Political Quarterly* 34 (September 1981): 359–71, esp. 366–70.

15. I say "often" because Rousseau allows that "the commands of leaders" can "pass for expressions of the general will, as long as the sovereign, being free to

oppose them, does not do so" (II, 1:59). See also *Political Economy,* included in Masters and Masters, *On the Social Contract,* p. 216.

16. The phrase translated as "private will" here might be better rendered as "particular opinion." See Jean-Jacques Rousseau, *Du Contrat Social,* ed. Ronald Grimsley (Oxford: Clarendon Press, 1972), p. 202.

17. In *Political Economy,* p. 216, Rousseau asks: "Must the whole nation be assembled at each unforeseen event? Such an assembly is all the less necessary because it is not sure its decision would be the expression of the general will."

18. For an elaboration of this point, which explains Rousseau's position in terms of Condorcet's Jury Theorem, see Barry, "The Public Interest," p. 122, and Levine, *The Politics of Autonomy,* pp. 63–72. For further developments, see Bernard Grofman and Scott L. Feld, "Rousseau's General Will: A Condorcetian Perspective," *American Political Science Review* 82 (June 1988): 567–76; their exchanges with David Estlund and Jeremy Waldron, "Democratic Theory and the Public Interest: Condorcet and Rousseau Revisited," *American Political Science Review* 83 (December 1989): 1317–40; and Trachtenberg, *Making Citizens,* pp. 220–30.

19. See, e.g., J. L. Talmon, *The Origins of Totalitarian Democracy* (New York: Praeger, 1960), chap. 3, and Lester Crocker, *Rousseau's Social Contract: An Interpretive Essay* (Cleveland, OH: The Press of Case Western Reserve University, 1968).

20. Jean-Jacques Rousseau, *Emile,* trans. Allan Bloom (New York: Basic Books, 1979), p. 85.

21. Note in this regard the contrast that Rousseau draws between big and small cities in *Politics and the Arts,* pp. 58–59.

22. For a survey of scholarly opinion on—and a provocative explanation of—Rousseau's civil religion, see Terence Ball, *Reappraising Political Theory: Revisionist Studies in the History of Political Thought* (Oxford: Clarendon Press, 1995), chap. 5.

23. "Soon enough," according to Riley (*The General Will before Rousseau,* p. 253; emphasis in original), "one finds Rousseau saying that the general will—the will one has as a citizen, when one thinks of the common good and of civic membership—is 'always right' (even if natural men lack a general will at the beginning of political time and must acquire such a will *over* time through a denaturing, antiparticularistic civic education supplied by a great legislator)."

24. Mary Wollstonecraft, *Vindication of the Rights of Woman,* ed. Miriam Brody (London: Penguin, 1985), p. 158.

CHAPTER SEVEN

1. See Peter Riesenberg, *Citizenship in the Western Tradition: Plato to Rousseau* (Chapel Hill: University of North Carolina Press, 1992), for a survey of citizenship, as a concept and an institution, until the French Revolution. *Theorizing Citizenship* (ed. Ronald Beiner [Albany: State University of New York Press, 1995]) is a useful collection of recent essays on citizenship, including a valuable review essay by Will Kymlicka and Wayne Norman.

2. Jean-Jacques Rousseau, *Discourse on the Arts and Sciences,* in *The Social Contract and Discourses,* trans. G. D. H. Cole (New York: E. P. Dutton, 1950), p. 169.

3. Pamela J. Conover, Ivor M. Crewe, and Donald D. Searing, "The Nature of Citizenship in the United States and Great Britain: Empirical Comments on Theoretical Themes," *Journal of Politics* 53 (1991): 800–832.

4. Jeffrey M. Berry, Kent E. Portney, and Ken Thompson, *The Rebirth of Urban Democracy* (Washington, DC: Brookings Institution, 1993), p. 2.

5. Alexis de Tocqueville, *Democracy in America,* trans. George Lawrence, ed. J. P. Mayer (Garden City, NY: Doubleday, 1969), pp. 526–27.

6. Sheldon Wolin, *Politics and Vision: Continuity and Innovation in Western Political Thought* (Boston: Little, Brown, 1960), p. 434.

7. For a trenchant statement of this view, see Louis Wirth's classic "Urbanism as a Way of Life," *American Journal of Sociology* 44 (July 1938): 1–24.

8. Dennis Thompson, *John Stuart Mill on Representative Government* (Princeton, NJ: Princeton University Press, 1976), pp. 43–50.

9. John Stuart Mill, *Three Essays: "On Liberty," "Representative Government," and "The Subjection of Women,"* ed. Richard Wollheim (Oxford: Oxford University Press, 1975), pp. 196–97.

10. Ibid., p. 196.

11. Ibid., pp. 197–98.

12. Tocqueville, *Democracy in America,* p. 506.

13. Joseph Schumpeter, *Capitalism, Socialism, and Democracy,* 3d ed. (New York: Harper and Row, 1962); Anthony Downs, *An Economic Theory of Democracy* (New York: Harper and Row, 1957). See also William Riker, *Liberalism against Populism* (San Francisco: W. H. Freeman, 1982), and Dennis Mueller, *Public Choice* (Cambridge: Cambridge University Press, 1979).

14. See Martin Hollis, "Friends, Romans, Consumers," *Ethics* 102 (October 1991): 27–41, for a critical comparison of the citizen as consumer to the two other conceptions of citizenship indicated in his essay's title. Note also David Selbourne, *The Principle of Duty: An Essay on the Foundations of the Civic Order* (London: Sinclair-Stevenson, 1994), p. 14: "Market theories of political exchange which reduce the citizen to a 'consumer' or 'customer' are not so much amoral—although they are that too—as trivial: a *reductio ad absurdum.*"

15. For critical discussions of the economic theory of democracy that trace its roots to Jeremy Bentham and James Mill, see Terence Ball, *Transforming Political Discourse: Political Theory and Critical Conceptual History* (Oxford: Basil Blackwell, 1988), chap. 6, and C. B. Macpherson, *The Life and Times of Liberal Democracy* (Oxford: Oxford University Press, 1977), chaps. 2 and 4.

16. Jon Elster, "The Market and the Forum: Three Varieties of Political Theory," in *Foundations of Social Choice Theory,* ed. J. Elster and A. Hylland (Cambridge: Cambridge University Press, 1986), pp. 103–32. See also Elster's *Sour Grapes: Studies in the Subversion of Rationality* (Cambridge: Cambridge University Press, 1987), pp. 33–42, and David Miller, *Market, State, and Community* (Oxford: Clarendon Press, 1989), chap. 10, in which he distinguishes "politics as *interest-aggregation*" from "politics as *dialogue*" (emphasis in original).

17. I refer to Kenneth Arrow's well-known "impossibility theorem," as demon-

strated in Arrow, *Social Choice and Individual Values,* 2d ed. (New York: John Wiley, 1963).

18. Miller, *Market, State, and Community,* pp. 255–56.

19. "The *Value,* or WORTH of a man, is as of all other things, his Price; that is to say, so much as would be given for the use of his Power: and therefore is not absolute, but a thing dependant on the need and judgment of another." Thomas Hobbes, *Leviathan,* ed. Richard Tuck (Cambridge: Cambridge University Press, 1991), p. 63.

20. Miller, *Market, State, and Community,* p. 257.

21. Thomas A. Spragens Jr., *Reason and Democracy* (Durham: Duke University Press, 1990), pp. 139–40.

22. Diego Gambetta, "Can We Trust Trust?," in *Trust: Making and Breaking Cooperative Relations,* ed. Diego Gambetta (Oxford: Basil Blackwell, 1988), pp. 220–21.

23. Mancur Olson, *The Logic of Collective Action,* rev. ed. (New York: Schocken Books, 1971), esp. p. 51.

24. Edna Ullmann-Margalit, *The Emergence of Norms* (Oxford: Clarendon Press, 1977), p. 37.

25. William Riker and Peter Ordeshook explain voting in terms of civic duty in "A Theory of the Calculus of Voting," *American Political Science Review* 62 (March 1968): 25–42, esp. 28. For criticisms of their argument as being inconsistent with their premises, see Brian Barry, *Sociologists, Economists, and Democracy* (London: Macmillan, 1970), pp. 15–19, and J. Donald Moon, "The Logic of Political Inquiry," in *Handbook of Political Science,* vol. 1, ed. F. I. Greenstein and N. W. Polsby (Reading, MA: Addison-Wesley, 1975), p. 202.

26. Michael Taylor, *Anarchy and Cooperation* (London: John Wiley, 1976), Section 7.2, revised and reissued as *The Possibility of Cooperation* (Cambridge: Cambridge University Press, 1987). See also Robert Axelrod, *The Evolution of Cooperation* (New York: Basic Books, 1984).

27. Taylor, *Anarchy and Cooperation,* p. 93.

28. Michael Taylor, *Community, Anarchy, and Liberty* (Cambridge: Cambridge University Press, 1982), p. 32.

29. "Conditional altruism" is a term Jon Elster uses in his valuable account of the assurance game. See Elster, *Ulysses and the Sirens: Studies in Rationality and Irrationality* (Cambridge: Cambridge University Press, 1979), pp. 21–22, 143–46. Amartya K. Sen seems to have "discovered" the assurance game. See his "Isolation, Assurance, and the Social Rate of Discount," *Quarterly Journal of Economics* 81 (1967): 112–24, and esp. *On Economic Inequality* (New York: W. W. Norton, 1973), pp. 96–99.

30. As Avital Simhony has pointed out to me, there is a sense in which "conditional altruism" is a misnomer. If the "conditional altruist" must be assured that he or she will not be played for a sucker before he or she will cooperate, then his or her motives hardly appear to be altruistic. Perhaps something like "solidarists" would be a better term. As Elster puts it: "Solidarity is *conditional altruism,* as distinct from the unconditional altruism of the categorical imperative and the unconditional egoism of capitalist society" (*Ulysses and the Sirens,*

pp. 21–22; emphasis in original). Certainly his conditional *altruism* bears a strong resemblance to Tocqueville's *self-interest* properly understood.

31. See, e.g., Amartya K. Sen, "Rational Fools: A Critique of the Behavioral Foundations of Economic Theory," *Philosophy and Public Affairs* 6 (Summer 1977): 317–44.

32. Elster, *Ulysses and the Sirens,* p. 146. Of course, a cynic might respond that "familiarity breeds contempt." Elster's claim seems borne out, however, by Robert Putnam's analysis of "social capital": that is, "features of social life—networks, norms, and trust—that enable participants to act together more effectively to pursue shared objectives." According to Putnam, the "theory of social capital presumes that, generally speaking, the more we connect with other people, the more we trust them, and vice versa. At least in the contexts I have so far explored, this presumption generally turns out to be true: social trust and civic engagement are strongly correlated." Robert D. Putnam, "Tuning In, Tuning Out: The Strange Disappearance of Social Capital in America," *PS: Political Science and Politics,* 28 (December 1995): 664–83, at 664, 665.

33. Montesquieu, *The Spirit of the Laws,* ed. and trans. Anne Cohler, Basia Miller, and Harold Stone (Cambridge: Cambridge University Press, 1989), Book VIII, Chapter 16, p. 124.

34. Olson, *The Logic of Collective Action,* chap. 2; Robyn Dawes, "Social Dilemmas," *Annual Review of Psychology* 31 (1980): 169–93. According to Dawes, "all experimenters who have made explicit or implicit comparisons of dilemma games with varying numbers of players have concluded that subjects cooperate less in larger groups than in smaller ones" (p. 186).

35. See Tocqueville, *Democracy in America:* "Local liberties, then, which induce a great number of citizens to value the affection of their kindred and neighbors, bring men constantly into contact, despite the instincts which separate them, and force them to help one another" (p. 511). For various federal and confederal schemes that are designed to overcome the size problem, see Taylor, *The Possibility of Cooperation,* pp. 4–5, 168–69; Russell Hardin, *Collective Action* (Baltimore: Johns Hopkins University Press, 1982), esp. p. 184; and Jonathan Bendor and Dilip Mookherjee, "Institutional Structure and the Logic of Ongoing Collective Action," *American Political Science Review* 81 (March 1987): 129–54.

36. Taylor, *Anarchy and Cooperation,* Section 7.2.

37. David Good, "Individuals, Interpersonal Relations, and Trust," in Gambetta, *Trust: Making and Breaking Cooperative Relations,* p. 35.

38. Elinor Ostrom, *Governing the Commons: The Evolution of Institutions for Collective Action* (Cambridge: Cambridge University Press, 1990), p. 88; see also pp. 34–35, 183–84.

39. Robert Putnam with Robert Leonardi and Rafaella Y. Nanetti, *Making Democracy Work: Civic Traditions in Modern Italy* (Princeton, NJ: Princeton University Press, 1993), pp. 88, 104–5.

40. John Rawls, *A Theory of Justice* (Cambridge, MA: Harvard University Press, 1971), esp. Section 13. In his study of the more and less "civic" regions of Italy, Putnam notes that income distribution is "more egalitarian in civic regions (r

= .81). Controlling for civic-ness, income inequality and performance are un-correlated, although multicollinearity shadows the result" (*Making Democracy Work*, p. 224, n. 52).

41. Good, "Individuals, Interpersonal Relations, and Trust," p. 36.

42. Tocqueville, *Democracy in America*, p. 515.

43. Putnam, *Making Democracy Work*, p. 183; see also pp. 89–99. According to Steven J. Rosenstone and John Mark Hansen, "Political analysts have long known that people who belong to clubs, organizations, and interest groups are more likely to participate in politics than people who do not, even after fac-toring out the influences that might cause people to do both" (*Mobilization, Participation, and Democracy in America* [New York: Macmillan, 1993], p. 83).

CHAPTER EIGHT

1. Shelley Burtt, "The Good Citizen's Psyche: On the Psychology of Civic Vir-tue," *Polity* 23 (Fall 1990): 23–38, at 24.

2. John Chubb and Terry Moe, *Politics, Markets, and America's Schools* (Wash-ington, DC: Brookings Institution, 1990), p. 54.

3. Ibid., p. 30.

4. Ibid., p. 55.

5. Ibid., pp. 219–25.

6. R. S. Peters elaborates the distinction between education and training in "Aims of Education—a Conceptual Inquiry," in *The Philosophy of Education*, ed. R. S. Peters (Oxford: Oxford University Press, 1973), esp. pp. 18–21.

7. For a brief history of "education," see R. S. Peters, "Further Thoughts on the Concept of Education," in ibid., p. 53.

8. For example, R. F. Dearden, "Autonomy as an Educational Ideal," in *Philoso-phers Discuss Education*, ed. S. Brown (Totowa, NJ: Rowman and Littlefield, 1975).

9. In this regard, it is interesting to note the renewal of interest in civic education on the part of political theorists. See, inter alia: Benjamin R. Barber, *An Aristoc-racy of Everyone: The Politics of Education and the Future of America* (New York: Ballantine Books, 1992); Richard Battistoni, *Public Schooling and the Education of Democratic Citizens* (Jackson: University Press of Mississippi, 1985); William Galston, *Liberal Purposes: Goods, Virtues, and Diversity in the Liberal State* (Cambridge: Cambridge University Press, 1991), chap. 11; and Amy Gutmann, *Democratic Education* (Princeton, NJ: Princeton University Press, 1987), and "Undemocratic Education," in *Liberalism and the Moral Life*, ed. Nancy L. Rosenblum (Cambridge, MA: Harvard University Press, 1989).

10. Quoted in Battistoni, *Public Schooling and the Education of Democratic Citi-zens*, p. 81.

11. As Gutmann remarks in *Democratic Education*, "[d]ependency is probably the primary harm that attends being functionally illiterate in our society" (p. 280).

12. Gutmann refers to these as "cooperative moral sentiments," part of "the moral-ity of association" (in Lawrence Kohlberg's terms) that "the most successful schools seem to teach" (ibid., p. 61). On the previous page, however, she re-

marks, "Although it is possible that there is a way that schools can teach autonomy, nobody has come even close to finding it." In this case, she refers specifically to the efforts of "liberal moralists" to make "moral autonomy" the goal
of "moral education"—that is, the belief that "education should produce in
children the desire and capacity to make moral choices based on principles that
are generalizable among all persons" (p. 59). The sense of "autonomy" here—
and the sense of "teach" too, I suspect—is narrower than mine. But her comments on "rational deliberation" in "Undemocratic Education" and on autonomy in "The Disharmony of Democracy" (in *NOMOS XXXV: Democratic
Community*, ed. John W. Chapman and Ian Shapiro [New York: New York
University Press, 1993], pp. 140–49), suggest that our views on the possibility
of promoting autonomy in the schools are closer than her remarks about the
teaching of autonomy indicate.

13. Battistoni, *Public Schooling and the Education of Democratic Citizens*, p. 121.
14. See ibid., pp. 185–96, for some interesting suggestions for improvement.
15. For a brief review, see Chubb and Moe, *Politics, Markets, and America's
Schools*, pp. 104–5.
16. Ibid., p. 105. But cf. Valerie E. Lee and Julia B. Smith, "Effects of High School
Restructuring and Size on Early Gains in Achievement and Education," *Sociology of Education* 68 (October 1995): 241–70: "Most research on the effect of
school size on students' development has supported a shift toward smaller high
schools" (p. 245). Lee and Smith's own study also supports this conclusion,
which they attribute to factors more likely to be found in small than in large
high schools: "[C]ollegiality among teachers, personalized relationships, and
less differentiation of instruction by ability (to name a few organizational features of schools) are more common and easier to implement in small schools"
(pp. 261–62).
17. Alyce Holland and Thomas Andre, "The Relationship of Self-Esteem to Selected Personal and Environmental Resources of Adolescents," *Adolescence* 29
(Summer 1994): 345–60: "[P]revious research has shown consistently that atten-
dance at smaller schools lead [*sic*] to increased high school extracurricular activity participation. . . , and that high school activity participation and self-esteem
are positively correlated" (p. 347 and the sources cited therein). See also E. P.
Willems, "Forces toward Participation in Behavior Settings," in *Big School,
Small School*, ed. R. G. Barker and P. V. Gump (Stanford: Stanford University
Press, 1964); A. W. Wicker, "Undermanning, Performances, and Students,"
Journal of Personality and Social Psychology 10 (1968): 255–61; and Leonard
Baird, "Big School, Small School: A Critical Examination of the Hypothesis,"
Journal of Educational Psychology 60 (August 1969): 253–60.
18. Chubb and Moe, *Politics, Markets, and America's Schools*, p. 219.
19. Ibid., p. 220.
20. Michael Walzer, *Spheres of Justice: A Defense of Pluralism and Equality* (New
York: Basic Books, 1983), p. 225.
21. For discussion of these cases, see, inter alia, Richard J. Arneson and Ian Shapiro, "Democratic Autonomy and Religious Freedom," in *NOMOS XXXVIII:
Political Order*, ed. Ian Shapiro and Russell Hardin (New York: New York
University Press, 1996), pp. 365–411; Shelley Burtt, "Religious Parents, Secular

Schools: A Liberal Defense of an Illiberal Education," *Review of Politics* 56 (Winter 1994): 51–70, and "In Defense of *Yoder:* Parental Authority and the Public Schools," in *NOMOS XXXVIII: Political Order,* ed. Ian Shapiro and Russell Hardin (New York: New York University Press, 1996), pp. 412–37; William Galston, "Two Concepts of Liberalism," *Ethics* 105 (April 1995): 516–34; Amy Gutmann, "Children, Paternalism, and Education," *Philosophy and Public Affairs* 9 (Summer 1980): 338–58, and "Civic Education and Social Diversity," *Ethics* 105 (April 1995): 557–79; Stephen Macedo, "Liberal Civic Education and Religious Fundamentalism: The Case of God v. John Rawls?," *Ethics* 105 (April 1995): 468–96; and Jeff Spinner, *The Boundaries of Citizenship: Race, Ethnicity, and Nationality in the Liberal State* (Baltimore: The Johns Hopkins University Press, 1994), chap. 5.

22. Gutmann reaches the same conclusion in "Children, Paternalism, and Education." Galston does not; see *Liberal Purposes,* chap. 11, and "Two Concepts of Liberalism." See also Arneson and Shapiro, "Democratic Autonomy and Religious Freedom," and Burtt's response, "In Defense of *Yoder.*"

23. Spinner, *The Boundaries of Citizenship,* p. 102.

24. Ibid., p. 91.

25. Ibid., p. 107.

26. Ibid., p. 98; emphasis added. Macedo follows the same tack in "Liberal Civic Education and Religious Fundamentalism," pp. 488–89.

27. Spinner, *The Boundaries of Citizenship,* p. 106.

28. On this point, Burtt's "Religious Parents, Secular Schools" is especially instructive.

29. Spinner points out that "many Amish men had been arrested in other states for not sending their children to public schools. In these circumstances, however, the Amish community and local school officials had usually worked out some arrangement, which often meant that Amish children received vocational training in high school by working on an Amish farm or in an Amish house" (*The Boundaries of Citizenship,* p. 87). Whether these arrangements could count as compromises, and not mere acquiescence to the Amish parents, is not clear.

30. See, e.g., Barber, *An Aristocracy of Everyone,* chap. 7, and Suzanne W. Morse, *Renewing Civic Capacity: Preparing College Students for Service and Citizenship* (Washington, DC: Clearinghouse on Higher Education, George Washington University, 1989), esp. pp. 38–44.

31. Burtt, "The Good Citizen's Psyche," p. 38. See also her "The Politics of Virtue Today: A Critique and a Proposal," *American Political Science Review* 87 (June 1993): 360–68, esp. 365.

CHAPTER NINE

1. Parts of this chapter draw on Richard Dagger and John Geer, "Apathy, Democracy, and Electoral Participation: The Case for Compulsory Self-Registration," *Journal of Social Philosophy* (forthcoming). I am grateful for Professor Geer for his permission to use this material here.

2. As one self-proclaimed defender of apathy insists, "[a] State which has 'cured'

apathy is likely to be a State in which too many people have fallen into the error of believing in the efficacy of political solutions for the problems of ordinary lives" (W. H. Morris-Jones, "In Defense of Apathy: Some Doubts on the Duty to Vote," *Political Studies* 2 [1954]: 37).

3. Ibid., p. 35.

4. Angus Campbell, Philip E. Converse, Warren E. Miller, and Donald Stokes, *The American Voter* (New York: John Wiley, 1960), p. 534.

5. According to Herbert McClosky, "[d]emocratic viability is . . . saved by the fact that those who are most confused about democratic ideas are also likely to be politically apathetic and without significant influence. Their role in the nation's decision process is so small that their 'misguided' opinions or non-opinions have little practical consequence for stability" ("Consensus and Ideology in American Politics," *American Political Science Review* 58 [June 1964]: 361–82, at 376).

6. John Mueller, "Democracy and Ralph's Pretty Good Grocery: Elections, Equality, and the Minimal Human Being," *American Journal of Political Science* 36 (1992): 995.

7. For "developmental democracy," see C. B. Macpherson, *The Life and Times of Liberal Democracy* (Oxford: Oxford University Press, 1977), esp. chaps. 3 and 5; David Held, *Models of Democracy* (Stanford, CA: Stanford University Press, 1987), esp. chap. 3. For "educative democracy," see Terence Ball, *Transforming Political Discourse: Political Theory and Critical Conceptual History* (Oxford: Basil Blackwell, 1988), chap. 6; and Dennis Thompson, *John Stuart Mill and Representative Government* (Princeton, NJ: Princeton University Press, 1976), p. 9, for Mill's emphasis on the "educative goal" of democracy. According to Carole Pateman's reading of Mill, Rousseau, and G. D. H. Cole (*Participation and Democratic Theory* [Cambridge: Cambridge University Press, 1970], chap. 2), democratic participation performs three functions: it educates people, it integrates them into the community, and it "aids the acceptance of collective decisions" (p. 43).

8. For an insightful discussion of landslides and mandates, see Stanley Kelley, *Interpreting Elections* (Princeton, NJ: Princeton University Press, 1983).

9. See, inter alia, James C. Miller III, "A Program for Direct and Proxy Voting in the Legislative Process," *Public Choice* 7 (Fall 1969): 107–13; Martin Shubik, "On Homo Politicus and the Instant Referendum," *Public Choice* 9 (Fall 1970): 79–84; Robert Paul Wolff, *In Defense of Anarchism* (New York: Harper and Row, 1970), pp. 34–37; Peter Singer, *Democracy and Disobedience* (Oxford: Oxford University Press, 1973), pp. 106–7; Ithiel de Sola Pool, "Citizen Feedback in Political Philosophy," in *Talking Back: Citizen Feedback and Cable Technology*, ed. Pool (Cambridge, MA: MIT Press, 1973), pp. 237–46; Kenneth Laudon, *Communications Technology and Democratic Participation* (New York: Praeger, 1977), chaps. 1–3; Keith Graham, "Democracy, Paradox, and the Real World," *Proceedings of the Aristotelian Society* 76 (1975/1976): 242; C. B. Macpherson, *The Life and Times of Liberal Democracy* (Oxford: Oxford University Press, 1977), pp. 94–98; and Richard Hollander, *Video Democracy* (Mt. Airy, MD: Lomond Publications, 1985).

10. I am grateful to Nannerl O. Keohane for impressing the importance of this point on me.

11. I refer to Wolff and Hollander, the latter of whom says, "Once the two-way cable or related technology is installed, then America has a true opportunity to reverse more than a generation of apathy. Politics can again be what those who dreamed about democracy had in mind. Civic affairs can be a part of everyday existence. Video democracy offers a new lease on life for a system noted more for lethargy than vigor" (*Video Democracy*, p. 106).

12. Those who think this too fanciful should read Hollander, *Video Democracy*, esp. chaps. 1 and 2, and John Wicklein, "Wired City, U.S.A.: The Charms and Dangers of Two-Way TV," *Atlantic Monthly* 243 (February 1979): 35–42.

13. Graham, "Democracy, Paradox, and the Real World," p. 242.

14. For the first suggestion, see Singer, *Democracy and Disobedience*, p. 107; for the second, see Wolff, *In Defense of Anarchism*, p. 35.

15. Dennis Mueller, *Public Choice* (Cambridge: Cambridge University Press, 1979), p. 66.

16. George Kateb, "The Moral Distinctiveness of Representative Democracy," *Ethics* 91 (April 1981): 373.

17. This point is made by Bernard Grofman, "Fair and Equal Representation," *Ethics* 91 (April 1981): 484. See also Jane Mansbridge, "Living with Conflict: Representation in the Theory of Adversary Democracy," *Ethics* 91 (April 1981): 475, n. 15.

18. Sidney Verba and Norman Nie, *Participation in America: Democracy and Social Equality* (New York: Harper and Row, 1972), pp. 79–80.

19. Macpherson, *The Life and Times of Liberal Democracy*, pp. 95–96.

20. Wolff, *In Defense of Anarchism*, pp. 36–37.

21. In "The Selfish-Voter Paradox and the Thrown-Away Vote Argument," *American Political Science Review* 71 (March 1977): 11, Paul Meehl concludes that his chances of casting the deciding vote in a presidential election "are of about the same order of magnitude as my chances of being killed driving to the polls." The same claim appears in B. F. Skinner's novel *Walden Two* (New York: Macmillan, 1976 [originally published 1948]), p. 249.

22. In *Teledemocracy: Can Technology Protect Democracy?* (Newbury Park, CA: Sage Publications, 1985), p. 161, F. Christopher Arterton concludes that "the available evidence [on turnout for referenda] contradicts the assertion by advocates of direct teledemocracy that once citizens realize their actions will really determine outcomes, rates of participation will rise."

23. Cf. Jane Mansbridge, *Beyond Adversary Democracy* (Chicago: University of Chicago Press, 1983), p. 301: "Most Americans experience democracy only in the voting booth. Citizens file into a curtained box, mark a preference, and file out. In special circumstances, if a big-city political machine is at work or if the community is small, they may see someone they know on the way in and out of the box, smile, and exchange a triviality. Most voters see no one they know. They sit in their homes; they consume information; they determine a preference; they go to the polling place; they register the preference; they return to their homes. Small wonder that the preferences so conceived and so expressed should tend toward the private and the selfish." See also Benjamin Barber, *Strong Democracy: Participatory Politics for a New Age* (Berkeley: University of California Press, 1984), p. 290, and Hollander, *Video Democracy*, chap. 9, in

which he acknowledges that video democracy poses a serious threat to face-to-face communication and the sense of community.

24. Hollander's conception of video democracy (*Video Democracy,* chap. 8) calls for the use of instant direct democracy only at the local level. Barber, *Strong Democracy,* chap. 10, proposes a variety of uses of teledemocracy, most of them at the local or regional level.

25. For a provocative example, see Miller, "A Program for Direct and Proxy Voting in the Legislative Process."

26. Steven J. Rosenstone and John Mark Hansen, *Mobilization, Participation, and Democracy in America* (New York: Macmillan, 1993), pp. 229–30.

27. For data on turnout, see G. Bingham Powell, "American Voter Turnout in Comparative Perspective," *American Political Science Review* 80 (March 1986): 17–43, and Robert W. Jackman, "Political Institutions and Voter Turnout in the Industrial Democracies," *American Political Science Review* 81 (June 1987): 405–23.

28. William Riker and Peter Ordeshook, "A Theory of the Calculus of Voting," *American Political Science Review* 62 (March 1968): 25–42.

29. Brian Barry, *Sociologists, Economists, and Democracy* (London: Collier-Macmillan, 1970), esp. chap. 2; J. Donald Moon, "The Logic of Political Inquiry," in *Handbook of Political Science,* vol. 1, *Political Science: Scope and Theory,* ed. Fred I. Greenstein and Nelson Polsby (Reading, MA: Addison-Wesley, 1975), pp. 200–204.

30. Powell, "American Voter Turnout in Comparative Perspective," p. 26.

31. Whether the penalty will be regarded as severe and whether it is likely to be enforced may be important considerations. As Jackman says, "I am unaware of any reports either that Australian authorities have shown an inclination or possess the resources to prosecute actively all nonvoters." In Italy, the penalty consists of a social stigma—for example, posting the names of nonvoters outside the town hall—rather than a fine. Jackman, "Political Institutions and Voter Turnout in the Industrial Democracies," p. 409.

32. Kenneth Arrow, *Social Choice and Individual Values,* 2d ed. (New York: John Wiley, 1963).

33. See Robert Dahl, *A Preface to Democratic Theory* (Chicago: University of Chicago Press, 1956), p. 128.

34. See, inter alia, Rosenstone and Hansen, *Mobilization, Participation, and Democracy in America,* pp. 234–48.

35. See Steven E. Finkel, "Reciprocal Effects of Participation and Political Efficacy: A Panel Analysis," *American Journal of Political Science* 29 (1985): 891–913.

36. As noted by Malcolm Feeley, "A Solution to the 'Voting Dilemma' in Modern Democratic Theory," *Ethics* 84 (1974): 235–42, and Alan Wertheimer, "In Defense of Compulsory Voting," in *NOMOS XVI: Participation in Politics,* ed. J. Roland Pennock and John W. Chapman (New York: Leiber-Atherton, 1975), pp. 276–96.

37. Jean-Jacques Rousseau, *Politics and the Arts: Letter to M. D'Alembert on the Theatre,* trans. Allan Bloom (Ithaca, NY: Cornell University Press, 1968), p. 24.

38. As amended in 1963, the law specifies a fine "not exceeding two pounds on a

first conviction" and "not exceeding five pounds on any subsequent conviction." More recently, an "Election Enrollment Information Leaflet," published in the late 1980s, does not even mention the penalty for failing to register.

39. Bruce E. Cain and Ken McCue, "The Efficacy of Registration Drives," *Journal of Politics* 47 (1985): 1221–30.

40. Two useful but different accounts of deliberative democracy are Joshua Cohen, "Deliberation and Democratic Legitimacy," in *The Good Polity: Normative Analysis of the State,* ed. Alan Hamlin and Philip Pettit (Oxford: Basil Blackwell, 1989), pp. 17–34; and Amy Gutmann, "The Disharmony of Democracy," in *NOMOS XXXV: The Democratic Community,* ed. John W. Chapman and Ian Shapiro (New York: New York University Press, 1993), pp. 126–60.

41. As proposed, for example, in Joshua Cohen and Joel Rogers, *On Democracy: Toward a Transformation of American Society* (New York: Penguin, 1983), pp. 154–57.

42. James Fishkin, *Democracy and Deliberation: New Directions for Democratic Reform* (New Haven: Yale University Press, 1991). See also *The Independent,* May 9, 1994, pp. 8–9, for an account of the first deliberative opinion poll in Great Britain.

43. Fishkin, *Democracy and Deliberation,* p. 4.

CHAPTER TEN

1. Charles M. Tiebout, "A Pure Theory of Local Expenditures," *Journal of Political Economy* 64 (October 1956): 416–24, at 418. See also Vincent Ostrom, Charles M. Tiebout, and Robert Warren, "The Organization of Government in Metropolitan Areas: A Theoretical Inquiry," *American Political Science Review* 55 (December 1961): 831–42; Robert Bish, *The Public Economy of Metropolitan Areas* (Chicago: Markham, 1971); and Paul Teske, Mark Schneider, Michael Mintrom, and Samuel Best, "Establishing the Micro Foundations of a Macro Theory: Information, Movers, and the Competitive Local Market for Public Goods," *American Political Science Review* 87 (September 1993): 702–13.

2. Jean-Jacques Rousseau, *Emile,* trans. Allan Bloom (New York: Basic Books, 1979), p. 59.

3. Norton Long, "An Institutional Framework for Responsible Citizenship," in Long, *The Polity,* ed. Charles Press (Chicago: Rand McNally, 1962), p. 179.

4. John C. Bollens and Henry J. Schmandt, *The Metropolis: Its People, Politics, and Economic Life,* 4th ed. (New York: Harper and Row, 1982), p. 140.

5. See Robert Dahl, "The City in the Future of Democracy," *American Political Science Review* 61 (December 1967): 953–70, for this comparison.

6. Robert Dahl and Edward Tufte provide a useful survey of claims and counterclaims regarding the desirable size of the polity in the first chapter of their *Size and Democracy* (Stanford, CA: Stanford University Press, 1973).

7. Aristotle, *The Politics,* ed. Stephen Everson (Cambridge: Cambridge University Press, 1988), p. 163, 1326b15–25. Cf. Jean-Jacques Rousseau, *The Government of Poland,* trans. Willmoore Kendall (Indianapolis, IN: Hackett, 1985), p. 25:

"Almost all small states, republics and monarchies alike, prosper, simply because they are small, because all their citizens know each other and keep an eye on each other, and because their rulers can see for themselves the harm that is being done and the good that is theirs to do and can look on as their orders are being executed."

8. For social-psychological evidence supporting this observation, see Warren B. Miller and R. Kenneth Godwin, *Psyche and Demos: Individual Psychology and Issues of Population* (New York: Oxford University Press, 1977), pp. 151–52, 203. Of the studies cited there, the most pertinent is probably Stanley Milgram, "The Experience of Living in Cities," *Science* 167 (1970): 1461–68. Note also Robert Levine, "Cities with Heart," *Responsive Community* 5 (Winter 1994–95): 59–67. On the basis of six experiments conducted in thirty-six cities of various sizes in the United States, Levine concludes that "the citizens of urban environments are clearly less likely to respond to the needs of strangers than are their counterparts in smaller communities" (p. 66). The chief culprit appears to be population density.

9. See A. John Simmons, *Moral Principles and Political Obligations* (Princeton, NJ: Princeton University Press, 1979), p. 137, and my discussion of Simmons's position in Chapter 5, supra.

10. See, e.g., Steven J. Rosenstone and John Mark Hansen, *Mobilization, Participation, and Democracy in America* (New York: Macmillan, 1993), pp. 43–45, 134–36.

11. Sidney Verba and Norman Nie, *Participation in America: Political Democracy and Social Equality* (New York: Harper and Row, 1972), chap. 13. An "isolated" community is one that is not caught in the orbit of a larger city—that is, one that has distinct boundaries and is not a suburb. See also the data Sidney Tarrow reports in "The Urban-Rural Cleavage in Political Involvement: The Case of France," *American Political Science Review* 65 (June 1971): 341–57.

12. See John Harrigan, *Political Change in the Metropolis*, 2d ed. (Boston: Little, Brown, 1976), pp. 139–46.

13. As reported in Bollens and Schmandt, *The Metropolis: Its People, Politics, and Economic Life*, pp. 88–89.

14. Verba and Nie, *Participation in America*, pp. 233–47.

15. Ibid., p. 247. Whether the authors' concern for the fate of "small and relatively independent communities" is warranted is difficult to say. In the 1970s, metropolitan areas in general lost population to nonmetropolitan areas in the United States, but the "1980s constricted migration flows from metropolitan to nonmetropolitan areas" (Patricia Gober, "Americans on the Move," *Population Bulletin* 48 [November 1993]: 1–40, at 32). Even if the trend is toward nonmetropolitan areas, the reason may be that people are moving just beyond the edge of metropolis. If so, they are simply extending urban sprawl, not preserving "small and relatively independent communities." On this possibility, see Harrigan, *Political Change in the Metropolis*, p. 375.

16. On this point, see Elinor Ostrom, *Governing the Commons: The Evolution of Institutions for Collective Action* (Cambridge: Cambridge University Press, 1990), pp. 34–35, 88, 183–84.

17. Thad A. Brown, *Migration and Politics: The Impact of Population Mobility on*

American Voting Behavior (Chapel Hill: University of North Carolina Press, 1988), p. 6.

18. Gober, "Americans on the Move," pp. 35–36.

19. Ibid., pp. 2–3, 6–7. See also Brown, *Migration and Politics,* p. 6.

20. Gober, "Americans on the Move," 3–4.

21. Jane Jacobs, *The Death and Life of Great American Cities* (New York: Modern Library, 1969), p. 138. Note also Michael Walzer's comments on geographical mobility as one of the "four mobilities" in his "The Communitarian Critique of Liberalism," *Political Theory* 18 (February 1990): 11: "Communities are more than just locations, but they are most often successful when they are permanently located."

   Several scholars have employed and extended Jacobs's idea of "social capital" in ways relevant to the purposes of this book, especially Robert Putnam, "Bowling Alone, Revisited," *Responsive Community* 5 (Spring 1995): 18–33, and "Tuning In, Tuning Out: The Strange Disappearance of Social Capital in America," *PS: Political Science and Politics* 28 (December 1995): 664–83, esp. 670.

22. Daniel Kemmis, *Community and the Politics of Place* (Norman: University of Oklahoma Press, 1990), pp. 122–23.

23. Stephen Elkin, *City and Regime in the American Republic* (Chicago: University of Chicago Press, 1987), p. 73.

24. Gober, "Americans on the Move," pp. 24–26.

25. Michael Taylor, *Anarchy and Cooperation* (New York: John Wiley, 1976), p. 93.

26. A. H. Birch, "The Habit of Voting," *Manchester School of Social and Economic Studies* 28 (January 1950): 82.

27. Raymond Wolfinger and Steven Rosenstone, *Who Votes?* (New Haven: Yale University Press, 1980), p. 54. For "community attachment," see John M. Strate, Charles J. Parrish, Charles D. Elder, and Coit Ford III, "Life Span Civic Development and Voting Participation," *American Political Science Review* 83 (June 1989): 443–64, esp. 458. See also Peverill Squire, Raymond E. Wolfinger, and David Glass, "Residential Mobility and Voter Turnout," *American Political Science Review* 81 (March 1987): 45–65, esp. 56; Verba and Nie, *Participation in America,* pp. 139–46; and Robert Alford and Eugene Lee, "Voting Turnout in American Cities," *American Political Science Review* 62 (September 1968): 796–813; but cf. Robert Alford and Harry Scoble, "Sources of Local Political Involvement," *American Political Science Review* 62 (December 1968): 1192–1206.

28. Garry Wills, *Confessions of a Conservative* (Garden City, NY: Doubleday, 1979), pp. 233–34; emphasis in original.

29. Christopher Lasch, *The True and Only Heaven* (New York: W. W. Norton, 1991), p. 83.

30. Alexis de Tocqueville, *Democracy in America,* trans. George Lawrence, ed. J. P. Mayer (Garden City, NY: Doubleday, 1969), p. 511.

31. Perhaps this is the place to note that suburbs are not all alike. In a review of John Brinckerhoff Jackson's *A Sense of Place, a Sense of Time,* Witold Rybczynski quotes the following passage from Jackson's book: "In theory, but

only in theory, we want to duplicate the traditional compact European community where everyone takes part in a rich and diverse public life. But at the same time most of us are secretly pining for a secluded hideaway, a piece of land, or a small house in the country, where we can lead an intensely private nonurban existence, staying close to home." Rybczynski then observes: "The compact nineteenth-century railroad suburb was in many ways a solution to this dilemma, providing private houses and gardens, leafy common streets, nearby shopping areas, and access to the city. But it was quickly usurped by the automobile, which did much to break the connection between the city and its suburbs." Witold Rybczynski, "Mysteries of the Mall," *New York Review of Books* 41 (July 14, 1994): 31–34, at 32.

32. According to the authors of *The Good Society,* "most Americans, like the citizens of other industrialized nations, would rather live in smaller settlements, something like an idealized Tocquevillean town." Robert N. Bellah, Richard Madsen, William M. Sullivan, Ann Swidler, and Steven M. Tipton, *The Good Society* (New York: Alfred A. Knopf, 1991), p. 266. On the basis of national surveys conducted in the United States in 1972 and 1988, Glenn V. Fuguitt and David L. Brown concluded that "if everyone were to live in the location that he or she preferred, the distribution of population would be different than current residence. In particular, there would be considerably fewer people in large cities [i.e., with more than 50,000 residents] and more people near large cities [i.e., within 30 miles]" ("Residential Preferences and Population Redistribution: 1972–1988," *Demography* 27 [November 1990]: 589–600, at 592–93). See also Niles M. Hansen, *The Challenge of Urban Growth* (Lexington, MA: Lexington Books, 1975), chap. 3, and James Sundquist, *Dispersing Population: What America Can Learn from Europe* (Washington, DC: Brookings Institution, 1975), pp. 24–30.

33. See Sundquist, *Dispersing Population,* chap. 1; Harrigan, *Political Change in the Metropolis,* chap. 12; and Gordon DeJong, "Population Redistribution Policies: Alternatives from the Netherlands, Great Britain, and Israel," *Social Science Quarterly* 56 (September 1975): 262–73.

34. For evidence on the connection between cities with active neighborhood assemblies, political participation, and the sense of community, see Jeffrey M. Berry, Kent E. Portney, and Ken Thompson, *The Rebirth of Urban Democracy* (Washington, DC: Brookings Institution, 1993). One of their conclusions is that "[p]olitical participation is clearly one of the most effective ways of building community among neighbors. And involvement in neighborhood associations is a particularly effective way of building community among those who are willing to participate in the political process" (p. 290).

35. All quotations in this paragraph are from Leon Eplan, "Atlanta: Planning, Budgeting, and Neighborhoods," *Personality, Politics, and Planning: How City Planners Work,* ed. Anthony Catanese and W. Paul Farmer (Beverly Hills, CA: Sage Publications, 1978), pp. 41–42.

36. For helpful discussions of this relationship and other constraints upon—and opportunities for—city governments, see Elkin, *City and Regime,* and Paul Peterson, *City Limits* (Chicago: University of Chicago Press, 1981).

37. Joseph E. Vitt Jr., "Kansas City: Problems and Successes of Downtown Devel-

opment," in Catanese and Farmer, *Personality, Politics, and Planning,* p. 109; emphasis in original.

38. See Peterson, *City Limits,* esp. p. 25.
39. See ibid., pp. 218–21, and Elkin, *City and Regime in the American Republic.*

CHAPTER ELEVEN

1. Iris Marion Young, *Justice and the Politics of Difference* (Princeton, NJ: Princeton University Press, 1990), p. 45. Further references to this book will appear in parentheses in the text. Young defines a social group as "a collective of persons differentiated from at least one other group by cultural forms, practices, or way of life. Members of a group have a specific affinity with one another because of their similar experience or way of life, which prompts them to associate with one another more than with those not identified with the group, or in a different way" (p. 43).
2. Young develops this theme in "Mothers, Citizenship, and Independence: A Critique of Pure Family Values," *Ethics* 105 (April 1995): 535–56, esp. 546–50.
3. Stephen Macedo, "Liberal Civic Education and Religious Fundamentalism: The Case of God v. John Rawls?," *Ethics* 105 (April 1995): 468–96, at 469.
4. Jeff Spinner, *The Boundaries of Citizenship: Race, Ethnicity, and Nationality in the Liberal State* (Baltimore: The Johns Hopkins University Press, 1994), pp. 31–32.
5. Anne Phillips, "Democracy and Difference: Some Problems for Feminist Theory," in *The Rights of Minority Cultures,* ed. Will Kymlicka (Oxford: Oxford University Press, 1995), p. 295.
6. Will Kymlicka, *Multicultural Citizenship* (Oxford: Clarendon Press, 1995), pp. 146–47.
7. Phillips, "Democracy and Difference," p. 294.
8. David Miller puts the point forcefully: "It is a major weakness of Young's argument that she does not consider how agreement is to be reached under the form of politics that she favours. She is preoccupied with the question of how oppressed groups are to find their authentic voice, and she does not ask what will happen when the (authentic) claims of some groups are confronted by the equally authentic but conflicting claims of others. There seems to be an unstated premise that when the groups she identifies as oppressed make their case, this case will overwhelm the opposition. As an understanding of politics, this seems naive in the extreme" ("Citizenship and Pluralism," *Political Studies* 43 [September 1995]: 432–50, at 446, n. 26). See also his discussion of "radical multiculturalism" in David Miller, *On Nationality* (Oxford: Clarendon Press, 1995), pp. 130–40.
9. In a subsequent article, Young writes of "the necessity and possibility of political togetherness in difference." Iris Marion Young, "Together in Difference: Transforming the Logic of Group Political Conflict," in Kymlicka, *The Rights of Minority Cultures.*
10. Miller, *On Nationality,* p. 151; Cass R. Sunstein, "Beyond the Republican Revival," *Yale Law Journal* 97 (1988): 1539–89, at 1587. For a thorough review of

the issues involved in group representation that leads to an admittedly "vague conclusion," see Kymlicka, *Multicultural Citizenship*, chap. 7.

11. Cynthia V. Ward, "The Limits of 'Liberal Republicanism': Why Group-Based Remedies and Republican Citizenship Don't Mix," *Columbia Law Review* 91 (April 1991): 581–607, at 600–601.

12. For a sample of the arguments in this debate, see, on the neutralist side, Ronald Dworkin, "Liberalism," in *Private and Public Morality*, ed. Stuart Hampshire (Cambridge: Cambridge University Press, 1978), pp. 113–43; Will Kymlicka, *Liberalism, Community, and Culture* (Oxford: Clarendon Press, 1989), esp. chaps. 3 and 5; and Charles Larmore, *Patterns of Moral Complexity* (Cambridge: Cambridge University Press, 1987), esp. chaps. 3 and 5. On the other side of the debate, see William Galston, "Defending Liberalism," *American Political Science Review* 76 (1982): 621–29, and "Liberal Virtues," *American Political Science Review* 82 (December 1988): 1277–90, both of which are incorporated into his *Liberal Purposes: Goods, Virtues, and Diversity in the Liberal State* (Cambridge: Cambridge University Press, 1991); Vinit Haksar, *Equality, Liberty, and Perfectionism* (Oxford: Clarendon Press, 1979); and Joseph Raz, *The Morality of Freedom* (Oxford: Clarendon Press, 1986), esp. chaps. 5 and 6.

13. I use "motivation" here in the first of the two senses that Ronald Dworkin distinguishes in "Foundations of Liberal Equality," in *The Tanner Lectures on Human Values*, vol. 11 (Salt Lake City: University of Utah Press, 1990), pp. 3–119, at 5, n. 1.

14. John Rawls, *Political Liberalism* (New York: Columbia University Press, 1993). I am particularly concerned with Chapter 5, in which Rawls elaborates and modifies the arguments of his essay, "The Priority of Right and Ideas of the Good," *Philosophy and Public Affairs* 17 (Fall 1988): 251–76.

15. Rawls, *Political Liberalism*, esp. pp. xvi–xvii. Further references to *Political Liberalism* will appear within parentheses in the text.

16. Rawls also cites Raz, *The Morality of Freedom*, chaps. 14 and 15, as a contemporary example.

17. This is a departure from "The Priority of Right and Ideas of the Good," p. 261, where Rawls states, "Justice as fairness is not, without important qualifications, procedurally neutral." He goes on to refer to "common, or neutral, ground" (p. 262) and contends that political liberalism "can be seen as neutral in procedure and in aim" (p. 263).

18. Galston, *Liberal Purposes*, pp. 273–74.

19. See J. G. A. Pocock, *The Machiavellian Moment: Florentine Humanism and the Atlantic Republican Tradition* (Princeton, NJ: Princeton University Press, 1975), and Quentin Skinner, "The Republican Ideal of Political Liberty," in *Machiavelli and Republicanism*, ed. Gisela Bock, Quentin Skinner, and Maurizio Viroli (Cambridge: Cambridge University Press, 1990), pp. 293–309.

20. Galston, *Liberal Purposes*, p. 225.

21. Skinner, "The Republican Ideal of Political Liberty," esp. pp. 301–2.

22. Ibid., p. 306.

23. Galston states: "Each of these contemporary liberal theories [including Rawls's] begins by promising to do without a substantive theory of the good; each ends by betraying that promise. All of them covertly rely on the same triadic theory

of the good, which assumes the worth of human existence, the worth of human purposiveness and of the fulfillment of human purposes, and the worth of rationality as the chief constraint on social principles and social actions. If we may call the beliefs in the worth of human existence and in the worth of purposes and their fulfillment the root assumptions of humanism, then the theory of the good presupposed by these neutralist liberals is the theory of rationalist humanism" (*Liberal Purposes,* p. 92).

24. Note also Charles Larmore's remarks on neutrality and equality of respect as the norms on which he bases his justification of liberalism in "Liberal Neutrality: A Reply to James Fishkin," *Political Theory* 17 (November 1989): 580–81.

25. John Rawls, *A Theory of Justice* (Cambridge, MA: Harvard University Press, 1971), esp. section 78.

26. Rawls does say that "the two moral powers do not exhaust the person, for persons also have a determinate conception of the good." He goes on to note, however, that "the role and exercise of these powers (in the appropriate instances) is a condition of the good" (*Political Liberalism,* p. 334). He also uses the two moral powers to identify the primary goods "by asking which things are generally necessary as social conditions and all-purpose means to enable persons to pursue their determinate conceptions of the good and to develop and exercise their two moral powers" (p. 307). For instance, he says of one of these primary goods, "Self-respect is rooted in our self-confidence as a fully cooperating member of society capable of pursuing a worthwhile conception of the good over a complete life. Thus self-respect presupposes the development and exercise of both moral powers and therefore an effective sense of justice" (p. 318). In short, the two moral powers are clearly vital to Rawls's conception of the person—and thus to his political liberalism.

27. Rawls comes close to making the connection explicit when he says that Dworkin's view (in "Foundations of Liberal Equality"), "like the comprehensive liberalisms of Kant and Mill, . . . has a proper place in the background culture and serves there in a supporting role for political liberalism" (*Political Liberalism,* p. 211, n. 42).

28. Kymlicka, *Liberalism, Community, and Culture,* p. 33.

29. Ibid., p. 254.

CHAPTER TWELVE

1. In *A Theory of Justice* (Cambridge, MA: Harvard University Press, 1971), p. 325, John Rawls defines the first "variant" of perfectionism as "a teleological theory directing society to arrange institutions and to define the duties and obligations of individuals so as to maximize the achievement of human excellence in art, science, and culture." The second and "more moderate" variant "is one in which a principle of perfection is accepted as but one standard among several in an intuitionist theory."

2. Shelley Burtt, "The Politics of Virtue Today: A Critique and a Proposal," *American Political Science Review* 87 (June 1993): 360–68, at 367.

3. David Miller argues that a national identity strengthens the obligations of reci-

procity among fellow citizens, but he does not define national identity in terms of blood or ethnicity. *On Nationality* (Oxford: Clarendon Press, 1995), pp. 65–73.

4. For related attempts to identify civic or political virtues, see William A. Galston, *Liberal Purposes: Goods, Virtues, and Diversity in the Liberal State* (Cambridge: Cambridge University Press, 1991), esp. chap. 10; Daniel Kemmis, *Community and the Politics of Place* (Norman: University of Oklahoma Press, 1990), pp. 118–19; Stephen Macedo, "Charting Liberal Virtues," in *NOMOS XXXIV: Virtue*, ed. John W. Chapman and William A. Galston (New York: New York University Press, 1992); and Thomas A. Spragens Jr., *Reason and Democracy* (Durham: Duke University Press, 1990), pp. 170–73.

5. Will Kymlicka, *Liberalism, Community, and Culture* (Oxford: Clarendon Press, 1989), pp. 12–13.

6. "State governments extoll the rewards of gambling and encourage the opposite of any work ethic. The Pennsylvania State Lottery claims, 'It pays to play every day.' The New York State Lottery advertises the dreams of ordinary people to live like aristocrats." Amy Gutmann, "The Disharmony of Democracy," in *NOMOS XXXV: The Democratic Community*, ed. John W. Chapman and Ian Shapiro (New York: New York University Press, 1993), p. 126.

7. See, inter alia, Morris Janowitz, *The Reconstruction of Patriotism: Education for Civic Consciousness* (Chicago: University of Chicago Press, 1983), chap. 7; Charles C. Moskos, *A Call to Civic Service: National Service for Country and Community* (New York: Free Press, 1988); Rogers M. Smith, "American Conceptions of Citizenship and National Service," in *New Communitarian Thinking: Persons, Virtues, Institutions, and Communities*, ed. Amitai Etzioni (Charlottesville: University Press of Virginia, 1995), pp. 233–58; Michael Walzer, *Spheres of Justice: A Defense of Pluralism and Equality* (New York: Basic Books, 1983), pp. 174–75; and *National Service: Pro and Con*, ed. Williamson M. Evers (Stanford, CA: Hoover Institution Press, 1990).

8. See, e.g., Susan Moller Okin, *Justice, Gender, and the Family* (New York: Basic Books, 1989), chaps. 7 and 8, and Iris Marion Young, "Mothers, Citizenship, and Independence: A Critique of Pure Family Values," *Ethics* 105 (April 1995): 535–56.

9. Robert Putnam's analysis of the (negative) relationship between television watching and "social capital" is worth noting in this regard: "Tuning In, Tuning Out: The Strange Disappearance of Social Capital in America," *PS: Political Science and Politics* 28 (December 1995): 664–83.

10. Manfred Riedel, *Between Tradition and Revolution: The Hegelian Transformation of Political Philosophy*, trans. Walter Wright (Cambridge: Cambridge University Press, 1984), chap. 6.

11. Antony Black, *Guilds and Civil Society in European Political Thought from the Twelfth Century to the Present* (Ithaca, NY: Cornell University Press, 1984), p. 32.

BIBLIOGRAPHY

Alford, Robert, and Eugene Lee, "Voting Turnout in American Cities," *American Political Science Review* 62 (September 1968): 796–813.

Alford, Robert, and Harry Scoble, "Sources of Local Political Involvement," *American Political Science Review* 62 (December 1968): 1192–1206.

Anderson, Charles, "The Place of Principles in Policy Analysis," *American Political Science Review* 73 (September 1979): 711–23.

Aristotle, *The Politics,* ed. Stephen Everson (Cambridge: Cambridge University Press, 1988).

Arneson, Richard, "The Principle of Fairness and Free-Rider Problems," *Ethics* 92 (July 1982): 616–33.

Arneson, Richard J., and Ian Shapiro, "Democratic Autonomy and Religious Freedom," in *NOMOS XXXVIII: Political Order,* ed. Ian Shapiro and Russell Hardin (New York: New York University Press, 1996).

Arrow, Kenneth, *Social Choice and Individual Values,* 2d ed. (New York: John Wiley, 1963).

Arterton, Christopher, *Teledemocracy: Can Technology Protect Democracy?* (Newbury Park, CA: Sage Publications, 1985).

Austin, J. L., *Philosophical Papers,* ed. J. O. Urmson and G. J. Warnock (Oxford: Oxford University Press, 1970).

———, "A Plea for Excuses," in Austin, *Philosophical Papers,* ed. J. O. Urmson and G. J. Warnock (Oxford: Oxford University Press, 1970).

Axelrod, Robert, *The Evolution of Cooperation* (New York: Basic Books, 1984).

Baird, Leonard, "Big School, Small School: A Critical Examination of the Hypothesis," *Journal of Educational Psychology* 60 (August 1969): 253–60.

Ball, Terence, *Reappraising Political Theory: Revisionist Studies in the History of Political Thought* (Oxford: Clarendon Press, 1995).

———, *Transforming Political Discourse: Political Theory and Critical Conceptual History* (Oxford: Basil Blackwell, 1988).

Ball, Terence, and J. G. A. Pocock, eds., *Conceptual Change and the Constitution* (Lawrence: University Press of Kansas, 1988).

Banning, Lance, "Jeffersonian Ideology Revisited: Liberal and Classical Ideas in the New American Republic," *William and Mary Quarterly* 43 (January 1986): 3–19.

——, "Some Second Thoughts on Virtue and the Course of Revolutionary Thinking," in *Conceptual Change and the Constitution,* ed. Terence Ball and J. G. A. Pocock (Lawrence: University Press of Kansas, 1988).

Barber, Benjamin, *An Aristocracy of Everyone: The Politics of Education and the Future of America* (New York: Ballantine Books, 1992).

——, *Strong Democracy: Participatory Politics for a New Age* (Berkeley: University of California Press, 1984).

Barker, R. G., and P. V. Gump, eds., *Big School, Small School* (Stanford, CA: Stanford University Press, 1964).

Barry, Brian, *Political Argument* (London: Routledge and Kegan Paul, 1965).

——, "The Public Interest," in *Political Philosophy,* ed. Anthony Quinton (Oxford: Oxford University Press, 1967).

——, *Sociologists, Economists, and Democracy* (London: Collier-Macmillan, 1970).

Battistoni, Richard, *Public Schooling and the Education of Democratic Citizens* (Jackson: University Press of Mississippi, 1985).

Becker, Lawrence C., *Reciprocity* (Chicago: University of Chicago Press, 1986).

Beiner, Ronald, "The Moral Vocabulary of Liberalism," in *NOMOS XXXIV: Virtue,* ed. John W. Chapman and William A. Galston (New York: New York University Press, 1992).

——, ed., *Theorizing Citizenship* (Albany: State University of New York Press, 1995).

Bell, Nora K., "Nozick and the Principle of Fairness," *Social Theory and Practice* 5 (1978): 65–73.

Bellah, Robert N., Richard Madsen, William M. Sullivan, Ann Swidler, and Steven M. Tipton, *The Good Society* (New York: Alfred A. Knopf, 1991).

Bendor, Jonathan, and Dilip Mookherjee, "Institutional Structure and the Logic of Ongoing Collective Action," *American Political Science Review* 81 (March 1987): 129–54.

Benn, Stanley, "Human Rights—for Whom and for What?," in *Human Rights,* ed. Eugene Kamenka and Alice Ehr-Soon Tay (New York: St. Martin's Press, 1978).

——, *A Theory of Freedom* (Cambridge: Cambridge University Press, 1988).

Bentham, Jeremy, "Anarchical Fallacies," in *Human Rights,* ed. A. I. Melden (Belmont, CA: Wadsworth, 1970).

——, *A Fragment on Government,* ed. Ross Harrison (Cambridge: Cambridge University Press, 1988 [originally published 1776]).

——, *An Introduction to the Principles of Morals and Legislation* (New York: Hafner, 1961 [originally published 1789]).

Beran, Harry, *The Consent Theory of Political Obligation* (London: Croom Helm, 1987).

Berlin, Isaiah, *Four Essays on Liberty* (Oxford: Oxford University Press, 1969).

——, "Two Concepts of Liberty," in Berlin, *Four Essays on Liberty* (Oxford: Oxford University Press, 1969).

Berry, Jeffrey M., Kent E. Portney, and Ken Thompson, *The Rebirth of Urban Democracy* (Washington, DC: Brookings Institution, 1993).

Birch, A. H., "The Habit of Voting," *Manchester School of Social and Economic Studies* 28 (January 1950): 75–82.

Bish, Robert, *The Public Economy of Metropolitan Areas* (Chicago: Markham, 1971).

Black, Antony, *Guilds and Civil Society in European Political Thought from the Twelfth Century to the Present* (Ithaca, NY: Cornell University Press, 1984).

Bock, Gisela, Quentin Skinner, and Maurizio Viroli, eds., *Machiavelli and Republicanism* (Cambridge: Cambridge University Press, 1990).

Bollens, John C., and Henry J. Schmandt, *The Metropolis: Its People, Politics, and Economic Life*, 4th ed. (New York: Harper and Row, 1982).

Branch, Taylor, *Parting the Waters: America in the King Years, 1954–1963* (New York: Simon and Schuster, 1988).

Bredvold, Louis, and Ralph Ross, eds., *The Philosophy of Edmund Burke: A Selection from His Speeches and Writings* (Ann Arbor: University of Michigan Press, 1967).

Brown, Peter, and Henry Shue, eds., *Food Policy: The Responsibility of the United States in Life and Death Choices* (New York: Free Press, 1977).

Brown, S., ed., *Philosophers Discuss Education* (Totowa, NJ: Rowman and Littlefield, 1975).

Brown, Thad A., *Migration and Politics: The Impact of Population Mobility on American Voting Behavior* (Chapel Hill: University of North Carolina Press, 1988).

Buchanan, Allen, "Assessing the Communitarian Critique of Liberalism," *Ethics* 99 (July 1989): 852–82.

Burke, Edmund, "Appeal from the New to the Old Whigs" (1791), in *The Philosophy of Edmund Burke: A Selection from His Speeches and Writings,* ed. Louis Bredvold and Ralph Ross (Ann Arbor: University of Michigan Press, 1967).

———, *Reflections on the Revolution in France,* ed. Conor Cruise O'Brien (Harmondsworth: Penguin, 1979 [originally published 1790]).

Burtt, Shelley, "The Good Citizen's Psyche: On the Psychology of Civic Virtue," *Polity* 23 (Fall 1990): 23–38.

———, "In Defense of *Yoder:* Parental Authority and the Public Schools," in *NOMOS XXXVIII: Political Order,* ed. Ian Shapiro and Russell Hardin (New York: New York University Press, 1996).

———, "The Politics of Virtue Today: A Critique and a Proposal," *American Political Science Review* 87 (June 1993): 360–68.

———, "Religious Parents, Secular Schools: A Liberal Defense of an Illiberal Education," *Review of Politics* 56 (Winter 1994): 51–70.

Cain, Bruce E., and Ken McCue, "The Efficacy of Registration Drives," *Journal of Politics* 47 (1985): 1221–30.

Campbell, Angus, Phillip E. Converse, Warren E. Miller, and Donald Stokes, *The American Voter* (New York: John Wiley, 1960).

Cassirer, Ernst, *Rousseau, Kant, and Goethe,* trans. James Gutmann, P. O. Kristeller, and J. H. Randall Jr. (New York: Harper and Row, 1963).

Catanese, Anthony, and W. Paul Farmer, eds., *Personality, Politics and Planning: How City Planners Work* (Beverly Hills, CA: Sage Publications, 1978).

Chapman, John W., and William A. Galston, eds., *NOMOS XXXIV: Virtue* (New York: New York University Press, 1992).

Chapman, John W., and J. Roland Pennock, eds., *NOMOS XVI: Participation in Politics* (New York: Leiber-Atherton, 1975).

Chapman, John W., and Ian Shapiro, eds., *NOMOS XXXV: Democratic Community* (New York: New York University Press, 1993).

Charvet, John, *The Social Problem in the Philosophy of Rousseau* (Cambridge: Cambridge University Press, 1974).

Chubb, John, and Terry Moe, *Politics, Markets, and America's Schools* (Washington, DC: Brookings Institution, 1990).

Cohen, Joshua, "Deliberation and Democratic Legitimacy," in *The Good Polity: Normative Analysis of the State,* ed. Alan Hamlin and Philip Pettit (Oxford: Basil Blackwell, 1989).

Cohen, Joshua, and Joel Rogers, *On Democracy: Toward a Transformation of American Society* (New York: Penguin, 1983).

Conover, Pamela J., Ivor M. Crewe, and Donald D. Searing, "The Nature of Citizenship in the United States and Great Britain: Empirical Comments on Theoretical Themes," *Journal of Politics* 53 (1991): 800–832.

Conway, Moncure D., ed., *The Writings of Thomas Paine* (New York: AMS Press, 1967).

Crittenden, Jack, "The Social Nature of Autonomy," *Review of Politics* 55 (Winter 1993): 35–65.

Crocker, Lester, *Rousseau's Social Contract: An Interpretive Essay* (Cleveland, OH: The Press of Case Western Reserve University, 1968).

Dagger, Richard, "Harm, Utility, and the Obligation to Obey the Law," *Archiv für Rechts- und Sozialphilosophie* 68 (1982): 102–8.

———, "Playing Fair with Punishment," *Ethics* 103 (April 1993): 473–88.

———, "Understanding the General Will," *Western Political Quarterly* 34 (September 1981): 359–71.

Dahl, Robert, "The City in the Future of Democracy," *American Political Science Review* 61 (December 1967): 953–70.

———, *A Preface to Democratic Theory* (Chicago: University of Chicago Press, 1956).

Dahl, Robert, and Edward Tufte, *Size and Democracy* (Stanford, CA: Stanford University Press, 1973).

Dawes, Robyn, "Social Dilemmas," *Annual Review of Psychology* 31 (1980): 169–93.

Dearden, R. F., "Autonomy as an Educational Ideal," in *Philosophers Discuss Education,* ed. S. Brown (Totowa, NJ: Rowman and Littlefield, 1975).

DeJong, Gordon, "Population Redistribution Policies: Alternatives from the Netherlands, Great Britain, and Israel," *Social Science Quarterly* 56 (September 1975): 262–73.

De Tocqueville, Alexis, *Democracy in America,* trans. George Lawrence, ed. J. P. Mayer (Garden City, NY: Doubleday, 1969).

Donnelly, Jack, *The Concept of Human Rights* (New York: St. Martin's Press, 1985).

Downs, Anthony, *An Economic Theory of Democracy* (New York: Harper and Row, 1957).

Dumbauld, Edward, ed., *The Political Writings of Thomas Jefferson: Representative Selections* (Indianapolis: Bobbs-Merrill, 1955).

Dunn, John, *Western Political Theory in the Face of the Future* (Cambridge: Cambridge University Press, 1979).

Dworkin, Gerald, "Paternalism," in *Morality and the Law,* ed. Richard Wasserstrom (Belmont, CA: Wadsworth, 1971).

————, *The Theory and Practice of Autonomy* (Cambridge: Cambridge University Press, 1988).

Dworkin, Ronald, "Foundations of Liberal Equality," in *The Tanner Lectures on Human Values,* vol. 11 (Salt Lake City: University of Utah Press, 1990).

————, "Liberalism," in *Private and Public Morality,* ed. Stuart Hampshire (Cambridge: Cambridge University Press, 1978).

————. *Taking Rights Seriously* (Cambridge, MA: Harvard University Press, 1977).

Elkin, Stephen, *City and Regime in the American Republic* (Chicago: University of Chicago Press, 1987).

Elster, Jon, "The Market and the Forum: Three Varieties of Political Theory," in *Foundations of Social Choice Theory,* ed. J. Elster and A. Hylland (Cambridge: Cambridge University Press, 1986).

————, *Sour Grapes: Studies in the Subversion of Rationality* (Cambridge: Cambridge University Press, 1987).

————, *Ulysses and the Sirens: Studies in Rationality and Irrationality* (Cambridge: Cambridge University Press, 1979).

Elster, Jon, and A. Hylland, eds., *Foundations of Social Choice Theory* (Cambridge: Cambridge University Press, 1986).

Eplan, Leon, "Atlanta: Planning, Budgeting and Neighborhoods," in *Personality, Politics, and Planning: How City Planners Work,* ed. Anthony Catanese and W. Paul Farmer (Beverly Hills, CA: Sage Publications, 1978).

Estlund, David, "Democratic Theory and the Public Interest: Condorcet and Rousseau Revisited," *American Political Science Review* 83 (December 1989): 1317–40.

Evers, Williamson M., ed., *National Service: Pro and Con* (Stanford, CA: Hoover Institution Press, 1990).

Feeley, Malcolm, "A Solution to the 'Voting Dilemma' in Modern Democratic Theory," *Ethics* 84 (1974): 235–42.

Feinberg, Joel, "The Nature and Value of Rights," in Feinberg, *Rights, Justice, and the Bounds of Liberty* (Princeton, NJ: Princeton University Press, 1980).

————, *Rights, Justice, and the Bounds of Liberty* (Princeton, NJ: Princeton University Press, 1980).

————, *Social Philosophy* (Englewood Cliffs, NJ: Prentice-Hall, 1973).

Feinberg, Joel, and Hyman Gross, eds., *Law in Philosophical Perspective* (Encino, CA: Dickenson, 1977).

Fink, Zera, *The Classical Republicans: An Essay in the Recovery of a Pattern of Thought in Seventeenth Century England* (Evanston, IL: Northwestern University Press, 1945).

Finkel, Steven E., "Reciprocal Effects of Participation and Political Efficacy: A Panel Analysis," *American Journal of Political Science* 29 (1985): 891–913.

Fishkin, James, *Democracy and Deliberation: New Directions for Democratic Reform* (New Haven: Yale University Press, 1991).

Flathman, Richard, *The Practice of Rights* (Cambridge: Cambridge University Press, 1976).

Fuguitt, Glenn V., and David L. Brown, "Residential Preferences and Population Redistribution: 1972–1988," *Demography* 27 (November 1990): 589–600.

Galston, William, "Defending Liberalism," *American Political Science Review* 76 (1982): 621–29.

———, "In Pursuit of Shared Purposes," *Responsive Community* 2 (Summer 1992): 58–61.

———, *Liberal Purposes: Goods, Virtues, and Diversity in the Liberal State* (Cambridge: Cambridge University Press, 1991).

———, "Liberal Virtues," *American Political Science Review* 82 (December 1988): 1277–90.

———, "Practical Philosophy and the Bill of Rights: Perspectives on Some Contemporary Issues," in *A Culture of Rights: The Bill of Rights in Philosophy, Politics, and Law—1791 and 1991,* ed. Michael J. Lacey and Knud Haakonssen (Cambridge: Cambridge University Press, 1991).

———, "Two Concepts of Liberalism," *Ethics* 105 (April 1995): 516–34.

Gambetta, Diego, "Can We Trust Trust?," in *Trust: Making and Breaking Cooperative Relations,* ed. Diego Gambetta (Oxford: Basil Blackwell, 1988).

———, ed., *Trust: Making and Breaking Cooperative Relations* (Oxford: Basil Blackwell, 1988).

Glass, David, Peverill Squire, and Raymond E. Wolfinger, "Voter Turnout: An International Comparison," *Public Opinion* 6 (1984): 49–55.

Glendon, Mary Ann, *Rights Talk: The Impoverishment of Political Discourse* (New York: Free Press, 1991).

Gober, Patricia, "Americans on the Move," *Population Bulletin* 48 (November 1993): 1–40.

Golding, Martin, "The Significance of Rights Language," *Philosophical Topics* 18 (Spring 1990): 53–64.

Good, David, "Individuals, Interpersonal Relations, and Trust," in *Trust: Making and Breaking Cooperative Relations,* ed. Diego Gambetta (Oxford: Basil Blackwell, 1988).

Goodin, Robert, *Political Theory and Public Policy* (Chicago: University of Chicago Press, 1982).

Goodin, Robert, and Philip Pettit, eds., *A Companion to Contemporary Political Philosophy* (Oxford: Basil Blackwell, 1993).

Gorovitz, Samuel, "Bigotry, Loyalty, and Malnutrition," in *Food Policy: The Responsibility of the United States in Life and Death Choices,* ed. Peter Brown and Henry Shue (New York: Free Press, 1977).

Graham, Keith, "Democracy, Paradox, and the Real World," *Proceedings of the Aristotelian Society* 76 (1975/1976): 227–45.

Green, Leslie, *The Authority of the State* (Oxford: Clarendon Press, 1988).

Green, T. H., *Lectures on the Principles of Political Obligation* (Ann Arbor: University of Michigan Press, 1967).

Greenstein, Fred I., and Nelson W. Polsby, eds., *Handbook of Political Science,* vol. 1 (Reading, MA: Addison-Wesley, 1975).

Grofman, Bernard, "Fair and Equal Representation," *Ethics* 91 (April 1981): 477–85.

Grofman, Bernard, and Scott Feld, "Democratic Theory and the Public Interest," *American Political Science Review* 83 (1989): 1317–40.

———, "Rousseau's General Will: A Condorcetian Perspective," *American Political Science Review* 82 (June 1988): 567–76.

Gutmann, Amy, "Children, Paternalism, and Education," *Philosophy and Public Affairs* 9 (Summer 1980): 338–58.

———, "Civic Education and Social Diversity," *Ethics* 105 (April 1995): 557–79.

———, "Communitarian Critics of Liberalism," *Philosophy and Public Affairs* 14 (Summer 1985): 308–22.

———, *Democratic Education* (Princeton, NJ: Princeton University Press, 1987).

———, "The Disharmony of Democracy," in *NOMOS XXXV: The Democratic Community,* ed. John W. Chapman and Ian Shapiro (New York: New York University Press, 1993).

———, "Undemocratic Education," in *Liberalism and the Moral Life,* ed. Nancy L. Rosenblum (Cambridge, MA: Harvard University Press, 1989).

Haksar, Vinit, *Equality, Liberty, and Perfectionism* (Oxford: Clarendon Press, 1979).

Hampshire, Stuart, ed., *Private and Public Morality* (Cambridge: Cambridge University Press, 1978).

Hansen, Niles M., *The Challenge of Urban Growth* (Lexington, MA: Lexington Books, 1975).

Hardin, Russell, *Collective Action* (Baltimore: The Johns Hopkins University Press, 1982).

Harrigan, John, *Political Change in the Metropolis,* 2d ed. (Boston: Little, Brown, 1976).

Hart, H. L. A., "Are There Any Natural Rights?," in *Human Rights,* ed. A. I. Melden (Belmont, CA: Wadsworth, 1970).

———, *The Concept of Law* (Oxford: Clarendon Press, 1961).

Haworth, Lawrence, *Autonomy: An Essay in Philosophical Psychology and Ethics* (New Haven: Yale University Press, 1986).

Held, David, *Models of Democracy* (Stanford, CA: Stanford University Press, 1987).

Herzog, Don, "Some Questions for Republicans," *Political Theory* 14 (August 1986): 473–93.

Hirsch, H. N., "The Threnody of Liberalism," *Political Theory* 14 (August 1986): 423–49.

Hobbes, Thomas, *Leviathan,* ed. Richard Tuck (Cambridge: Cambridge University Press, 1991).

Hohfeld, Wesley N., *Fundamental Legal Conceptions* (New Haven: Yale University Press, 1964 [originally published 1919]).

Holland, Alyce, and Thomas Andre, "The Relationship of Self-Esteem to Selected Personal and Environmental Resources of Adolescents," *Adolescence* 29 (Summer 1994): 345–60.

Hollander, Richard, *Video Democracy* (Mt. Airy, MD: Lomond Publications, 1985).

Hollis, Martin, "Friends, Romans, and Consumers," *Ethics* 102 (October 1991): 27–41.

Horton, John, *Political Obligation* (Atlantic Highlands, NJ: Humanities Press, 1992).

Isaac, Jeffrey C., "Republicanism vs. Liberalism?: A Reconsideration," *History of Political Thought* 9 (Summer 1988): 349–77.

Jackman, Robert W., "Political Institutions and Voter Turnout in the Industrial Democracies," *American Political Science Review* 81 (June 1987): 405–23.

Jacobs, Jane, *The Death and Life of Great American Cities* (New York: Modern Library, 1969).

Janowitz, Morris, *The Reconstruction of Patriotism: Education for Civic Consciousness* (Chicago: University of Chicago Press, 1983).

Jefferson, Thomas, Letter to Henry Lee, May 8, 1825, in *The Political Writings of Thomas Jefferson: Representative Selections,* ed. Edward Dumbauld (Indianapolis, IN: Bobbs-Merrill, 1955).

Kamenka, Eugene, and Alice Ehr-Soon Tay, eds., *Human Rights* (New York: St. Martin's Press, 1978).

Kateb, George, "The Moral Distinctiveness of Representative Democracy," *Ethics* 91 (1981): 357–74.

Kelley, Stanley, *Interpreting Elections* (Princeton, NJ: Princeton University Press, 1983).

Kemmis, Daniel, *Community and the Politics of Place* (Norman: University of Oklahoma Press, 1990).

Klosko, George, *The Principle of Fairness and Political Obligation* (Lanham, MD: Rowman and Littlefield, 1992).

———, "Reformist Consent and Political Obligation," *Political Studies* 39 (December 1991): 676–90.

Kymlicka, Will, *Contemporary Political Philosophy: An Introduction* (Oxford: Clarendon Press, 1990).

———, *Liberalism, Community, and Culture* (Oxford: Clarendon Press, 1989).

———, *Multicultural Citizenship* (Oxford: Clarendon Press, 1995).

———, ed., *The Rights of Minority Cultures* (Oxford: Oxford University Press, 1995).

Lacey, Michael J., and Knud Haakonssen, eds., *A Culture of Rights: The Bill of Rights in Philosophy, Politics, and Law—1791 and 1991* (Cambridge: Cambridge University Press, 1991).

Larmore, Charles, "Liberal Neutrality: A Reply to James Fishkin," *Political Theory* 17 (November 1989): 580–81.

———, *Patterns of Moral Complexity* (Cambridge: Cambridge University Press, 1987).

Lasch, Christopher, *The True and Only Heaven* (New York: W. W. Norton, 1991).

Laudon, Kenneth, *Communications Technology and Democratic Participation* (New York: Praeger, 1977).

Lee, Valerie E., and Julia B. Smith, "Effects of High School Restructuring and Size on Early Gains in Achievement and Education," *Sociology of Education* 68 (October 1995): 241–70.

Levine, Andrew, *The Politics of Autonomy: A Kantian Reading of Rousseau's Social Contract* (Amherst: University of Massachusetts Press, 1976).

Levine, Robert, "Cities with Heart," *Responsive Community* 5 (Winter 1994–95): 59–67.

Lindley, Richard, *Autonomy* (London: Macmillan, 1986).

Long, Norton, "An Institutional Framework for Responsible Citizenship," in Long, *The Polity*, ed. Charles Press (Chicago: Rand McNally, 1962).

Lyons, David, *Forms and Limits of Utilitarianism* (Oxford: Clarendon Press, 1965).

Macedo, Stephen, "Charting Liberal Virtues," in *NOMOS XXXIV: Virtue*, ed. John W. Chapman and William A. Galston (New York: New York University Press, 1992).

———, "Liberal Civic Education and Religious Fundamentalism: The Case of God v. John Rawls?," *Ethics* 105 (April 1995): 468–96.

MacIntyre, Alasdair, *After Virtue*, 2d ed. (Notre Dame, IN: University of Notre Dame Press, 1984).

———, *Whose Justice? Which Rationality?* (Notre Dame, IN: University of Notre Dame Press, 1988).

Macpherson, C. B., *The Life and Times of Liberal Democracy* (Oxford: Oxford University Press, 1977).

Mansbridge, Jane, *Beyond Adversary Democracy* (Chicago: University of Chicago Press, 1983).

———, "Living with Conflict: Representation in the Theory of Adversary Democracy," *Ethics* 91 (April 1981): 466–86.

Marx, Karl, "Critique of the Gotha Programme," in *The Portable Karl Marx*, ed. Eugene Kamenka (Harmondsworth: Penguin, 1983).

———, "On the Jewish Question," in *The Portable Karl Marx*, ed. Eugene Kamenka (Harmondsworth: Penguin, 1983).

———, *The Portable Karl Marx*, ed. Eugene Kamenka (Harmondsworth: Penguin, 1983).

McClosky, Herbert, "Consensus and Ideology in American Politics," *American Political Science Review* 58 (June 1964): 361–82.

Meehl, Paul E., "The Selfish Voter and the Thrown-Away Vote Argument," *American Political Science Review* 71 (March 1977): 11–30.

Melden, A. I., *Rights in Moral Life* (Berkeley: University of California Press, 1988).

———, ed., *Human Rights* (Belmont, CA: Wadsworth, 1970).

Milgram, Stanley, "The Experience of Living in Cities," *Science* 167 (1970): 1461–68.

Mill, John Stuart, *Three Essays: "On Liberty," "Representative Government," and "The Subjection of Women,"* ed. Richard Wollheim (Oxford: Oxford University Press, 1975).

Miller, David, "Citizenship and Pluralism," *Political Studies* 43 (September 1995): 432–50.

———, *Market, State, and Community* (Oxford: Clarendon Press, 1989).

———, *On Nationality* (Oxford: Clarendon Press, 1995).

Miller, David, Janet Coleman, William Connolly, and Alan Ryan, eds., *The Blackwell Encyclopedia of Political Thought* (Oxford: Basil Blackwell, 1987).

Miller, James C., III, "A Program for Direct and Proxy Voting in the Legislative Process," *Public Choice* 7 (Fall 1969): 107–13.

Miller, Warren B., and R. Kenneth Godwin, *Psyche and Demos: Individual Psychology and Issues of Population* (New York: Oxford University Press, 1977).

Montesquieu, *The Persian Letters,* trans. C. J. Betts (Harmondsworth: Penguin, 1973).

———, *The Spirit of the Laws,* ed. and trans. Anne Cohler, Basia Miller, and Harold Stone (Cambridge: Cambridge University Press, 1989).

Moon, J. Donald, "The Logic of Political Inquiry," in *Handbook of Political Science,* vol. 1, *Political Science: Scope and Theory,* ed. Fred I. Greenstein and Nelson W. Polsby (Reading, MA: Addison-Wesley, 1975).

Morris-Jones, W. H. "In Defense of Apathy: Some Doubts on the Duty to Vote," *Political Studies* 2 (1954): 25–37.

Morse, Suzanne W., *Renewing Civic Capacity: Preparing College Students for Service and Citizenship* (Washington, DC: Clearinghouse on Higher Education, George Washington University, 1989).

Moskos, Charles C., *A Call to Civic Service: National Service for Country and Community* (New York: Free Press, 1988).

Mueller, Dennis, *Public Choice* (Cambridge: Cambridge University Press, 1979).

Mueller, John, "Democracy and Ralph's Pretty Good Grocery: Elections, Equality, and the Minimal Human Being," *American Journal of Political Science* 36 (1992): 983–1003.

Murphy, Jeffrie, "Consent, Coercion, and Hard Choices," *Virginia Law Review* 67 (1981): 78–95.

Nozick, Robert, *Anarchy, State, and Utopia* (New York: Basic Books, 1974).

Okin, Susan Moller, *Justice, Gender, and the Family* (New York: Basic Books, 1989).

Oldfield, Adrian, *Citizenship and Community* (London: Routledge, 1990).

Olson, Mancur, *The Logic of Collective Action,* rev. ed. (New York: Schocken Books, 1971).

Ostrom, Elinor, *Governing the Commons: The Evolution of Institutions for Collective Action* (Cambridge: Cambridge University Press, 1990).

Ostrom, Vincent, Charles M. Tiebout, and Robert Warren, "The Organization of Government in Metropolitan Areas: A Theoretical Inquiry," *American Political Science Review* 55 (December 1961): 416–24.

Paine, Thomas, *The Rights of Man,* in *The Writings of Thomas Paine,* vol. 2, ed. Moncure D. Conway (New York: AMS Press, 1967).

Pateman, Carole, *Participation and Democratic Theory* (Cambridge: Cambridge University Press, 1970).

Peters, R. S. "Aims of Education—a Conceptual Inquiry," in *The Philosophy of Education,* ed. R. S. Peters (Oxford: Oxford University Press, 1973).

———, "Authority," in *Political Philosophy,* ed. Anthony Quinton (Oxford: Oxford University Press, 1967).

——, "Further Thoughts on the Concept of Education," in *The Philosophy of Education*, ed. R. S. Peters (Oxford: Oxford University Press, 1973).

——, ed., *The Philosophy of Education* (Oxford: Oxford University Press, 1973).

Peterson, Paul, *City Limits* (Chicago: University of Chicago Press, 1981).

Phillips, Anne, "Democracy and Difference: Some Problems for Feminist Theory," in *The Rights of Minority Cultures*, ed. Will Kymlicka (Oxford: Oxford University Press, 1995).

Plant, Raymond, "Community," in *The Blackwell Encyclopedia of Political Thought*, ed. David Miller, Janet Coleman, William Connolly, and Alan Ryan (Oxford: Basil Blackwell, 1987).

Pocock, J. G. A., *The Machiavellian Moment: Florentine Humanism and the Atlantic Republican Tradition* (Princeton, NJ: Princeton University Press, 1975).

Pool, Ithiel de Sola, "Citizen Feedback and Political Philosophy," in Pool, *Talking Back: Citizen Feedback and Cable Technology* (Cambridge, MA: MIT Press, 1973).

——, ed., *Talking Back: Citizen Feedback and Cable Technology* (Cambridge, MA: MIT Press, 1973).

Powell, G. Bingham, "American Voter Turnout in Comparative Perspective," *American Political Science Review* 80 (March 1986): 17–43.

Putnam, Robert D., "Bowling Alone, Revisited," *Responsive Community* 5 (Spring 1995): 18–33.

——, "Tuning In, Tuning Out: The Strange Disappearance of Social Capital in America," *PS: Political Science and Politics* 28 (December 1995): 664–83.

Putnam, Robert D., with Robert Leonardi and Rafaella Y. Nanetti, *Making Democracy Work: Civic Traditions in Modern Italy* (Princeton, NJ: Princeton University Press, 1993).

Quinton, Anthony, ed., *Political Philosophy* (Oxford: Oxford University Press, 1967).

Rahe, Paul, *Republics Ancient and Modern: Classical Republicanism and the American Revolution* (Chapel Hill: University of North Carolina Press, 1992).

Rawls, John, *Political Liberalism* (New York: Columbia University Press, 1993).

——, "The Priority of Right and Ideas of the Good," *Philosophy and Public Affairs* 17 (Fall 1988): 251–76.

——, *A Theory of Justice* (Cambridge, MA: Harvard University Press, 1971).

Raz, Joseph, *The Authority of Law* (New York: Oxford University Press, 1979).

——, *The Morality of Freedom* (Oxford: Clarendon Press, 1986).

Reidel, Manfred, *Between Tradition and Revolution: The Hegelian Transformation of Political Philosophy*, trans. Walter Wright (Cambridge: Cambridge University Press, 1984).

Riesenberg, Peter, *Citizenship in the Western Tradition: Plato to Rousseau* (Chapel Hill: University of North Carolina Press, 1992).

Riker, William, *Liberalism against Populism* (San Francisco: W. H. Freeman, 1982).

Riker, William, and Peter Ordeshook, "A Theory of the Calculus of Voting," *American Political Science Review* 62 (March 1968): 25–42.

Riley, Patrick, *The General Will before Rousseau: The Transformation of the Divine into the Civic* (Princeton, NJ: Princeton University Press, 1986).

Ritchie, D. G., *Natural Rights* (London: George Allen and Unwin, 1952 [originally published 1894]).

Rosenblum, Nancy, ed., *Liberalism and the Moral Life* (Cambridge, MA: Harvard University Press, 1989).

Rosenstone, Steven J., and John Mark Hansen, *Mobilization, Participation, and Democracy in America* (New York: Macmillan, 1993).

Rousseau, Jean-Jacques, *Discourse on the Arts and Sciences,* in *The Social Contract and Discourses,* trans. G. D. H. Cole (New York: E. P. Dutton, 1950).

———, *Du Contrat Social,* ed. Ronald Grimsley (Oxford: Clarendon Press, 1972).

———, *Emile,* trans. Allan Bloom (New York: Basic Books, 1979).

———, *The Government of Poland,* trans. Willmoore Kendall (Indianapolis, IN: Hackett, 1985).

———, *On the Social Contract,* ed. Roger D. Masters and trans. Judith R. Masters (New York: St. Martin's Press, 1978).

———, *Politics and the Arts: Letter to M. D'Alembert on the Theatre,* trans. Allan Bloom (Ithaca, NY: Cornell University Press, 1968).

———, *The Social Contract and Discourses,* trans. G. D. H. Cole (New York: E. P. Dutton, 1950).

Ryan, Alan, "The Liberal Community," in *NOMOS XXXV: Democratic Community,* ed. John W. Chapman and Ian Shapiro (New York: New York University Press, 1993).

———, "Liberalism," in *A Companion to Contemporary Political Philosophy,* ed. Robert Goodin and Philip Pettit (Oxford: Basil Blackwell, 1993).

Rybczynski, Witold, "Mysteries of the Mall," *New York Review of Books* 41 (July 14, 1994): 31–34.

Sandel, Michael J., *Democracy's Discontent: America in Search of a Public Philosophy* (Cambridge, MA: Harvard University Press, 1996).

———, *Liberalism and the Limits of Justice* (Cambridge: Cambridge University Press, 1982).

———, ed., *Liberalism and Its Critics* (London: Basil Blackwell, 1984).

Sartorius, Rolf, "Political Authority and Political Obligation," *Virginia Law Review* 67 (1981): 3–17.

Schumpeter, Joseph, *Capitalism, Socialism, and Democracy,* 3d ed. (New York: Harper and Row, 1962).

Selbourne, David, *The Principle of Duty: An Essay on the Foundations of the Civic Order* (London: Sinclair-Stevenson, 1994).

Sen, Amartya K., "Isolation, Assurance, and the Social Rate of Discount," *Quarterly Journal of Economics* 81 (1967): 112–24.

———, *On Economic Inequality* (New York: W. W. Norton, 1973).

———, "Rational Fools: A Critique of the Behavioral Foundations of Economic Theory," *Philosophy and Public Affairs* 6 (Summer 1977): 317–44.

Senor, Thomas, "What If There Are No Political Obligations?: A Reply to A. J. Simmons," *Philosophy and Public Affairs* 16 (Summer 1987): 260–68.

Shubik, Martin, "On Homo Politicus and the Instant Referendum," *Public Choice* 9 (Fall 1970): 79–84.

Shue, Henry, *Basic Rights: Subsistence, Affluence, and U.S. Foreign Policy* (Princeton, NJ: Princeton University Press, 1980).

Simmons, A. John, "The Anarchist Position: A Reply to Klosko and Senor," *Philosophy and Public Affairs* 16 (1987): 269–79.

———, *Moral Principles and Political Obligations* (Princeton, NJ: Princeton University Press, 1979).

Singer, Peter, *Democracy and Disobedience* (Oxford: Oxford University Press, 1973).

Sinopoli, Richard C., *The Foundations of American Citizenship: Liberalism, the Constitution, and Civic Virtue* (New York: Oxford University Press, 1992).

Skinner, B. F., *Walden Two* (New York: Macmillan, 1976 [originally published 1948]).

Skinner, Quentin, "The Republican Ideal of Political Liberty," in *Machiavelli and Republicanism,* ed. Gisela Bock, Quentin Skinner, and Maurizio Viroli (Cambridge: Cambridge University Press, 1990).

Smith, M. B. E., "Is There a Prima Facie Obligation to Obey the Law?," in *Law in Philosophical Perspective,* ed. Joel Feinberg and Hyman Gross (Encino, CA: Dickenson, 1977).

Smith, Rogers M., "American Conceptions of Citizenship and National Service," in *New Communitarian Thinking: Persons, Virtues, Institutions, and Communities,* ed. Amitai Etzioni (Charlottesville: University Press of Virginia, 1995).

Spinner, Jeff, *The Boundaries of Citizenship: Race, Ethnicity and Nationality in the Liberal State* (Baltimore: The Johns Hopkins University Press, 1994).

Spragens, Thomas A., Jr., *Reason and Democracy* (Durham: Duke University Press, 1990).

Squire, Peverill, Raymond E. Wolfinger, and David Glass, "Residential Mobility and Voter Turnout," *American Political Science Review* 81 (March 1987): 45–65.

Strate, John M., Charles J. Parrish, Charles D. Elder, and Coit Ford III, "Life Span Civic Development and Voting Participation," *American Political Science Review* 83 (June 1989): 443–64.

Sullivan, Daniel, "Rules, Fairness, and Formal Justice," *Ethics* 85 (1975): 322–31.

Sullivan, William M., *Reconstructing Public Philosophy* (Berkeley: University of California Press, 1982).

Sumner, L. W., *The Moral Foundations of Rights* (Oxford: Clarendon Press, 1987).

Sundquist, James, *Dispersing Population: What America Can Learn from Europe* (Washington, DC: Brookings Institution, 1975).

Sunstein, Cass R., "Beyond the Republican Revival," *Yale Law Journal* 97 (1988): 1539–89.

Talmon, J. L., *The Origins of Totalitarian Democracy* (New York: Praeger, 1960).

Tarrow, Sidney, "The Urban-Rural Cleavage in Political Involvement: The Case of France," *American Political Science Review* 65 (June 1971): 341–57.

Taylor, Charles, "Cross-Purposes: The Liberal-Communitarian Debate," in *Liberalism and the Moral Life,* ed. Nancy L. Rosenblum (Cambridge, MA: Harvard University Press, 1989).

———, *Philosophy and the Human Sciences: Philosophical Papers,* vol. 2 (Cambridge: Cambridge University Press, 1985).

Taylor, Michael, *Anarchy and Cooperation* (New York: John Wiley, 1976).

———, *Community, Anarchy, and Liberty* (Cambridge: Cambridge University Press, 1982).

———, *The Possibility of Cooperation* (Cambridge: Cambridge University Press, 1987).

Teske, Paul, Mark Schneider, Michael Mintrom, and Samuel Best, "Establishing the Micro Foundations of a Macro Theory: Information, Movers, and the Competitive Local Market for Public Goods," *American Political Science Review* 87 (September 1993): 702–13.

Thompson, Dennis, *John Stuart Mill and Representative Government* (Princeton, NJ: Princeton University Press, 1976).

Tiebout, Charles M., "A Pure Theory of Local Expenditures," *Journal of Political Economy* 64 (October 1956): 416–24.

Trachtenberg, Zev M., *Making Citizens: Rousseau's Political Theory of Culture* (London: Routledge, 1993).

Ullmann-Margalit, Edna, *The Emergence of Norms* (Oxford: Clarendon Press, 1979).

Verba, Sidney, and Norman Nie, *Participation in America: Political Democracy and Social Equality* (New York: Harper and Row, 1972).

Viroli, Maurizio, *Jean-Jacques Rousseau and the "Well-Ordered Society,"* trans. Derek Hanson (Cambridge: Cambridge University Press, 1988).

Vitt, Joseph E., Jr., "Kansas City: Problems and Success of Downtown Development," in *Personality, Politics, and Planning: How City Planners Work*, ed. Anthony Catanese and W. Paul Farmer (Beverly Hills, CA: Sage Publications, 1978).

Vlastos, Gregory, "Justice and Equality," in *Social Justice*, ed. R. B. Brandt (Englewood Cliffs, NJ: Prentice-Hall, 1962).

Waldron, Jeremy, "Democratic Theory and the Public Interest: Condorcet and Rousseau Revisited," *American Political Science Review* 83 (1989): 1317–40.

———, ed., *Theories of Rights* (Oxford: Oxford University Press, 1984).

Walzer, Michael, "The Communitarian Critique of Liberalism," *Political Theory* 18 (February 1990): 6–23.

———, *Spheres of Justice: A Defense of Pluralism and Equality* (New York: Basic Books, 1983).

Ward, Cynthia V., "The Limits of 'Liberal Republicanism': Why Group-Based Remedies and Republican Citizenship Don't Mix," *Columbia Law Review* 91 (April 1991): 581–607.

Wasserstrom, Richard, ed., *Morality and the Law* (Belmont, CA: Wadsworth, 1971).

Weale, Albert, *Political Theory and Social Policy* (New York: St. Martin's Press, 1983).

Wertheimer, Alan, "In Defense of Compulsory Voting," in *NOMOS XVI: Participation in Politics*, ed. J. Roland Pennock and John W. Chapman (New York: Leiber-Atherton, 1975).

Wicker, A. W., "Undermanning, Performances, and Students," *Journal of Personality and Social Psychology* 10 (1968): 255–61.

Wicklein, John, "Wired City, U.S.A.: The Charms and Dangers of Two-Way TV," *Atlantic Monthly* 243 (February 1979): 35–42.

Willems, E. P., "Forces toward Participation in Behavior Settings," in *Big School,*

Small School, ed. R. G. Barker and P. V. Gump (Stanford, CA: Stanford University Press, 1964).

Wills, Garry, *Confessions of a Conservative* (Garden City, NY: Doubleday, 1979).

Wirszubski, Ch., *Libertas as a Political Idea at Rome During the Late Republic and Early Principate* (Cambridge: Cambridge University Press, 1960).

Wirth, Louis, "Urbanism as a Way of Life," *American Journal of Sociology* 44 (July 1938): 1–24.

Wolff, Robert Paul, *In Defense of Anarchism* (New York: Harper and Row, 1970).

Wolfinger, Raymond, and Steven Rosenstone, *Who Votes?* (New Haven: Yale University Press, 1980).

Wolin, Sheldon, *Politics and Vision: Continuity and Innovation in Western Political Thought* (Boston: Little, Brown, 1960).

Wollstonecraft, Mary, *Vindication of the Rights of Woman,* ed. Miriam Brody (London: Penguin, 1985).

Young, Iris Marion, *Justice and the Politics of Difference* (Princeton, NJ: Princeton University Press, 1990).

———, "Mothers, Citizenship, and Independence: A Critique of Pure Family Values," *Ethics* 105 (April 1995): 535–56.

———, "Together in Difference: Transforming the Logic of Group Political Conflict," in *The Rights of Minority Cultures,* ed. Will Kymlicka (Oxford: Oxford University Press, 1995).

Young, Robert, *Personal Autonomy: Beyond Negative and Positive Liberty* (London: Croom Helm, 1986).

INDEX

Agenda Committee, 138–39
allegiance, 107
altruism. *See* conditional altruism
Amish, 127–31
Anderson, Charles, 211 n.4
Andre, Thomas, 221 n.17
apathy, 132–35, 142, 156
Aristotle, 15, 28, 51, 99, 155–56
Arneson, Richard, 73
Arrow, Kenneth, 147, 217 n.17
Arterton, F. Christopher, 224 n.22
assurance game, 108–16, 166–67
atomism, 53–55, 76
Austin, J. L., 75
authority, 62–66, 68–69
autonomy
   as ability, 30–31, 38
   and assistance, 54–60
   and authority, 62–66
   as capacity, 66–68
   and choice, 32, 38–39, 67, 129–31
   and civic virtue, 13–18, 175
   and common good, 15–16
   and community, 36–40, 48, 64–68
   as contextual, 35–36
   and cooperation, 18, 36–40, 66
   defined, 30–31
   and the difference principle, 34–35
   and diversity, 127
   and duty, 16, 30–31, 33, 35
   and education, 117–31
   and general rights, 31–32
   and heteronomy, 16
   as individualistic, 36–40, 66–67

   and oppression, 177–81
   and political obligation, 62–68
   right of, 5, 28, 30–31, 180
   and right to be free, 28–29
   and special rights, 31, 36
   as virtue, 16

Ball, Terence, 216 n.22
Banning, Lance, 11–12, 18–19, 204 n.2
Barry, Brian, 84, 87, 91, 215 n.13
Battistoni, Richard, 122
Becker, Lawrence C., 213 n.14
Bellah, Robert N., et al., 229 n.32
Benn, Stanley, 208 n.8
Bentham, Jeremy, 12, 18–19, 25, 105
Beran, Harry, 211 n.5
Berlin, Isaiah, 37–38
Berry, Jeffrey M., et al., 229 n.34
Birch, A. H., 163
Black, Antony, 198
Brown, David L., 229 n.32
Budd, Billy, 38
Burger, Warren, 128
Burke, Edmund, 19–20
Burtt, Shelley, 117

capitalism, 11
Census of Governments, 159
Chubb, John, 118, 123, 125–26
citizenship, 6, 98–116
   active, 104
   and civic virtue, 98–99, 195–96
   and collective action, 108–16
   and the common good, 99